8,000 Miles
Across Alaska

A Runner's Journeys
on the Iditarod Trail

By Jill Homer
and Tim Hewitt

Edited by Diana Miller

Arctic Glass Press

www.arcticglasspress.com

2240 Homestead Court, No. 307,
Los Altos, California, 94024

© 2014 by Jill Homer and Tim Hewitt
All rights reserved
First edition, 2014

Distributed in the United States by Arctic Glass Press, www.arcticglasspress.com

Manufactured in the United States

Editor: Diana Miller
Cover Design: Jill Homer
Interior Design: Jill Homer
Photographers: Mike Curiak, Beat Jegerlehner, Tim Hewitt, and Jill Homer

Cover: Tim and Loreen Hewitt approach the Alaska Range during the 2011 Iditarod Trail Invitational. Photo by Mike Curiak.

Back Cover: Tim Hewitt crosses the sea ice over the Norton Sound in 2014. Photo by Beat Jegerlehner.

Adjacent page: Rainy Pass in 2014. Photo by Beat Jegerlehner.

ISBN 978-0692263365

This is a work of narrative nonfiction. Dialogue and events herein have been recounted to the best of the subject's memory.

For Alaska

Contents

The Iditarod Trail

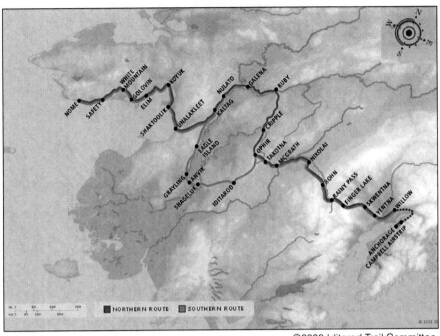

©2008 Iditarod Trail Committee

The following is a rough estimate of distances between checkpoints on the Iditarod Trail.

Northern Route

	Distances between checkpoints	Total distance from Knik
Knik to Yentna Station	57	57
Yentna Station to Skwentna	30	87
Skwentna to Finger Lake	40	127
Finger Lake to Rainy Pass	35	162
Rainy Pass to Rohn	40	202
Rohn to Nikolai	75	277
Nikolai to McGrath	52	329
McGrath to Takotna	18	347
Takotna to Ophir	23	370
Ophir to Cripple	73	443
Cripple to Ruby	70	513
Ruby to Galena	50	563
Galena to Nulato	37	600
Nulato to Kaltag	47	647
Kaltag to Unalakleet	85	732
Unalakleet to Shaktoolik	40	772
Shaktoolik to Koyuk	50	822
Koyuk to Elim	48	870
Elim to Golovin	28	898
Golovin to White Mountain	18	916
White Mountain to Safety	55	971
Safety to Nome	22	993

Southern Route

	Distances between checkpoints	Total distance from Knik
Knik to Yentna Station	57	57
Yentna Station to Skwentna	30	87
Skwentna to Finger Lake	40	127
Finger Lake to Rainy Pass	35	162
Rainy Pass to Rohn	40	202
Rohn to Nikolai	75	277
Nikolai to McGrath	52	329
McGrath to Takotna	18	347
Takotna to Ophir	23	370
Ophir to Iditarod	80	450
Iditarod to Shageluk	55	505
Shageluk to Anvik	25	530
Anvik to Grayling	18	548
Grayling to Eagle Island	62	610
Eagle Island to Kaltag	60	670
Kaltag to Unalakleet	85	755
Unalakleet to Shaktoolik	40	795
Shaktoolik to Koyuk	50	845
Koyuk to Elim	48	893
Elim to Golovin	28	921
Golovin to White Mountain	18	939
Safety to Nome	22	1016

A Brief History of the Iditarod Trail

1910
The Alaska Railroad Commission completes construction on a new southern mail route from Seward to Nome.

1925
A diphtheria outbreak in Nome prompts the governor to launch a "Great Race of Mercy" to shuttle serum to the village with a relay of dog sled teams.

1932
Airplanes become the preferred method of delivery for mail and supplies, reducing trail use.

1945
Joe Redington and his family move to Alaska and establish a homestead in Knik near the Iditarod Trail.

1953
After moving to Flathorn Lake, Redington becomes interested in dog sled racing.

1960s
Snowmobiles begin to replace dog teams.

1964
An Alaska Centennial committee plans a 56-mile dog sled race on the Iditarod Trail to commemorate the occasion.

1973
After years of planning, Joe Redington and others launch the first thousand-mile Iditarod Dog Sled Race.

1983
Redington starts the first human-powered race on the trail, a 200-mile ski race called Iditaski.

1987
On Redington's prompting, the Mountain Bikers of Alaska host the first Iditabike.

2000
Iditasport holds the first thousand-mile race for cyclists, skiers, and runners.

Iditarod Sport Records

Iditarod Trail Invitational (since 2002)

Men's 350-mile race to McGrath:
Bicycle: Kevin Breitenbach of Alaska: 2 days 4 hours 43 minutes; 2014
Foot: David Johnston of Alaska: 4 days 1 hour 38 minutes; 2014
Ski: Jim Jaeger of Alaska: 4 days 8 hours; 2002

Women's 350-mile race to McGrath:
Bicycle: Heather Best of Alaska: 2 days 14 hours 13 minutes; 2014
Foot: Anne Ver Hoef of Alaska: 6 days 12 hours 20 minutes; 2013
Ski: Gail Koepf of Alaska; 7 days 6 hours 18 minutes; 2005

Men's 1,000-mile race to Nome, Northern Route:
Bicycle: Jeff Oatley of Alaska: 10 days 2 hours 53 minutes; 2014 (overall)
Foot: Tom Jarding of Pennsylvania: 20 days 14 hours 45 min; 2010

Women's 1,000-mile race to Nome, Northern Route:
Bicycle: Ausilia Vistarini of Italy: 17 days 6 hours 25 minutes; 2014 (overall)
Foot: Loreen Hewitt of Pennsylvania: 26 days 6 hours 59 minutes; 2014 (overall)

Men's 1,000-mile race to Nome, Southern Route:
Bicycle: Jay Petervary of Idaho: 17 days 6 hours, 2011
Foot: Tim Hewitt of Pennsylvania: 20 days 7 hours 17 minutes; 2011 (overall)

Women's 1,000-mile race to Nome, Southern Route:
Bicycle: Tracey Petervary of Idaho: 18 days 6 hours 30 minutes; 2011
Foot Shawn McTaggart of Alaska: 30 days 12 hrs 10 min: 2013

Iditasport (1990-2001) *Times include a mandatory overnight

350-mile race to McGrath:
Bicycle: John Stamstad, 3 days 8 hours 15 minutes; 1998
Foot: Tom Possert, 6 days 2 hours 50 minutes: 1998
Ski: Mel Strauch, 6 days 7 hours 5 minutes; 1997
Women's Bicycle: Chloe Lanthier, 4 days 23 hours 50 minutes; 1998

1,000-mile race to Nome, Northern Route:
Bicycle: Mike Curiak, 15 days 1 hour 15 minutes; 2000

1,000-mile race to Nome, Southern Route:
Bicycle: Andrew Heading and Mike Estes, 26 days 5 hours 7 minutes; 2001
Foot: Tom Jarding and Tim Hewitt, 26 days 20 hours 46 minutes; 2001
Ski: Bob Baker and Tim Kelley, 23 days 5 hours 4 minutes; 1990
Women's Foot: Janine du Plessis, 41 days 10 hours 30 minutes; 2000

Source: Alaska Ultrasport

Iditarod Gear List

The contents of Tim Hewitt's sled have changed throughout the years, with the evolution of gear technology and shifts in perspective about what items are necessary to survive for a month in the Alaska wilderness. The fundamentals, however, remain the same — food, fuel, hydration, medicine, warm clothing, and shelter. The following is a list of items that Tim Hewitt carried with him for his trek across Alaska with his wife, Loreen, in 2014:

Gear:

- Four-foot pulk, home-made from ultra-high molecular weight polyethylene
- Hip belt with carabiners and extra buckle
- Rope and two strips of PVC pipe to connect the sled
- Thermarest Z-lite closed-cell foam ground pad
- Western Mountaineers Hotsac vapor barrier
- Feathered Friends Expedition down sleeping bag (850 fill weight) rated to -60°
- Atlas dual track race snowshoes
- Kelty duffel bag, extra large
- Black Diamond C-3 carbon trekking poles
- MSR Whisperlite International stove with windscreen and base
- MSR fuel bottles
- White gas
- Titanium pot and lid
- Titanium spork
- REI insulated mug
- Waterproof matches
- Small toothbrush and floss
- Camera
- Two Carmex lip balms
- Padded moleskin
- Knife with scissors
- Leukotape-P
- Neosporin
- Keflex
- Z-pack antibiotics
- Cipro
- Safety pin
- Vitamins
- Aleve
- Duct tape
- Goggles
- Sunglasses (Julbo Glacier photochromatic polarized)
- REI flash backpack
- Montrail midheight Mountain Masochist Outdry trail-running shoes
- Carbide studs, made to specifications by Aggressive Grinding Services
- Insulated sole inserts
- MP3 with earbuds
- Garmin GPS
- Two Headlamps
- Lithium batteries
- Two Sea-to-Summit dry bags
- One trash compactor bag
- Wiggy's hip waders
- Plastic baggies for feet

Clothing:

- Heavy windstopper balaclava
- Fleece neck gaiter
- REI primaloft vest

Tim Hewitt in the Dalzell Gorge in February 2014.　Photo by Jill Homer

- Mountain Hardware Dome Perignon Gore-Tex tassel cap
- Under Armour long sleeved mock turtleneck top
- Patagonian R-1 fleece quarter zip top
- Patagonia nanopuff full-zip hoodie jacket
- Go-Lite Bitterroot down jacked with hood (850-fill weight)
- Feathered Friends Rock and Ice Expedition Parka with hood (850-fill weight)
- Black Diamond liner gloves with leather palms
- Outdoor Research primaloft Alti-Mitts with primaloft removable inner mitts
- Heavy-weight Hind Drylete tights
- Second layer running tights
- Mountain Hardware full-zip primaloft compressor pants
- Go-Lite Pac-lite shell pants
- Outdoor Research gaiters
- Drymax socks, three pairs
- Patagonia briefs

Food and Hydration:

- Geigerrig three-liter hydration pack with insulator, in-line filter and clip for hose.
- Lemonade mix in a one-liter Nalgene bottle with Outdoor Research insulated zip-top holder.
- Beef and ostrich jerky and sticks from Ostrim
- Crunchy peanut butter
- Freeze-dried fruit
- Smoked salmon
- Various nuts
- Chocolate
- Candy – Gummy bears, Swedish Fish, Mike & Ikes
- Trail Mix
- Vita-fuel bars
- Chewing gum
- Cliff blocks
- Other food picked up from villages or left behind by mushers

Introduction

1

*"Beyond the very extreme of fatigue and
distress, we may find amounts of ease and
power we never dreamed ourselves to own,
sources of strength never taxed at all because
we never push through the obstruction."*
~William James, philosopher

Few moments will make a person feel more alone than stopping at random in a snow-covered wilderness to sleep. And yet, few moments will make one feel more alive than waking up in that wilderness to pink sunlight and piercing cold, wholly independent in a beautiful and terrifying world.

For Tim Hewitt, dozens of these moments consolidate in memories, infusing a typically hectic life with quiet refrain. The sky opens up in penetrating darkness, with a clarity that pulls the curtain from unknowable depths of the universe. Stars shimmer like spotlights behind a ballet of Northern Lights, as green waves of aurora glide above the horizon. The boreal forest stands in rapt attention, with clusters of spruce trees leaning away from the prevailing wind, giving the appearance that they, too, are gazing up at the sky. This is where Tim spreads out his sleeping bag — in a bed of clean snow, beside the protection of trees, and away from the tracks of territorial moose. On calm and cold nights, ice crystals jingle in the air like tiny bells. More often than not, sleep battles a clamorous wind that roars through this symphony of solitude.

Exhaustion has a way of amplifying isolation and vice versa, and walking a thousand miles across Alaska can rattle a person to pieces. A shattered body sometimes revolts against its tyrannical mind, and there were nights when Tim nearly lost life's most crucial battles. At its worst, sleep just forced its way in — as though his body suddenly went on strike even when his conscience screamed to keep moving.

There was one such night on the jumbled ice of Golovin Bay, a small pocket of the Bering Sea just a hundred miles from Nome. A fierce storm charged through the night, a blitzkrieg of hurricane-force winds that pushed a jet stream of snow across the white expanse. Tim battled the blizzard to the edge of a pressure ridge — a broken wall of ice slabs lifted by ocean currents like concrete after an earthquake. Blowing snow streamed over the slabs and Tim could see, on the leeward side, a depression with clear air — the tiniest sliver of protection. Against all remaining logic, Tim unhooked from his sled and spread out his sleeping bag against the eighteen-inch barrier — hardly higher than his reclined body. His movements were emotionless and mechanical, as though he was observing his body act independently of his mind while he surrendered in the bowels of a subzero cyclone. As wind continued to pummel the sleeping bag, his body soon began to thrash with shivering convulsions. It was impossibly cold, with wind chill approaching 100 below zero.

In these conditions, the only orders that make any sense are "do not stop." Yet Tim felt helpless against a desperate fatigue. He wasn't certain that he could physically take another step into the storm, and yet he was certain that he wouldn't survive if he stayed. The wind chill and exhaustion drained heat from his body, leaving skin icy and extremities numb. It felt like dying, and yet some base instinct still demanded rest against the odds of survival. Tim's thoughts echoed through the hollow chamber where his body held them hostage: "If you fall asleep, you will never wake up."

His mind conjured up images of a corpse frozen inside an ice-encrusted sleeping bag, wedged where the wind had driven it between slabs of ice. If he was lucky, Alaska Natives would find his body before spring came and the Bering Sea swallowed what was left. He imagined a group standing over his rigid remains, speculating at the circumstances that would cause a man to end up alone on the sea ice without a snowmobile or even sled dogs.

"Must've gotten lost in the storm," one would say.

"Sure," another would reply. "But what was he doing out in that blizzard?"

Even Tim had a difficult time answering this question — why did he run and walk and trudge a thousand miles across Alaska on the Iditarod Trail? "Because it's there" wasn't adequate. "As a challenge" or "for the adventure of it" were closer, but still too vague. The thousand-mile dog sled race on the Iditarod Trail is often called "The Last Great Race" — but there's another, much more obscure race, where participants don't even have the help of dogs. Formerly called the Iditasport and now the Iditarod Trail Invitational, this race challenges cyclists, skiers, and runners to complete the distance under their own power and without much in the way of outside support. It's more of an expedition than a race, and Tim Hewitt is the only person to have completed it more than three times. His actual number? An astonishing eight. Six of those, he won or tied.

But no one who sees Tim on the street near his law firm in Pittsburgh would ever suspect that battling hurricane-force blizzards is something he does in his spare time. Fifty-nine years old with a slim build, a bright smile, and cropped gray hair, Tim isn't the stereotype of a grizzled Arctic explorer. He's an employment lawyer, a talented amateur runner, a father to four daughters, and a husband to an equally adventurous wife. But his well-kept home on a lake outside Pittsburgh harbors subtle evidence of another life: an Iditarod Trail marker attached to the mail box, a photograph of the white-capped mountains surrounding Rainy Pass, and a few screen-printed T-shirts and hats that were the only tangible "prizes" for participation in the race beyond The Last Great Race.

These objects serve as mementos of a truly unique accomplishment. Far more people have reached the summit of Mount Everest than Nome under their own power, and it's incredibly unlikely that another person will ever try for eight (or more — Tim hasn't shown any inclination toward stopping just yet).

"Why?" remains a valid question. The Iditarod Trail Invitational is a race that has no prize money, no spectators cheering at the finish, no awards, no trophies. There are no logical reasons to participate in such a race, and so participants must find motivation from within. Tim thrives amid adversity, remains cool-headed in the face of great dangers, and relishes in testing his already expansive limits. He also enjoys the mental rewards of every small victory: the many times he wanted to quit and didn't, the lessons he learned, the struggles and successes in simply surviving. Out on windswept ice of Golovin Bay, he knew the stakes were as high as they had ever been. If he emerged from this challenge victoriously, the reward would be the most valuable of all — his life.

Visualizing the scene of defeat — people discovering his corpse frozen against blocks of ice — boosted his exhausted and defiant body out of the sleeping bag. The ten-minute stop carried a steep price; his core temperature had dropped substantially, and his motor functions were firing at a fraction of their usual capabilities. Packing up his sled with his back to the wind, he became so wracked with shivering that his arms barely worked. Numb fingers and violent limb convulsions added an urgent impossibility to the simplest chores. Sheer willpower accomplished these tasks, and he turned to face the blizzard with renewed resolve — he would get out of this one alive. He always did.

* * * * *

After six successful journeys to Nome between 2001 and 2011, the last of which culminated in a long-term goal of breaking the overall speed record, Tim formulated the ultimate challenge for the trail — something that had never been done before, and likely would never be done again. In 2013, he would launch an unsupported expedition on foot across Alaska, traveling completely autonomously with all of the food and supplies he needed for a thousand miles. He would not purchase or accept any food along the way. He would carry all of the fuel needed to melt snow for drinking water, as well as for cooking. He would not go inside of a single building. He would not even pick up discarded morsels of food that he found on the trail.

Tim's plan echoed Arctic expeditions in the Golden Age of Exploration — an era before the World Wars when complete autonomy was the only option, when Robert Scott and Ernest Shackleton raced against their own dwindling provisions toward the South Pole. At a thousand miles, the distance of Tim's expedition would rival the longest known unsupported polar expeditions of modern times, and surpass the longest known distance for a person traveling solo and unsupported on foot. Unlike most polar explorers, who work in teams, Tim would be traveling alone for much of the journey.

At the start of the 2013 race in Knik, Tim hooked himself to a sled that weighed one hundred and ten pounds — the equivalent of dragging a full-grown woman across the Alaska wilderness, and just marginally lighter than his own body weight. His provisions included 5,000 calories per day of energy-dense foods such as peanut butter, and were rationed out for a twenty-four-day timeline. Any longer than that, and Tim would run out of food and fuel. Every labored step in front of that bulging sled was a race against the clock.

That year, the middle segment of the trail was plagued with a challenge that polar explorers rarely face — a prolonged mid-winter thaw. Temperatures a few degrees above freezing, sleet, and rain rendered the packed snow on the trail into soft slush, soaked crucial survival gear, and opened previously frozen waterways. Self-imposed rules prevented Tim from going inside buildings to dry his clothing, and his twenty-four-day time limit discouraged stopping to wait for better conditions. Hunger gnawed at his stomach and food consumed his thoughts as he trudged through the miserable slush.

As he made his way across steeply undulating climbs and descents in a region known as the Shageluk Hills, Tim approached a cluster of snowmobiles idling at the mouth of a ravine just beyond the Moose Creek shelter cabin. He had seen this group earlier, and thought it strange that they had bypassed the cabin only to stop a quarter mile later. It was a few hours after sunset, and their machines' headlights burned bright spots onto the slope of the next hill, illuminating a swirl of snow flurries. Curious as to why they were just idling there, Tim broke into a jog down the soft trail. At the bottom, his headlamp revealed a wide barrier of open water, the color and consistency of a margarita. Warm temperatures had broken up the surface ice of Moose Creek and unleashed a river of what Northerners refer to as overflow — water sitting on top of snow and ice. The snowmobiles were parked on the other side of the overflow, and several men with thick Australian accents were conversing loudly as they repacked trailer sleds. In the red glow of their taillights, Tim could see jumbles of ice and slush flowing in swift current. This clearly wasn't a thin skim of water on top of ice.

"How deep is the river?" Tim yelled over the hum of idling engines across the river.

"We don't know," one of the men yelled back to him. "We skipped across" — meaning they revved up their machines and skimmed the surface of the water with their snowmobiles' caterpillar tracks, similar to skipping stones. "We didn't hit bottom."

Another driver suggested Tim camp out on the shore and hope the slurry would freeze overnight so he could walk across in the morning. Tim already knew this wasn't going to happen; temperatures were barely below freezing as it was, and snow flurries meant overcast skies, which would retain warmth. Even if he had the time to wait for new ice to form, it might take days.

"Good luck, mate," the first driver called out before the group drove away. Tim paced the shoreline, mulling his options. It was too early to stop for the night, and he had no desire to wake up to this mess first thing in the morning. There was no sense in traveling up or down river looking for a more narrow or shallow section, as flows indicated a volume of water clearly too large for a reasonable crossing. No, he was going to have to ford this river with his hulking sled. Just over ten days into his journey, the duffel bag was twenty-five pounds lighter, but still well over seventy pounds — more than he could reasonably carry on his back while wading through swift-flowing water. Based on the grade of the bank, he guessed the river was about three feet deep. He hoped the river was only three feet deep — any deeper than that, and there would be no possible way to stay dry during a crossing. Any deeper than three feet, and the river might as well be a hundred-foot-high brick wall.

Experience served as an important guide. First he put on his down coat to preserve his core temperature; even though the night was "warm," temperatures were still below freezing, and this was going to be an extended stop. He removed his snowshoes and pulled on a pair of lightweight hip waders — waterproof nylon overboots designed to keep his shoes and pants dry during water crossings. Before ferrying any gear, he would need to gauge the water's depth to determine how heavy of a load he could manage. He also needed an unloaded run to determine how well he could balance in the current. If he fell over, he would soak all of his clothing. This would be bad enough on its own, but the danger would be compounded if he also soaked his sleeping bag and other survival gear.

He tentatively stepped off the embankment into the fast-flowing slush. Ice-cold water surged to his thighs, and the temperature differential sparked an involuntary yelp. The bottom was slick and uneven, and the waders provided no traction. Tim used his trekking poles to gauge water depth, as well as stabilize his body against the swift current and collisions with floating chunks of ice. The water level rose near the top of his waders. His heart pounded, and he moved as though he were walking barefoot over a bed of nails. A slip or a step into a marginally deeper hole would flood his hip waders and undoubtedly result in falling over. He wouldn't drown in a hip-deep stream, but the consequence of fully submerging his body in ice water could ultimately be the same with extended suffering.

When Tim reached the far side of the stream with legs still dry and everything else intact, he retreated for his first load of gear. First he shuttled the duffel loaded with the food, which weighed fifty pounds. He needed both hands to hoist the heavy bag, and the necessary grip forced him to leave his trekking poles on the far side of the river. This crossing was an exercise in core stability, leaning into the flow to avoid being pushed over. Once across, he dumped the load on the bank and returned for the rest of his provisions — sled, sleeping bag, mat, clothing, fuel, snowshoes, and other items — again tiptoeing carefully through the slurry. Adrenaline pulsed through his blood, and he felt an invigorating surge of satisfaction at overcoming an obstacle that for most would have seemed impassable.

After Tim removed his waders, he discovered that they had taken on some water. Whether water had seeped through the seams or splashed over the top, he couldn't be sure, but the result was the same — his shoes and two of his three pairs of socks were wet. One foot was just damp while the other was soaked. Back in Anchorage, Tim and his wife had discussed the problem of putting dry socks and feet into wet shoes, and she suggested he add a few plastic ice-bucket liners from the hotel to his kit. Since the thin bags weighed almost nothing, he stuffed a few into the zippered side pocket of the duffel. The conversation came back to him as he wrung out the wet socks, and a felt a wave of relief. Now he wouldn't have to soak his last pair of dry socks to keep his feet warm. He pulled the baggies over his bare skin and the wet socks over the baggies. Innovation triumphs over intimidation. Tim packed his sled and commenced the climb up the next hill.

With the threat and thrill of adversity abated, his adrenaline surge wore off quickly. The satisfaction of victory only clung on a little bit longer, replaced by an inevitable energy crash and crushing sleepiness. Snow flurries continued to float through his headlamp beam in hypnotic patterns, lulling Tim to a walking semi-consciousness. The flickering logical side of his brain told him the river crossing had eaten up a lot of time, and he needed to make up for the delay by marching through the night. But almost independently of his mind, his eyes began scanning for a tree-protected place to rest for a few hours. With robotic motions, he set up camp and crawled inside his sleeping bag even as his deadline-stressed mind continued to conjure protests.

These mind-body disputes happen with some regularity on the Iditarod Trail, to Tim and others who push themselves to the limits of strength and fatigue. Maybe if his life was at risk, as it had been on Golovin Bay, Tim's brain would win the battle. But these were not dire conditions — just terribly exhausting conditions — and he felt a warm peace as he drifted to sleep beneath gently falling snowflakes. Nobody knew he was here, and the forest itself would scarcely feel the impact of his presence. He was alone and infinitely small in the embrace of wilderness. But he was also a fully actualized human, capable of making his own decisions, and thus free. He could sleep for as long or as little as he chose. And when he woke up, he'd still be here — in Alaska. Nothing else mattered for now. He was going to Nome. Again.

What brings Tim and others back to the Alaska wilderness, year after year? In order to grasp the allure of the Iditarod Trail, it's important to understand the trail's history — all the way back to the beginning.

History

2

*When I went out to the villages where there
were beautiful dogs once, a snowmachine
was sitting in front of a house and no dogs.
It wasn't good. I didn't like that. I've seen
snowmachines break down and fellows
freeze to death out there in the wilderness.
But dogs will always keep you warm and
they'll always get you there.*
  ~Joe Redington, "Father of the Iditarod"

The Alaska Railroad Commission authorized the construction of
the Iditarod Trail in the early 1900s, after gold was discovered in the remote
Bering Sea community of Nome and the Interior village of Iditarod, a name
said to mean "distant place" in the local indigenous language. During the winter
months, when northern ports were icebound, miners used dog sleds to shuttle
mail, gold ore, and supplies to the villages. More than a thousand miners settled
in Iditarod; an even greater number were located in Nome. The Iditarod Trail
was finished in 1910; there was a roadhouse every twenty miles, or about a day's
walk for a man. Even as the Gold Rush began to fizzle, the Iditarod Trail continued to serve as the main mail route through the Interior until airplanes became
the preferred cargo carrier in 1932.

In 1925, Nome was gripped with a diphtheria outbreak in the depth of winter. By late January, the only doctor in Nome had confirmed twenty cases, with
fifty more at risk. At the time Nome had a population of 10,000, and without
serum the mortality rate of diphtheria was 100 percent. With bush piloting still
in its infancy and no planes readily available for use, the territory's governor
launched a "Great Race of Mercy" to shuttle antitoxin by train from Anchorage
to Nenana, and then by dog sled to Nome on a northern mail route — several
hundred miles north of the Iditarod Trail — that at the time was the shortest
overland distance to the Bering Sea town. Just before midnight on January 27,

the first of twenty mushers took the twenty-pound cylinder of serum and set out on a 674-mile relay involving more than a hundred dogs.

The first musher in the relay was "Wild Bill Shannon," who placed the twenty-pound package of serum on a sled driven by a team of nine inexperienced dogs. Horse-made holes in the trail forced the team onto the Tanana River, where the temperature dropped to sixty-two below. Despite jogging alongside his sled to stay warm, Shannon developed hypothermia. When he reached Minto at 3 a.m., patches of frostbite blackened his face, and three of his dogs were dying. After resting by the fire for four hours, Shannon continued down the trail with six dogs, finishing the seventy-mile leg at 11 a.m. A half-Athabaskan man named Edgar Kallands took over from there, in temperatures that had risen to fifty-six below. Reportedly, the owner of the roadhouse at Manley Hot Springs had to pour hot water over Kallands' hands to pry them from the sled's handlebar when he arrived five hours later.

Temperatures remained perilously low during the race through the Interior. Two more dogs died, succumbing to groin frostbite, on the next leg of the route. As a Native musher named Victor Anagick approached the coast, a swirling storm prompted him to portage around the dangerous sea ice on the hilly coast. Whiteout conditions drove the wind chill to minus seventy, and "the eddies of drifting, swirling snow passing between the dogs' legs and under the bellies made them appear to be fording a fast-running river," Anagick later recounted.

A Norwegian named Gunnar Kassen, along with his soon-to-be famous lead dog, Balto, arrived on Front Street in Nome just five and a half days after the relay departed Nenana. Historians estimate that several dozen children and adults were saved by the prompt arrival of the serum. And while Balto became the public symbol of the 1925 serum run, most mushers consider Leonhard Seppala and his lead dog, Togo, to be the true heroes of the relay. Seppala's team covered 91 miles — the farthest distance — on the most hazardous section of the route, including a treacherous crossing of the frozen Norton Sound. The crossing significantly shortened the overland route, but a low-pressure weather system moved in over Seppala's team. Having crossed the sea ice before, Seppala made the decision to charge into the violent storm, encountering wind chills estimated at eighty-five below and gale-force gusts so loud that he could no longer hear potential warning sounds from the shifting sea ice. By the time the team returned to land, the ice had broken up altogether and drifted out to sea.

Kassen collected the serum and transported it on the final leg of the relay, continuing to fight winds so severe that a gust flipped his sled over and nearly discharged the serum. Visibility was so poor that he often couldn't see the dogs harnessed closest to his sled. But together, the dog teams covered the 674 miles in 127.5 hours, a monumental effort given the extreme subzero temperatures, blizzard conditions and hurricane-force winds. A number of dogs died during and after the grueling journey.

Several mushers went on to receive international recognition, and Kassen and Balto were widely heralded as heroes. The media largely ignored the Native mushers, who covered two-thirds of the distance to Nome during the serum relay. According to Edgar Kallands, "it was just an everyday occurrence as far as we were concerned."

✳ ✳ ✳ ✳ ✳

The Iditarod Trail itself slowly fell into disuse as the Gold Rush waned, boom towns cleared out, and aircraft became more widely used to deliver mail and supplies to villages. The thin white line across Alaska might have disappeared altogether, were it not for a homesteader named Joe Redington. The future Alaskan was born February 1, 1917, in a tent on the banks of the Cimmaron River in Oklahoma. His mother left when he was just a few years old. His father was a farm laborer who spent the warm seasons following the wheat harvest from Texas to Nebraska to Canada. In the winter they sought temporary housing, at times burning corn cobs for warmth in the drafty quarters of a granary as temperatures plunged to 14 below zero.

With no anchored sense of home, young Redington was drawn to the lore of the Alaskan frontier. Despite only itinerant schooling, Redington loved to read and devoured the works of Jack London and tales about Leonhard Seppala, a musher who came to Nome in 1900 and became Alaska's most prominent dog driver in the first half of the 20th century. Redington was eight years old when Seppala and other mushers ran the dog-team relay across Alaska with diphtheria medicine. As a boy, he was enthralled.

"A dog team, that's what I wanted," remembered Redington.

Although he never attended school beyond the sixth grade, Redington joined the Army in 1940, and served as a motor pool sergeant for the paratroopers in World War II. He married and had a son in 1943, although the relationship with his wife, Cathy, quickly became tense. After he was released from the Army in 1945, Redington and his family, along with his brother Ray and Ray's wife, Vi, moved to Pennsylvania, where Redington became a jeep salesman. Returning home from work one evening, he made a snap decision to leave the eastern United States and move to Alaska.

"I decided that wasn't what I wanted. I decided overnight to go to Alaska."

The crew loaded a vehicle and headed up the Alaska Highway. They established a homestead in Knik — a tiny community in the Susitna Valley — paying thirteen dollars to lay claim to 101 acres. It was all Redington could afford. The federal government didn't ask much of Alaska homesteaders — only that they pay their filing fee, move in, and make some effort to improve the property. Right away, the two families started accumulating huskies.

Before he came to Alaska, Redington admitted that he had no specific knowledge of the Iditarod Trail. One could say it was fate that he happened to settle land just a few hundred feet away from the historic route.

"When I first came to Alaska, I didn't know anything about anything, really," he said. "I was very fortunate to meet an old-timer who was the last sled-dog mail carrier here in Knik. He always seemed to talk to me about dog mushing, and he gave me a lot of history of the Iditarod Trail. I fell in love with the Iditarod immediately. I felt it was a trail that should continue to be used."

After just a few years in Alaska, the two couples' marriages began to unravel and both were divorced. Joe became estranged from his brother, Ray, and married Vi in 1953. Years after the painful dissolution of marriages and melding of families, Joe joked about the circumstances surrounding his and Vi's love affair.

"I think I had a choice of Cathy or the dogs," he said. "I took the dogs."

After World War II, fascination with motor and air transportation gripped the nation. Redington went the other way, clinging to an already outdated way of life. Lee Ellexson, a former mail carrier whose job ended in 1920, took Redington on his first mushing trip on the Iditarod Trail. Redington devoured Ellexson's stories and imagined a life where he could travel like Ellexson across the length of Alaska, traversing the tundra and back again. During this time, he also started to tune in to broadcasts of dog sled championships on radio. There hadn't been any serious dog racing in Alaska since the 408-mile All-Alaska Sweepstakes had ended in 1917, however, a new style of racing was coming into prominence — sprint mushing. Although Redington didn't race his work dogs, he became a fan.

Joe and Vi Redington established a second homestead at Flathorn Lake in 1953, and until they moved back to Knik in 1968, lived the hardscrabble life of an early 19th century frontier family. For months at a time they managed a pure subsistence lifestyle, though Joe took a variety of jobs to supplement their income. He worked self-imposed long hours, going for years sleeping only four hours a night, sometimes only one hour in the summer.

"I never found anyone who could go like I could," Redington said. "I used to be pretty tough. That was a long time before the Iditarod."

* * * * *

Through the 1960s, many rural Alaskans and homesteaders still used dog teams to run freight across the frozen tundra. However, the advent of the snowmobile had a wildfire effect on the already fading way of life, and dog teams began to disappear from the trails in favor of the "iron dog." Redington felt a sense of loss surrounding a lifestyle he'd grown to love, and became one of the state's most vocal mushing advocates. The future of sled dogs, he concluded, was in recreational use — specifically, racing.

In 1964, a committee formed to look into events to commemorate the centennial of Alaska's establishment as a U.S. territory. Dorothy Page, the group's chairman, conceived the idea of a sled dog race on the historic Iditarod Trail. Redington enthusiastically signed onto the idea, and led a volunteer effort to establish a sprint race and clear nine miles of the Iditarod Trail near his Knik homestead. A fifty-six-mile Centennial Race between Knik and Big Lake was held in 1967 and again in 1969. After the celebrations ended, public interest waned.

Redington, on the other hand, was more fired up than ever. He had amassed a grand vision for an endurance race of a distance no one had yet conceived — one thousand miles across Alaska. Mushers would race through the day and night, carrying their own supplies and sometimes breaking their own trails through subzero cold and blizzards. As a reward, he said, the race would offer a purse of $50,000. Redington's mushing group didn't have a dime. Critics questioned the irresponsibility of sending dozens of mushers into the uninhabited Alaska backcountry. Newspapers called him the "Don Quixote of Alaska." All but two of his supporters walked away.

A small, wiry man with boundless energy, Redington countered with optimism. "If you don't have a plan," he liked to say, "That's one less thing that can go wrong."

Redington mortgaged his home and sold a piece of his land near Flathorn Lake to help finance his dream event's start-up costs. Two school teachers, Gleo Huyck and Tom Johnson, began planning and fundraising in October 1972. Howard Farley and other Nome residents help establish the northern segment of the Iditarod Trail, and the U.S. Army opened up more than 200 miles of trail from Farewell Lake to Knik as part of a winter exercise. Thanks to these efforts, the first official Iditarod Dog Sled Race launched in March 1973 with thirty-four mushers, twenty-two of whom completed the race. While his dogs ran with other mushers in the race, Redington continued his efforts to raise money for the promised $50,000 purse for the duration of the event. Dick Wilmarth and his lead dog, Hotfoot, won the first Iditarod in what today would be considered a leisurely twenty days.

Although Redington and his group couldn't offer the same purse prize in 1974, Iditarod fever had taken hold and the second race drew a field of forty-four. Corporate sponsorship was established in 1975, when Emmitt Peters brought the winning time from twenty days down to fourteen and a half. The first musher to finish in less than ten days was Jeff King in 1996. In 2014, a third-generation family legacy musher named Dallas Seavey established the fastest winning time so far in eight days, thirteen hours, and four minutes. Joe Redington went on to race the Iditarod several times over the years. His best finish was fifth place, which he achieved in 1988 at the age of seventy-one.

Despite financial ups and downs over the years, the Iditarod dog sled race has only grown in popularity since its first year. The Iditarod draws an annual field of fifty to seventy mushers and more than a thousand dogs, and is supported by a similarly large workforce of volunteers. People who were otherwise ordinary, hard-working Alaskans went on to become household heroes — names such as Rick Swenson, a five-time winner, and four-time winners Susan Butcher, Lance Mackey, Jeff King, and Montana resident Doug Swingley. Highly successful family legacies were established in the Redington, Seavey, and Mackey clans. Libby Riddles was the first woman to win the race in 1985. Swiss musher Martin Buser became the first international winner in 1992, and went on to win the race four times. To prepare for the thousand-mile journey, mushers train with their dogs year-round, running them with four-wheelers on dirt paths in the summertime. Dogs are subject to drug screenings and are tracked using GPS and microchips implanted under the skin.

As the dog sled race gained traction, Redington sought to entice other user groups to the Iditarod Trail. In 1983, Redington and others launched "Iditaski," the first human-powered endurance race in Alaska. The 210-mile cross-country ski race took skiers over the first hundred miles of the Iditarod Trial and back. In the mid-1980s, a hundred-mile snowshoe race launched. But human-powered Iditarod Trail racing took a turn toward international fame in 1987 when Redington approached a group called the Mountain Bikers of Alaska with an idea to launch a bicycle race on the Iditaski route. Mountain biking was still a fledgling sport at the time, and no one had ever conceived that bikes could be raced on winter trails. But the MBA accepted the challenge, and Iditabike was born.

"We don't have any idea what's going to happen, but we're willing to give this thing a try," race organizer Dan Bull told a reporter.

The Mountain Bikers of Alaska figured ten Anchorage-area riders might take on the challenge. But after a cycling publication picked up the story, the race drew twenty men and six women, most of them sponsored or semi-pro mountain bikers, from six different states and as far away as Los Angeles. Although small in terms of participants, the extreme nature of Iditabike drew sponsors and international media attention before the word "extreme" was even embedded in mountain biking's nomenclature.

Race organizers required racers to bring an array of survival gear needed to camp out in twenty below temperatures and blizzards. Since there was no set standard for carrying such gear on bicycles in the winter, each racer adopted their own strategy — some dragging sleds, some wearing backpacks, others strapping panniers to racks.

Thirteen of the twenty-six starters finished the race. Dave Zink of Minnesota and Mike Kloser of Colorado went on to cross the finish line together in thirty-three hours and fifty minutes, although Kloser would insist that Zink won in the finishing sprint. Martha Kennedy of Minnesota was the first woman to finish Iditabike in forty-two hours and fifty-nine minutes.

In 1988, fifty-three riders lined up for the second annual Iditabike. The event drew filmmaker Mark Forman, who made a twenty-four-minute documentary that aired on the Discovery Channel. The 1988 race also drew higher-profile riders such as Race Across America finisher Chris Kostman. As an experienced ultra-distance racer, Kostman expected to dominate the event, but struggled with soft snow and tire punctures. After finishing in tenth place in 45:53, Kostman received a special award for the racer who showed the most humility. The "Laddie Shaw Award" was named in honor of a first-year Iditaski racer who coined a phrase that is now famous in Iditarod Trail racing — "Cowards won't show and the weak will die." Shaw went on to drop out first in that race, inspiring the award for the most glaring hubris to be humbled by the Iditarod Trail.

Iditabike drew a similar number of riders in 1989. That same year, race organizer Dan Bull, along with Les Matz, Roger Cowles, and Mark Frise, launched the first mountain bike expedition along the thousand-mile length of the Iditarod Trail, reaching Nome in twenty-one days.

In 1991, Bull merged ski, bike, and foot races into the combined race Iditasport, held concurrently under all three disciplines, along with a "triathlon" division. In 1992 he added a running division for those who didn't want to wear snowshoes. The event drew more racers as interest in endurance events grew in the 1990s, tripling to as many as 200 participants and boasting purses of $50,000 to $80,000 for winners.

Dominating the 1990s Iditasport was Mountain Bike Hall of Famer John Stamstad, who at the time was sponsored by Chevy Trucks. Stamstad won the 170-mile version of the race in 1993, 94, 95 and 96. In 1997, the race organization began offering a 350-mile race to McGrath called the Iditasport Extreme, which Stamstad won that year and in 1998, 99, and 2000.

Bull took the organized race to its inevitable big step in 2000 with the Iditasport Impossible, an official thousand-mile race to Nome. Colorado cyclist Mike Curiak won the race on the Iditarod Trail's Northern Route in fifteen days, one hour, and fifteen minutes. This record stood as the fastest human-powered traverse of the Iditarod trail for fourteen years. In 2014, Jeff Oatley of Fairbanks took advantage of a low-snow season and hard-packed trails to shave an astonishing five days off this record, finishing in a time that would be respectable for an entire team of well-trained Iditarod dogs — ten days, two hours, and fifty-three minutes.

While human-powered Iditarod travel on a bicycle or skis seemed extreme, travel without any mechanical aid — on foot — was almost unfathomable. The Iditasport offered a foot division that generally attracted a small field of runners and trekkers. Ed Kelly was the first person to walk the entire Iditarod trail in modern times, taking forty-five days to complete the distance in 1989. In 1998, Tom Possert established the 350-mile Iditasport Extreme foot record at six days, two hours, and fifty minutes. And in 2000, the newly married couple Janine Duplessis and John Wagner of Gig Harbor, Washington, walked to Nome as a rather unconventional honeymoon, and established the thousand-mile foot record at forty-one days, ten hours, and thirty minutes.

✳ ✳ ✳ ✳ ✳

Also caught up in the allure of the Iditarod Trail was an employment lawyer from Pennsylvania named Tim Hewitt.

Tim was born October 18, 1954, in Tarentum, Pennsylvania, and grew up in the small town of Latrobe. His father worked as a director of industrial relations at a local corporation, and his mother stayed at home with Tim, his older brother, and three younger sisters. Tim's father was a standout cross-country athlete at Adrian College, and Tim became a pole vaulter in high school. He excelled at the sport, but had little interest in running.

Tim studied business administration at Northern Michigan University, where he met Loreen. He went on to law school at Stetson University College of Law in St. Petersburg, Florida. Loreen transferred to the University of Southern Florida, and they married in August 1978. Tim began a career in employment law, representing employers in negotiating collective bargaining agreements with unions, and defending employers against charges related to employment, among other cases. He and Loreen have four daughters: twins Amanda and Brittany, and Caitlin and Abby.

In law school, Tim would run with friends as a way to stay in shape, and also ran with Loreen as she trained for her first 10K race. He found running came naturally, but didn't break into racing until his early thirties, when he entered his first marathon. Even then, Tim didn't take his athletic hobby all that seriously at first, and only began training on a more competitive level in his late thirties.

Just as Tim's interest in racing gained traction, he discovered ultramarathons. His first ultra-distance race was the Laurel Highlands 70, a 70.5-mile trail race along the spine of the Laurel Highlands in Pennsylvania, which he now co-directs. Since he started racing more seriously, Tim had done well in a number of marathons; he thought he had a reasonable shot at a win in his first ultramarathon. Tom Possert — who went on several years later to set a 350-mile foot record during the Iditasport Extreme — was the reigning course record holder and had won the race seven times. Tim considered this runner from neighboring Ohio to be the main competition, and formed a strategy that revolved around staying on Tom Possert's heels.

A young runner named Eric Clifton took off from the start; Tim assumed Eric didn't know what he was doing and stayed with Tom, shadowing his every step. To keep up with Tom's long walking stride, Tim shuffled up the steep climbs, and then took off barely in control on every rocky descent. At one point, Tom stumbled and fell. Tim stepped around him and increased the pace until Tom was no longer behind him. This was a mental strategy against the reigning champion — as long as Tim stayed out of sight, Tom might lose hope that he could catch him.

Six hours in, Tim had been racing longer than he had ever raced. The day was heating up and afternoon thunderstorms arrived. Tim was nauseated and unable to hold down any food. After rain showers drenched the trail, he was careful to only vomit in puddles so Tom wouldn't know he was sick, and made extended strides through the mud to give the appearance of a healthy runner. Despite his physical distress, Tim managed to hold off Tom to the end, but never did catch Eric — although he had significantly closed the distance over the last trail section. Tim was upset that he'd become so sick, and realized that body management, strategy, and mental toughness were just as important — if not more important — as speed and fitness in an ultramarathon. Ultras were a thinking man's sport. Tim was hooked.

Although a late bloomer in competitive running, Tim has amassed an astounding race history over the past two decades. He's lost count of the number of marathons and ultramarathons he's run, but estimates the tally to be well over one hundred.

When he was fifty years old, he completed the JFK fifty-mile race in 6:29, and has more top ten finishes in JFK — the United States' longest-running ultramarathon — than anyone else. He was a U.S. 100K Masters Champion, and finished in the top ten of the USATF 100K championships in four out of four efforts. He's run nine Boston Marathons, and is one of only a handful of runners to complete all twenty-five Pittsburgh Marathons. His personal records include 16:47 for five kilometers, just under thirty-two minutes for ten kilometers, and 2:38 in the marathon. He finished what's widely considered to be the toughest hundred-mile mountain race in North America, the Hardrock 100 in Colorado, while suffering from altitude sickness so severe that a fellow competitor was convinced Tim wouldn't survive. Tim possesses above-average natural speed, but considers the mental challenge of tough ultramarathons to be his field of expertise.

"I've always been able to bend without breaking," Tim says.

In 2000, Tim competed in the Badwater Ultramarathon, a 135-mile race through Death Valley in the heat of summer — running from the lowest to highest points of North America. At mile forty-two of the race, the temperature was 127 degrees in the shade, and heat reflecting off the pavement was a scorching 186 degrees — hot enough to cook a roast. Tim was facing a fifteen-mile climb, so he opted to climb into his support car for a short break in order to take in some food and allow his body temperature to cool. This turned out to be a mistake; not only did his stomach reject all the food he ate, but when he emerged from the car to start running, the sand-blasting wind hit his skin like needles of fire. He didn't realize that cooling his skin would sensitize it further to the brutal heat. Tim ducked back into the car, ready to quit, but stubborn determination prompted him to try running one more time.

Tim is well-versed in dealing with the devil on his shoulder, the voice that feeds doubt and frustration. He engaged self-bargaining techniques, forcing himself back outside with promises that his next adventure would take place in a much cooler climate. Dreams of Alaska swirled through his heat-addled mind. Earlier that year, Tim had traveled to Alaska to run a hundred-mile race on the Iditarod Trail, setting a new course record in the process. Racing through the snow and sharply cold air of the Susitna River Valley during the Iditasport 100 had been an invigorating experience, and Tim was intrigued by a much longer distance connected to that race — the Iditasport Impossible. The Impossible traveled the length of the Iditarod Trail, more than a thousand miles across Alaska wilderness, from a town just a few miles north of Anchorage all the way to historic town of Nome on the western coast. Several cyclists had completed the thousand-mile race the previous year, but no one had yet competed in the Iditasport Impossible on foot. As it was, less than a handful of people had ever walked to Nome, and no one had done it faster than the Washington couple's journey of forty-one days.

As Tim ran up the long climb out of Death Valley, skin roasting and vision blurring, he thought that anything, even an "Impossible" race across Alaska, had to be better than what he was enduring. He finished the Badwater 135 in thirty hours and fourteen minutes, and went on to climb all the way to the summit of Mount Whitney, the highest point in North America at 14,500 feet. Standing at the crest of the Sierra Nevada and looking over the stark desert he had just crossed, Tim felt a sense of invincibility,. He thought that everything else from that point on would seem easy.

He couldn't have been more wrong, and yet this catalyst of tundra dreams in the desert would prove to be one of the most significant turning points of his life. It was out of the frying pan, and into the icebox.

The Beginning

3

The woods are lovely, dark and deep
But I have promises to keep
And miles to go before I sleep.
And miles to go before I sleep.

~Robert Frost,
"Stopping By Woods
on a Snowy Evening"

"Something is wrong," Tim thought. "It's too quiet."

A wash of stars filled the midnight sky, framed by the skeletal branches of hardwood trees — a rare sight in the inhospitable climate of Interior Alaska. Tim's plastic sled, affectionately named "Cookie," scraped quietly along the icy surface of the Iditarod Trail. Cookie nudged over the undulating moguls in the trail, pushing her forty-five pounds of momentum into Tim's back as he crested the next mound. The jerky rhythm had become familiar to Tim, peaceful, after nearly two weeks of relentless marching toward Nome. The temperature, which Tim estimated to be around minus ten, gave some teeth to the air, but didn't saturate it with cold.

"And there's no wind," Tim thought, as though he'd suddenly arrived at the conclusion of exactly what was wrong. "There's always wind."

Tim wondered if he had simply forgotten to pay attention to the wind; for several hours he'd been preoccupied with thoughts of Anvik, a tiny Athabascan village on the banks of the Yukon River that was his next checkpoint destination. There, he would enter the jarring warmth of a school, find his drop bag to refill his sled with food and fuel, and maybe, if he could reach the village by 2 a.m., even call his wife Loreen in Pennsylvania before she went for her weekend morning run. Memories of home filled his thoughts, and he became lost in them. It would soon be early morning on the East Coast; friends and family would be pulling back the soft covers of their beds, frying bacon and eggs in their kitchens, walking dogs on dry sidewalks, getting into cars to drive on paved streets with an ease of movement that was almost unfathomable. Cookie tugged on her harness and Tim's thoughts swung back to his own immediate future: the darkened windows of Anvik and the intimidating expanse of white beyond — referred by those who know the Iditarod Trail only with the utmost reverence as "The Mighty Yukon."

The Yukon River — the great waterway that cuts through the heart of Alaska on its journey to the Bering Sea — is more than a mile wide where the Southern Route of the Iditarod Trail joins it for one hundred and fifty miles atop windswept ice. The banks are more than a hundred feet high, but are usually far enough away to appear tiny. Wind blows furiously and unceasingly down the river corridor on its own roaring journey to the sea. The Southern Route of the Iditarod Trail travels upriver. In preparation for his first attempt to complete the thousand-mile journey to Nome, Tim anticipated this headwind with trepidation. How would he manage to push into hurricane-force gusts for one hundred and fifty miles? Just how cold would it be?

But now, at the entrance to the Mighty Yukon, the air was as calm as a spring morning. Tom Jarding, a friend of Tim's from Pennsylvania and now a fellow competitor in the Iditasport Impossible race to Nome, shadowed Tim about a hundred yards back. They had seen signs staked by Iditarod Dog Sled Race volunteers indicating that the Yukon was just two miles away.

"Why is this so comfortable?" Tim wondered. "This feels too easy."

Almost as soon as he started to feel uneasy about his own complacency, a breeze swirled through the trees and stirred up puffs of powder snow. The trail continued to meander through the deep forest, and Tim wondered if they'd entered a slough or stream above the Yukon. The flatter terrain surrounding the massive river made it impossible to distinguish whether the packed snow they traveled was over water or over land, but the new breeze led Tim to suspect they had dropped into a drainage. The low moaning of the wind became more persistent, and the branches of trees above them began swishing back and forth. Wind is indeed the default condition in Alaska, Tim thought, and his mind continued to drift four thousand miles away to his wife and four daughters in their warm beds.

But as the trail widened and the forest retreated into the distance, the wind became more persistent. Snow swirled around Tim's feet, occasionally lifting high enough to obscure his vision — a phenomenon known as a "ground blizzard." The gusts seemed to be pushing at his back, which confused Tim. In talking to dog sled mushers before the race, Tim was told that the headwind on the Yukon was so constant that "if you find the wind at your back, turn around because you're going the wrong way." But he was still following forward-facing trail markers, and when he looked down, he could see the tracks of husky paws pressing into the trail in the same direction. The tracks were even more comforting than the trail markers. Tim trusted dogs. Not surprisingly, he felt more kinship with the dogs of the Iditarod Trail than he did with the mushers.

The trail emerged from the woods and plummeted down a twenty-foot river bank, then made an abrupt turn, becoming perpendicular with the wind. Blowing snow pelted Tim's side and the thirty-mile-per-hour persistent crosswind drove needles of frigid air through the foam-covered vents of his neoprene face mask. Even with the mask, a thermal balaclava, goggles and three hoods, the icy wind still stung his face and eyes. Tim lifted his gloved hand to shield his face; he had no more layers to add.

As Tim expected of the Mighty Yukon, the wind-chill factor was off the charts. But something still didn't seem right about this quartering crosswind. As he turned around to check on Tom's progress, Tim saw a light approaching from behind. Lights on the frozen Yukon River after midnight are a rare enough sight to be alarming for most of the winter. However, Tim and Tom were also traveling in the midst of the Iditarod Dog Sled Race, and shared the trail with sixty-some mushers who were attempting to drive dog teams to Nome. They'd watched half of the field pass in the preceding days, and this musher seemed to be overtaking at a much slower pace than the race leaders. Tim looked over his shoulders and waited as long as he could to yield the narrow trail by stepping into the knee-deep snow to the side. When the musher finally passed, she greeted Tim with an indecipherable grunt — just enough for Tim to realize that this driver buried in bulky clothing was a woman — and continued into the encompassing night.

As they approached the west bank, Tim realized that the forest they were heading toward wasn't the river bank — it was an island. The trail had been cut to go around the island rather than directly across the cluster of trees. They'd been traveling south on the Yukon River, which is why the wind felt "wrong" to him, and as the trail made another sharp turn, his intuition was validated. They faced due north into a direct onslaught of tumultuous wind.

As he pressed into the tunnel of blowing snow, Tim saw the musher's headlight about a half mile ahead, jerking back and forth. Was she looking for something? Had she lost a dog? After a few minutes, her headlight circled back and headed directly toward him. The light stopped, started, swung around, and stopped again. As the distance between them shortened, Tim saw the stalled sled and a string of fourteen dogs sitting in the snow.

"Gee, gee Louie!" the musher shouted over the roar of the wind. "Louie, gee!"

Louie must be the lead dog, Tim thought. Louie appeared to be in the midst of a mutiny supported by the rest of the team. Tim couldn't say he blamed them — he'd pulled his own sled six hundred miles at that point, and he could understand the dogs' reluctance to push into the driving wind with no reward in sight. He'd probably plop down on the trail himself if his brain weren't wired to make higher commands against his body's wishes. In the case of the dogs, the higher commands were in the musher's brain, and she had clearly lost control.

Tim pulled up beside her and asked if there was anything he could do to help. He half expected her to wave him off — accepting outside assistance is prohibited by Iditarod race rules, both in the dog sled race and the human-powered version. So he was surprised by her plea to "grab Louie?"

In preparing for the thousand-mile race to Nome, Tim steeled himself to expect the unexpected, to be flexible and bend with the circumstances. He was in this race for adventure, and adversity was adventure. But he hadn't expected to intervene in a standoff between a surly dog and its frenzied owner. Still, what else could he do? Tim wrapped his mittens around the dog's harness while calling to Louie, in the hope that knowing the right name would prevent the animal from sinking its teeth into his arm. Louie crouched into a huddle. Tim felt a rush of guilt, as though he were betraying a fellow lead dog. But Louie seemed eager to give up his command and obeyed as Tim started pulling him up the trail. The other dogs followed obediently, and soon the team broke free of Tim's grasp and continued up the trail.

Filled with satisfaction at his good deed, Tim proceeded into the wind with renewed vigor. But within minutes the musher's headlight rotated back toward him. Fueled by a fierce tailwind, the dogs streaked back down the trail with reckless abandon. Tim dove sideways to avoid the canine stampede, followed by Tom, who was now directly behind him. As the dogs streamed past, Tim reached out to grab Louie and force him to a halt. The musher and Tim untangled the dogs, and Tim took his position back at the front of the pack to pull the team forward. Like launching a kite, Louie and the team were off again. The third dog on the line leapt over Tim's sled, tangling itself in the harness and pulling Tim off of his feet. In an instant he felt the stampede of dog feet over his legs as the team dragged his tangled body and sled through a blast of cold snow. The musher yelled something, but Tim couldn't hear what she said and wasn't interested anyway.

As Tom ran toward them, Tim screamed, "Grab Louie!" His mind, attached to the helpless body being dragged along the cold ice of the Mighty Yukon like a piece of road kill, couldn't help but seize on the curiosity of it all, that defining point of origin that he was continuously trying to retrace. The question wasn't just how he got there — but where did he think he was going?

✳ ✳ ✳ ✳ ✳

A logical mind like Tim Hewitt's knows that completing a thousand-mile journey across frozen Alaska hinges on successfully solving a series of equations:

preparation, adaptation, and execution. Sure, in the Alaskan backcountry —
where weather can turn on a breath and trail conditions fluctuate just as rapidly
— there was an undeniable percentage of luck involved. However, even the most
unexpected and uncontrollable variables could be mitigated by arriving at the
start line as prepared as possible.

But how does one prepare for something that, even thirteen years later, only
a few dozen people have achieved? In 2001, that number was markedly smaller — fewer than twenty people had completed the human-powered journey to
Nome, and most of them were on double-rimmed bicycles or skis. It was the
second year of the Iditasport Impossible, the first "full-distance" bicycle, ski, and
foot race that ran concurrently with the 350-mile Iditasport Extreme from Knik
to McGrath, and the 130-mile Iditasport to Finger Lake. Although seventeen
racers had started with the intention of traveling the full distance across Alaska,
by the time Tim arrived at the Yukon River that number had fallen to four —
himself and Tom Jarding on foot, and Andy Heading and Mike Estes on bicycle.

In an endeavor where everyone was a novice and the attrition rate was high,
Tim knew that he needed to be fully self-sufficient and use his imagination to
prepare for a number of possibilities. At the same time, he couldn't let himself
be weighed down by over-preparation. As climbers say, people pack their inse-
curities. Tim knew from his experience in the hundred-mile race in 2000, along
with stories of failures among others, that excess weight exponentially reduces
chances of success. The proper balance of enough, but not too much, had to be
attained. Survival gear such as a sleeping bag, bivy sack, and medical supplies
were necessities, as were a stove, fuel, and pot to melt snow for drinking water,
in addition to food, warm clothing, matches, a headlamp, and spare batteries.
Food, fuel, batteries, and other restocked necessities would be sent ahead in drop
bags to twelve checkpoints along the course. For Tim, the ultimate question
wasn't "What do I need to get myself to Nome?" but "What can I do without?"

For competitors on foot, a sled is the most logical way to carry supplies. The
additional weight of a backpack causes runners to sink deeper into the snow or
more frequently break through thin crust on the packed trail. Backpacks also
add to the strain on legs and feet. In addition to pulling gear, sleds also can be
used as a shovel to quickly build a snow shelter, a protective wall against the
wind, or a bed. Tim, being a meticulous planner, tested a number of plastic sleds
designed for use as children's toys before settling on a four-foot "ugly turquoise"
platform of molded plastic that was one-eighth of an inch thick with two runners pressed into the base. It weighed about four pounds and connected to a
backpack hip belt through bungee cords run through two five-foot lengths of
light gauge, half-inch-diameter plastic pipe. "Cookie" was born.

On the floor of the plastic sled, Tim used a permanent marker to record trail
notes — the checkpoints listed in order, the distance between each one, and the
distance between drop bags. The last column listed special items in the drop

bags at each checkpoint, such as fuel or spare shoes. Food for one day weighed three to four pounds. At that weight, Tim could only afford to carry one day's worth of spare food, so knowing the items in each drop bag would be key. While having this information readily available seemed like a good idea at the time, the duffel inside of the sled shifted relentlessly during the race, rubbing away most of the ink within days.

Instead the duffel was everything Tim needed to survive in the frozen Alaska wilderness for four weeks — a four-pound, 900-fill down sleeping bag rated to twenty-five below zero, a Gore-Tex bivy sack that weighed one and a half pounds, a closed-cell foam ground pad cut to two feet by seven feet, two headlights, batteries, a two-quart aluminum pot with the handle removed to reduce weight, an MSR WhisperLite stove, white gas fuel, overflow boots for navigating open water, a small first-aid kit, "Don's Trail Notes" for the Iditarod Trail, and spare clothing, including a number of socks: two pairs wool sock liners, one pair heavy wool socks, neoprene socks, and Gore-Tex over-socks. Clothing consisted of a pair of Hind Drylete tights, Polypro briefs, Gore-Tex wind pants, a Capilene long-sleeve top base layer, a Polypro top mid-layer, and a polar fleece thermal layer. The fourth layer was a hooded stretch polar fleece jacket with a zipper to turn the hood into a balaclava. For a fifth layer, Tim carried a Marmot windproof polar fleece vest with many pockets, and the sixth layer was a windproof ultralight hooded Patagonia jacket. The seventh layer was a Gore-Tex expedition-weight hooded shell, extra large in size. Last was a Marmot down jacket for emergencies, and for comfort while stopped. For his hands, Tim had stretch polar fleece gloves and a windproof outer layer, as well as wool liner mittens and Gore-Tex mitten shells. An insulated hat, neoprene face mask, and ski goggles completed the outfit. Over the years, Tim would make marked changes and reductions to his clothing, but this gives an idea of the system he used during his first year on the trail.

For water, he carried a seventy-ounce insulated bladder on his back, supplemented by a two one-liter plastic bottles inside insulated pouches. This worked to keep the liquid from freezing quickly, and gave him a day's supply of water until he could again melt snow. Food consisted of beef jerky, freeze-dried meals, ramen noodles, trail mix, nuts, sesame seeds, candy, peanut butter, tuna, smoked salmon, sausage, chocolate, cheese, dried fruit, and occasionally fruit pies. Altogether, the sled and supplies weighed about forty-five pounds. If this appears excessive, Tim assures that for that first year on the trail, it wasn't. There were times on the trail that he wore every stitch of clothing he carried, and lost weight despite his steady diet of high-calorie food. Later, as he gained more experience and confidence, he would steadily refine everything about his supplies.

✳ ✳ ✳ ✳ ✳

Before the start of the 2001 Iditasport, Tim made it clear that he was in the race to win — in all three distances if possible. Tom Jarding, Tim's friend from Pennsylvania who had previously completed the 100-mile and 350-mile versions of the Iditasport, hoped he and Tim would form a partnership and travel together.

Tom and Tim had known each other for about five years, since Tom dialed Tim's phone out of the blue in 1996 and offered to crew for Tim at a hundred-mile ultramarathon called the Vermont 100, which Tim had run the previous year as his first hundred-mile race. Tom was a stranger to Tim but seemed to know all about him — races run, finishing times, records. Tom seemed something of a fan; Tim joked with his wife that Tom came across as a stalker. But he agreed to join him in Vermont, where Tim finished second in the race.

After the race, they drove back to Pennsylvania in a van with several other runners. Tom regaled Tim with stories of the Iditasport in Alaska. He described his finish in the 350-mile Extreme, when he spent much of the race sick and alone, and arrived in McGrath after the race banner had already been removed. Before meeting Tom, Tim had never heard of the Iditasport, but was immediately intrigued. He'd long been a fan of the dog sled race, and the thought of a human-powered race on the same course was irresistible.

Tom is a postal worker with a foot delivery route. He held all of the speed records on his route — not a trait that endeared him to his co-workers, Tim joked, but did make him a good old-school ultrarunner. They shared other common interests; Tom is one year younger, loves bluegrass music, and lived about half hour away with his wife, Deb, and daughter, Leah. Tim and Loreen ended up traveling with Tom to Alaska for the 2000 Iditasport 100. During that race, Tom caught up while Tim was experiencing a bout of stomach sickness. Even as Tim began to feel better, Tom persuaded him to stick together so they could tie for the foot record in the hundred-mile race. Tim agreed, but after they finished he still felt strong enough to return to mile ninety of the course to meet his wife and run the final ten miles with her.

This was the root of their complicated dynamic as friends and competitors — Tom sought to latch on to the stronger runner to fuel his competitive ambitions, and Tim believed in the advantages of camaraderie and working as a team. As both men became interested in the thousand-mile Iditasport Impossible, Tim knew that Tom already had experience finishing the 350-mile race to McGrath, and hoped to benefit from that experience. He also knew a race that would take three weeks or more to complete would be difficult to manage entirely alone — as the saying goes, misery loves company. But Tim also knew he had a chance of winning the race and wasn't going to let Tom hold him back.

Tom argued that pushing hard in the early miles was too risky for competitors in the long race. Tim agreed that staying together in such dangerous conditions would be mutually beneficial, but he wasn't willing to make any promises.

He had only tapped the edge of his strength while racing the hundred-mile Iditasport in twenty-two hours, and felt confident that he could stay competitive while saving energy for the later stages. He knew he needed to move slower than the limit his body could tolerate at any given moment of a multi-week endeavor, and felt that sixty to seventy percent effort was the most efficient level for the distance.

Pulling a forty-five-pound sled, however, is a great equalizer. Aerobic capacity and leg speed do not pay the same dividends on snow as they do on trails or roads. Even with all of his past successes in running, Tim understood the limitations as well. First and foremost he wanted to finish the race, but he set an ambitious target of twenty-six days. Prior to 2001, the fastest anyone had completed the distance on foot was nearly forty-two days.

During the pre-race briefing, Tim and Tom listened to reports about lack of snow in the Interior and unstable sea ice on the Norton Sound crossing. Tim fretted about the sturdiness of his sled if he was required to pull it across rocks and open tundra, and whether the sea ice would freeze solid before he reached that point on the course. Race director Dan Bull joked that while no one had yet died during the Iditasport, it was likely to happen and would probably be good for publicity. The light-hearted jab rang true and sent an air of uneasiness through the crowd.

After a too-short review of notes about a thousand miles of trail, Tim left the briefing with an unsettling sense that he knew even less than before. But his resolve remained unscathed. He knew before arriving in Alaska that there were imminent and unpredictable dangers, but his prior participation in the hundred-mile race and extensive ultrarunning background gave him confidence that he knew his own limits and was up to the task. He never seriously considered that he would not finish the race. The only question in his mind was how long it would take.

The 2001 Iditasport launched at 3 p.m. from the Knik Bar, a log cabin watering hole on a dead-end highway near Wasilla, Alaska. While driving to the start, Tim and Tom traveled from a blue-sky day in Anchorage into an ice cloud just a few miles north.

"This can't be a good sign," Tim thought. The Knik Bar looked like a scene from "Star Wars," with dozens of racers huddled in their high-tech athletic gear while locals in snowmobile suits, Carhartt work jackets, and winter boots guzzled mugs of beer and eyed the racing crowd suspiciously. The air temperature was a brisk ten degrees, but Tim felt more comfortable waiting outside.

Since Tim had won the hundred-mile race the previous year, several foot racers approached him to ask for advice. Tim offered them what he considered false assurances. "Why not?" he thought. "These people look like they're awaiting execution." Little could be said or done that would make a difference now.

As the minutes ticked toward 3 p.m., bundled-up athletes emerged from the bar and began to congregate on the frozen shoreline of Knik Lake. Nervous chatter streamed up from the crowd in clouds of condensed breath. Sled dogs tied near the starting line contributed their own barks and howls to the building chorus. A rushed ten-second countdown launched the foot racers into a mad dash across the hard ice, or at least as much of a mad dash as they could muster while dragging forty-five-pound sleds. Tim and Tom clawed up the steep bank on the other side of the lake and emerged on a narrow trail surrounded by a cluster of birch trees. This trail — a ribbon of packed snow carved by snowmobiles and dog sleds through a sweeping expanse of untrammeled powder — would be their sole guiding beacon for the next nine hundred and ninety-nine miles.

As part of his strategy to win all three legs of the race, Tim believed he needed to maintain an early lead to the first checkpoint on Flathorn Lake, about thirty miles from the race start. At Flathorn, the Iditasport organization instituted a mandatory rest and camp-out to ensure each racer had adequate gear and supplies to survive a cold night out on the trail. A restart the following morning would launch the nonstop race, and times to Flathorn would be added to the total. A "stage" win going into Flathorn would give Tim a crucial edge in the mental game against his competitors.

After the initial climb, the trail meandered through the woods over low-rolling hills, with gentle grades. Tim settled in behind a group of skiers and increased his pace to stay with them as they glided over the snow.

"Tim!" Tom yelled from behind. "We're going to Nome!" Tim let the words wash over him as pre-race jitters melted into a comfortable flow. The egg-yolk-colored sun hovered above the tip of Mount Susitna on its lazy winter arc along the southern horizon. In just two more short hours, its weak rays would be entirely extinguished, and Tim knew that long winter nights meant slower progress. Daylight meant speed, and he would take advantage of his abundant energy and ease of movement while he still had it.

With Tom behind and no other runners ahead, Tim traded positions with some of the faster cross-country skiers as well as mid-pack cyclists. While climbing hills, he would lean forward and power-walk up the steep grades, passing others with ease, only to be passed again on hard-packed descents by those with wheels and skis to glide. On long flat sections, he kept pace with the skiers, and soon passed more cyclists as the snow surface became softer. He treated this first segment of trail like a competitive marathon, even though there were few similarities. Still, he relished in the challenge of competing head to head with athletes who possessed tools he did not. Tim didn't fret about going out too hard — he was still in his comfort zone, and either way, there was no question in his mind that he was going to Nome.

As he settled into a sustainable race pace, the fatigue of jet lag and limited sleep before the race began to creep into his consciousness. His stomach churned as he ran. Before the race Tom had supplied him with a hot, cinnamon-flavored gel called "Fireballs." Although such a strong flavor seemed like a good idea before the race, Tim was now reeling with the fiery alcohol aftertaste of cinnamon Schnapps, accompanied by cold shivers every time he forced one down. The cinnamon gels were all he had to eat for this first leg of the race, as he planned to stick to performance food for this "fast" stage. There was little he could do but endure the assault on his throat and stomach.

Tim marched onto another steep ascent just as a dog team crested the hill and plunged down the other side. The banks of the trail were too steep to step off the path, and his sled drifted into the middle of the trail even as he jumped to the edge. The lead dog passed with tongue flapping, sprinting like a greyhound at the track. Tim froze. The musher screamed something at his dogs and leaned downhill to lift his sled onto one runner. The maneuver worked in avoiding Tim, but as the dog sled came back down it hooked Tim's sled, with Tim attached, and yanked him backward. While sliding downhill, Tim somehow managed to stay on his feet until the sled released, causing his body to slingshot forward into a snowdrift. After checking to make sure nothing was damaged, he called it a lucky break and continued climbing. Dog team tangles were one obstacle he hadn't anticipated before the race, but he was sure there would be more unexpected surprises.

As darkness fell, Tim emerged from the woods onto an open swamp, where the surface of the trail deteriorated. First came a layer of sugary drifted snow, and then a thin crust that collapsed into knee-deep powder as Tim walked. He strapped on his snowshoes and continued marching past cyclists who had been forced off their bikes. One was thirteen-year-old Ben Coutier, who had gained some publicity by being the youngest person to attempt the 350-mile Iditasport Extreme, which he was riding with his father. "Look, Dad, a walker is passing us," Ben complained as Tim edged by them.

As darkness settled, snow began to fall in large amounts, accumulating on the trail. Cookie tugged heavily in the thick powder, and Tim's energy was flagging. All of the excitement of the race start had faded; this was real now. Tim's core temperature was dropping and shivers gripped his limbs. Although the air temperature had dipped below zero, his body was working far too hard to feel as cold as he felt. He needed real food to replenish his energy stores, which would in turn reboot his internal furnace.

But Flathorn Lake did not arrive easily. Tim dropped onto an open slough, a frozen arm of the lake still several miles from the checkpoint. His headlight was dying, but he was too anxious about the thought of another foot racer catching him to stop and change batteries. A cyclist passed, churning over the fragile crust, and Tim followed using the cyclist's light as a beacon. As the surface changed to hard ice, the bike pulled away and Tim was left alone in the dark. He wandered off the main trail and edged toward a flickering light in the distance. As he approached, he saw snowmobiles, a campfire, and another foot racer and cyclist making their way toward the group on the main trail. Tim sprinted through knee-deep snow and managed to arrive at the checkpoint just seconds ahead of the second-place runner, David Dent of Portland, Oregon.

The scene at the checkpoint was straight out of an apocalyptic movie — a party happening at the end of the world. On a wide, frozen lake steeped in ice fog and expansive darkness, five raging bonfires flickered and popped. Surrounding the flames was a junkyard of camping equipment and snowmobiles. Volunteers and spectators cooked hamburgers on charcoal grills. Racers moved zombie-like through the crowds and surrounded the campfires, or sprawled out in sleeping bags in the snow. A crew from the television show "Ripley's Believe It Or Not" was filming. Tim took all of it in with amazement.

He didn't stand still for long. It was ten below zero and he was soaked in sweat. Within minutes he was wracked with violent shivering, and his fingers were rigid with cold. His hands moved in slow motion as he attempted to unpack his sled and unload his sleeping bag. Tim dove inside the down cocoon and worked on changing out of his wet clothing, then emerged to stand by the campfire and wait for Tom.

By 2 a.m., more than two hundred people had congregated at the encampment. Some could not stay warm in their bags and remained huddled beside the fire. Most did not have tents, and the camp resembled a post-battle graveyard with bodies wrapped in bivy sacks. Tim tossed and turned for several hours before giving up on sleep. From inside his sleeping bag, he fired up his stove on an extension of his sleeping pad to cook a breakfast of cheddar mashed potatoes. He tore open the cellophane bag only to watch freeze-dried potato powder fly everywhere — into his sleeping bag, between the bag and his bivy sack, into the snow. Undaunted, he spooned potato-flavored snow into his pot. It would be many hours before the race restart would release Tim from this anxious waiting. He passed time by eating slowly and writing in his journal, and trying not to fixate on the nine hundred and seventy miles ahead.

At 10 a.m., the field restarted in a strong headwind and drifting snow. Runners, skiers, and hiking cyclists formed a single-file line to march through the calf-deep powder. The route crossed an open swamp and dropped onto the Yentna River, where snowdrifts didn't align with the trail. Markers were sporadic. Pressure ridges — large slabs of broken ice pushed vertically out of the river — created short but almost impossibly steep climbs. Tim traveled with Tom, a Montanan named Andrew Matalonis, and a six-foot-four veteran of the Extreme race who had styled himself as the "Italian Moose," Roberto Ghidoni. As Tom and Roberto drifted back, Tim and Andrew took turns breaking trail, running when they could. Tim still had his eyes on the prize, a thousand dollar purse for the first runner to reach the 130-mile point at a remote lodge on Finger Lake.

Accumulating snow eventually made it impossible to run. Tim and Andrew made a quick stop at Yentna Station checkpoint, mile fifty-seven, to eat soup and dry their wet clothes, and were again on their way as the whiteout storm morphed almost imperceptibly into darkness. Cyclists and skiers had slowed to the point that the runners were passing nearly everyone who had been ahead.

The group faced another thirty-five miles of trudging through deep snow before reaching the next outpost on the trail. Going into his third night without real sleep, Tim found his concentration waning, and he frequently drifted off the trail into the bottomless powder to the side. Snowshoes did little to support the effort; instead, they anchored his feet in such a way that he couldn't lift his legs high enough to clear the powder. They were more like snowplows than snowshoes. He decided to take them off and battle every thigh-deep plunge without fins attached to his feet. Unnerving hallucinations began to appear in his peripheral vision.

At about midnight, Tim's leg punched through the snow crust into a sink of icy water below. In a panic he lunged forward and dove onto his stomach just as the water rose to mid-thigh level. In Alaska, uneven freezes on large and fast-flowing rivers often cause a phenomenon called "overflow," where liquid water is pushed on top of ice. The water is covered in snow before it has a chance to re-freeze, insulating the pools and hiding them from sight. These icy puddles can be deep, and present what is perhaps the most dangerous hazard for winter travelers in Alaska — the prospect of becoming soaked in subzero temperatures. Tim struggled out of the hole as the outer layer of his wind pants froze in a shell of ice. As he pulled himself to his hands and knees, his left leg crashed through the thin ice, soaking the other leg in ice water. Again he collapsed onto his belly, feeling sick.

Andy also had broken through the ice, soaking one leg. While lying horizontal, Tim strapped his snowshoes back on, because the platforms would better distribute his weight. Together Tim and Andrew crawled through this overflow-drenched section for more than an hour just to make a few hundred yards of progress back to the primary trail. There they saw the headlight of The Italian Moose, who was also having difficulties locating the trail beneath the deepening snow. The packed trail was the only known safe zone to bypass overflow, and the three agreed that they should stick together in these dire conditions.

Night deepened. The three men could hear wolves howling in the distance, but couldn't trust their eyes to alert them of danger. For Tim, hallucinations started as phantom people lurking on the trail, and then morphed to walls and buildings. Andrew expressed sightings of similar hallucinations. A couple of times, Tim experienced the rude awakening of hitting the snow after falling asleep on his feet. They attempted to sit on the duffel bags strapped to their sleds and take five-minute power naps, but the cold — now about twenty below zero — wouldn't allow them to stop for more than a minute. Tim wasn't sure that he would ever wake up if he fell into a sound sleep.

They continued to grope through the darkness, searching for signs of the snow-buried trail. A pack of wolves lurked in close range, howling intermittently through the night. Too many hours had passed since they left Yentna Station, and Roberto was certain they were lost. As dawn approached, they crept past funnel-shaped "siphons" where swirling eddies in the river prevented ice from forming. Tim hadn't noticed these whirlpools as frequently during the night, but he recognized them instantly as snow-blanketed slides to certain death. One misplaced step. That's all it would take.

In the mid-afternoon, they finally reached a welcoming sign of civilization, a wooden tripod planted on the river ice. Tim brushed snow away from a sign that read "Skwentna Roadhouse, 3 miles." It had taken them fifteen hours to travel thirty-two miles. "Unbelievable," Tim thought.

The roadhouse was a beacon in the storm, a red cabin nestled in the woods near the Skwentna River. Tim ordered pancakes and used a satellite phone to call his wife. Roberto collapsed his hulking frame on a small couch and gave instructions to the checkers to awaken him in exactly two hours. Tim and Andrew struggled to fall asleep despite exhaustion. Tim tried so hard to force sleep that it just wouldn't come. Two hours passed and Roberto indicated that he would snooze another hour. The Italian Moose knew the importance of sleep in the long run.

Upon leaving the roadhouse, the Iditarod Trail veered away from the Skwentna River and crossed a windswept swamp before rising into the steeper climbs and descents of the Shell Hills. These white-tipped hills were dwarfed by the craggy peaks of the Alaska Range, still far in the distance, but becoming closer with every mile. A day and a half had passed since Tim had left Flathorn Lake, and strength, focus, and morale were all waning. But this was a race. The finish of the 130-mile event was still forty-five miles ahead, and Tim wasn't going to ease his pace until he reached it.

"This is a race," he repeatedly reminded himself.

Night fell as Andrew and Tim trudged through the hills and descended into a new series of open swamps broken by thin stands of scrawny pines. Hallucinations returned — at first outlines among the trees took the shape of cabins, and then individual trees morphed into people and animals. Andrew also saw people who weren't there, and Tim found it frustrating that intruders would appear next to the side of the trail and then just flicker out of existence the second he reached them. Although they posed no real threat, he knew each sighting meant his brain was not processing information correctly. In this environment, with this many hazards, he could not afford bad decisions. A childhood poem cycled through his thoughts — "As I was walking up a stair, I met a man who wasn't there. He wasn't there again today. I wish, I wish he'd stay away."

To combat the mounting fatigue, Tim and Andrew stopped for a meal at the Shell Lake Lodge, about eighteen miles past Skwentna. As they ate, Roberto was spotted crossing the lake a half mile from the lodge. Tim and Andrew quickly packed up and left, but not before Roberto caught back up to them. He didn't even enter the lodge, gaining close to an hour by not stopping. Tim felt a surge of desire to hold onto the lead, and pushed hard, running at close to his marathon pace when the trail permitted. He ran as though his race was ending at Finger Lake. Andrew's race would end there, but both he and Tim realized that working side-by-side helped them both move faster, so they stuck together. Tim imagined Roberto as the bounty hunter from "Butch Cassidy and the Sundance Kid." He aimed to build just enough of a lead to disappear from sight — hopefully that would be enough to crush The Italian Moose's morale.

Snow began coming down hard again just as the flat gray light darkened into a purple twilight. More than a foot of fresh powder re-buried the trail and terrain started to repeat itself — up a long grade to a wooded knoll, a hard right at the top, and down a steep slope to another frozen lake. Repeat.

In the fresh snow they could no longer see the tracks of the competitors in front of them, and their own tracks were obscured within minutes. Tim was certain his sense of direction was failing him; surely they were going in circles. To alleviate his concerns, he made a slash in a snow bank with his glove, which he would recognize on the next rotation if they truly were returning to the same points. Seconds later, Andrew walked up from behind and cursed loudly. He had also been concerned about walking in circles, and had made his own similar mark in the snow. When Andrew saw Tim's mark, he recognized it as his own and became convinced they really had looped back to where they were before. Tim spent several minutes trying to persuade Andrew that he had made that mark in the snow. Andrew was still skeptical, but they both had a good laugh — it was exactly what they needed to break the tension and they continued on. With heavy cloud cover there was no moonlight, and wolves continued to howl in close range.

At 11:45 p.m., Andrew and Tim arrived in Finger Lake, mile 135 of the Iditasport. Tim was given a winning time of two days, eight hours, and forty-five minutes. Because he had arrived a half hour later than Tim to Flathorn Lake, Andrew took second place. They were fifth and sixth overall, only three hours behind the lead cyclist, who had to push his bike through deep snow for much of the distance. Tim received prize money for that finish as well; he never considered the possibility of finishing the "sprint" distance in the top five overall while competing on foot, but the bad weather was working to his advantage.

The checkpoint was located in Winter Lake Lodge, a polished log building with high timbered ceilings that offers customers the thrill of luxury accommodations in the Alaska wilderness. Tim and Andrew enjoyed a big meal, and then were pointed to a shed where the lodge owners stored dog food, and told they could sleep there. A few cyclists were already sacked out in sleeping bags while a small wood stove flickered in the corner. Tim decided that this humble shed couldn't be any finer and if it was, such luxury would have been lost on him. He was so exhausted that he could have fallen asleep on a bed of nails.

A Race at 1 MPH

4

We will go to the moon. We will go to the moon and do other things, not because they are easy but because they are hard.

~John F. Kennedy Jr.

Tom arrived in Finger Lake more than ten hours behind Tim, ready for sleep. Although trail breakers had not yet passed through since the storm had deposited two feet of fresh powder on the trail, Tim opted to press forward at a comfortable pace and wait for Tom at the next checkpoint.

Roberto had left Finger Lake several hours earlier, and Tim followed his punchy tracks as the route began to climb a steep ravine. Punching into knee-deep snow on the side hill, Tim couldn't keep his sled from turning over on its side. As the grade steepened, his sled would tunnel into the snow like a submarine. Tim fished a piece of spare rope out of his duffel bag and threaded it through the sled, making a loop that he wrapped around his shoulders to hoist the tip of the sled out of the snow. Although the rig worked, the extra weight on his back made him heavier, which caused him to punch deeper into the powder. After six hours, he had made perhaps four miles of progress. But Tim felt more resignation than frustration. The full journey to Nome was just beginning.

Snow continued to swirl over the trail, masking the tracks of those who had come before him. Tim wondered how far ahead Roberto might be; already his thoughts were returning to racing. He weighed the advantages of holding back and waiting for Tom so they could work together, or chasing Roberto to

McGrath and possibly garnishing a two-thousand-dollar purse for winning the Extreme race. Without question, arriving in Nome was far more important, and he couldn't risk his chance of completing the distance by pushing too hard in these early stages. Still, as he wallowed in the knee-deep powder, he doubted Roberto was making much better progress. Theirs was a race happening at less than one mile per hour.

In the late afternoon, Tim became aware of the first sound he had heard in hours — the whine of a distant snowmobile. As the machine approached, the rumbling engine cut out and then started again, a pattern of sputtering and bursts of silence. After thirty minutes of this, the snowmobile driver finally caught up to Tim. Tim stepped tentatively from the knee-deep snow of the packed trail into the bottomless snow off to the side, sinking nearly to his chest. He didn't dare wallow any farther for fear he would become stuck.

"Boy am I glad to see you," Tim called out to the driver. "Finally, a trail I can follow."

"Thanks for breaking trail," the driver responded. "But without you in front, I'm not sure I can continue."

Surely he was joking. Tim was one man on snowshoes, breaking trail for a half-ton machine? The man explained that his engine started overheating after snow packed around the submerged front end. Without Tim's tracks burrowing a notch in the trail, it would likely bury itself deeper and shut the engine down altogether. But, like Tim, the snowmobile driver was stranded unless he tried. He again fired up the engine and sputtered away, stopped after a hundred yards, and fired up again just before Tim again caught him a minute later. Tim heard the snowmobile leaving for as long as it took to approach, but now it was his turn to enjoy the spoils of a broken trail.

Nine miles after leaving Finger Lake, Tim arrived at the notorious Happy River Steps. The series of steep descents into the Happy River Gorge is infamous among dog mushers for hairpin turns and near-vertical drop-offs, which can be terrifying behind a team of sixteen dogs. A small group of Iditarod trail breakers were parked at the top of the first hill, shoveling snow onto the higher side of the sharp turn to create a smoother run for the dogs. It wouldn't be a cakewalk for Tim, either, with a forty-five-pound sled threatening to mow him down. Tim launched down the drop-off at a full sprint, but the careening sled caught and passed him within twenty yards, whipping Tim's hip belt around and pulling him head-first down the slope. The group of trail breakers whistled and cheered as Tim stood back up at the bottom of the hill, unscathed.

After the second descent, Tim encountered a fracture in the ice on the Happy River, with clear, slushy water oozing out. The resulting pool of overflow was at least a foot deep and spread across the entire river to the vertical banks on both sides. There was no way around. Tim fished out a pair of nylon hip waders that he had brought for this purpose, removed his shoes, and set out timidly in his new foot gear. The ice underneath the water was uneven, and the waders flopped around as he skittered over the slippery surface. He waded deeper to prevent his floating sled from overturning in the icy slurry. The overflow pool was twenty yards long, and would likely be refrozen to a solid sheen within a couple of hours. Like many obstacles on the ever-changing Iditarod Trail, Tim's struggles were his alone.

After the third steep descent, the trail turned back onto the north bank of the Skwentna River. Snowmobiles had cut deep grooves into the trail during aggressive accelerations for the climb up the embankment ahead. The resulting track was smooth and packed, the first runnable section of trail Tim had seen since the first day. He launched into a gallop, relishing the simple pleasure of running after the interminable tractor pull. Within seconds of changing his stride, Tim heard an audible crack and felt an electric shock reverberating from his left ankle. He collapsed onto his back and clasped his injured foot, writhing and nauseated with pain.

He pulled down his sock to examine his ankle, which had swollen to softball size and was turning a sickly shade of purple. Tim wasn't sure whether the color was from the sprain or the cold, which was already seeping into his core like an ice bath. He was injured but he wouldn't be able to lie here for long — not without crawling into his sleeping bag. Gingerly, he climbed to his feet and hobbled a few more yards down the trail. He stopped again to let the new shock of pain seep through his body, and glanced at the fading light over the top of the gorge, nearly a thousand feet above him. The sky was turning the same color as his ankle. Night had arrived.

"Only eight hundred and fifty miles to go on a sprained ankle," Tim thought. "What next?"

The sprained ankle reluctantly gained flexibility as Tim hobbled out of the steep canyon, grabbing brush with his hands to prevent his feet from sliding backward down near-vertical snow walls. Hours crept along. An undulating wave of pastel lights glowed on the northeastern horizon. Tim is somewhat colorblind, and the vibrancy of the greens and blues in the light resonated as truly distinct. The North Star shimmered brightly, like a street light in a Van Gogh painting. Tim unclipped his harness and sat on his duffel, marveling at the sky.

"How blessed I am," he thought, "to be ascending the Alaska Range at midnight." A low moan sounded in the distance, growing to a chorus of howls from a pack of wolves. "They're announcing midnight," Tim thought, and sure enough, when he looked at his watch it was 11:57 p.m.

As Tim rested, a dim light appeared on the trail in the distance. He sat and waited, and as he expected, the light belonged to his friend. Tom announced he couldn't sleep at Finger Lake and left three hours after Tim. The snowmobile had left in front of Tom, and with a better trail and Tim's hobbled pace, Tom had closed the gap quickly. They continued together and arrived at Puntilla Lake, mile one hundred and sixty-five, just before 3 a.m.

The checkpoint was a small log cabin, a double room of no more than two hundred square feet with a wood stove, four bunk beds, and a picnic table. Dim light from a propane lantern did little to cut through the night's long darkness, and the wood stove crackled and popped weakly with logs of gnarled dwarf spruce that populated this lake shore at the cusp of the tree line. A race checker offered the men a bowl of stew with a ladleful of rice in the bottom. The provision did almost nothing to satisfy Tim's gnawing hunger, but when he asked for more, the checker refused, informing him that portions were limited by weight restrictions on the ski plane. Tim and Tom dug into their drop bags and procured their own supplies — energy bars and drink mixes that made Tim feel sick to his stomach. He yearned for a hearty, hot meal as he gnawed on a frozen food brick and fretted about his calorie supply, which now seemed too minimal for the task at hand.

They slept for three hours, until the fire in the wood stove burned down and Tim woke up, shivering in the cold and feverish. His knee joints ached and his sprained ankle throbbed with renewed pain as endorphins faded. Outside, strong winds swept shards of snow into the frigid air. The men encased themselves in goggles and most of their available layers of clothing for the long ascent to the spine of the Alaska Range at Rainy Pass.

The trail out of Puntilla Lake ascended a steep grade. Tim and Tom soon passed the last dwarf spruce trees and continued onto the windswept tundra, which was covered in a sheen of hard ice. Without tree protection, the headwind blasted them like a cold furnace. The drinking water in Tim's backpack froze, despite resting next to his skin under five layers of clothing. As they marched, Tim frequently looked up to scan the landscape for wooden tripods, which were the only landmarks to discern the trail from anything else. If Tim strayed from the invisible trail, the hard crust would eventually collapse under his weight and leave him crawling on all fours through the powder, grasping the surface crust, which was like the broken pieces of an egg shell.

As the weak daylight faded again to twilight, the men continued to climb. All day they had been gaining elevation consistently, and the final rolling ascents were the steepest. The surrounding mountains closed in and rock outcroppings framed what Tom was certain had to be the top of Rainy Pass, finally. Standing in the dead center of this formidable scene was a man slumped over his bike, not moving. The ashen-faced cyclist introduced himself as Rocky Reifenstuhl, a semi-professional endurance racer from Fairbanks and perennial participant in the Iditasport. Tim had read Rocky's article on the Iditasport Extreme in Alaska Magazine just a few weeks earlier. He didn't look so tough out here, Tim thought.

Tim and Tom offered Rocky food, which he accepted. Rocky agreed that it was a cold evening but not as cold as the prior year, when he burned his backpack for heat. Tim wondered why any person with any mobility wouldn't do everything in their power to escape the brutal exposure of this windswept plain. They needed to return to the relative shelter of trees at lower elevations. The roaring wind swept away their words as they spoke, and communication was reduced to blunt shouting. Snow tore off the mountain ridges in a white jet stream — a visual reminder of the avalanche danger that lurked over their heads. Tim wanted nothing more than to get out of there, fast. The determined Rocky was uninjured and forged ahead, following the faint lead of Roberto's tracks down the Dalzell Gorge.

As the ravine closed in, cliffs towered over them like a fortress, buffeted by the blue ice of frozen waterfalls. The trail snaked through a tunnel-like corridor of trees, so narrow that alder branches grabbed Tim's sled as he walked. Ice bridges spanned the creek, and steep drops continued to pull Tim onto his backside. The gorge emptied onto the Tatina River, a wide plain of ice blown clear of snow. Tim and Tom broke into an awkward slide run and arrived at the remote outpost of Rohn at 2 a.m., twenty-one hours after they had left Puntilla Lake. Roberto had arrived just twenty minutes earlier. The Italian Moose looked ragged and, Tim noted, not particularly pleased to see them.

Rohn is nothing more than an unmaintained air strip and a single-room Bureau of Land Management cabin pressed against the western front of the Alaska Range. It's unoccupied and unused for most of the year until the Iditarod Dog Sled Race, when volunteers fly in from Anchorage to assist mushers. Perennial volunteers Jasper, the self-proclaimed "mayor" of Rohn and his "deputy," Terry, had gathered up a wooden barrel full of food left over from the previous year's Iditarod race — mostly ramen noodles. Tim slurped up multiple helpings and collapsed in the bottom half of one of the only two bunk beds in the building. Since the volunteers and Roberto occupied the other three beds, Tom nuzzled up beside him.

Rocky arrived one hour later, awakening Tim, who was anxious to get back on the trail. Tom wouldn't even consider it. "We're going to Nome," he hissed at Tim. "There's no way we can survive at this pace." Tim knew it was true but fretted about Roberto leaving before them. If Roberto stole away with another three-hour head start, Tim would feel compelled to spend yet another day chasing him. The Extreme win and its prize money were still in his grasp, and he was reluctant to let that go.

Tim lay back down and dozed off for another two hours, awakening with first light. Roberto was still at the cabin, packing his sled. Just outside Rohn, the trail veered onto the South Fork of the Kuskokwim River, which was also a slick of glare ice with gravel bars and softball-sized rocks protruding through the ice. Driftwood littered the shoreline, and air bubbles created a mesmerizing display of abstract art beneath the blue ice. Tim was amazed. Just eighty miles back, Finger Lake Lodge was buried under twenty-two feet of snow, and here there was almost none. The massive Alaska Range creates a storm wall that prevents moisture from reaching the western slope. What little snow falls there is carried away by constant winds, leaving a stark, brown landscape of frozen tundra and twisted spruce trees.

As they skittered over the ice, Tim heard Tom scream and turned around just in time to watch Tom's head smack the ice with an audible crack. Tom went down so hard that Tim was certain he'd suffered serious head trauma, but Tom stood up quickly, shook his head, and insisted they keep walking.

"Now I know just how hard-headed you can be," Tim joked.

Ten miles west of Rohn, a steeply sloped stream flowed toward the Post River and then the South Fork of the Kuskokwim, creating a large waterfall at the confluence that mushers refer to in nervous tones as "The Post River Glacier." The frozen cascade is nearly two hundred feet high and often slicked in a thin film of flowing water where overflow oozes out of the ice. At the bottom of the waterfall was a pool of slushy overflow that the men opted to wade through without taking the time to put on waders. Tim's Gore-Tex shoes kept his feet dry, but Tom's feet got wet.

After they had bypassed the worst of the overflow, Tom stopped to stuff his shoes with dry grass. While Tom was wicking his shoes, Roberto arrived, appearing in much better spirits than the night before. At this point, Tim thought it would be awkward to continue racing Roberto, so he concluded that they should all travel together. Although Roberto spoke no English and Tim spoke no Italian, their communication through hand gestures gave Tim a deeper affection for the quiet giant of a man.

The trail veered straight up the Post River Glacier, which as far as Tim could tell, wasn't climbable without crampons. They opted to bypass the ice by scrambling up a steep embankment, using rock ledges as handholds while their sleds dragged at precarious angles below them. Near the top, rock outcroppings forced them onto the edge of the ice, an extremely treacherous section that they had to skitter across as fast as they could while praying they didn't lose their balance.

Once off the ice, the three men began the laborious task of dragging their sleds over frozen clumps of grass, rocks, and even petrified bison dung. As they marched, Tim listened to the worrisome sound of rocks scraping across the sled bottom, gouging the plastic. Curls of blue plastic shreds clung to the rocks after he passed. While training in the Laurel Highlands of Pennsylvania, Tim had seen sleds fail from the bottoms being torn out in better conditions than this. At least Pennsylvania had some snow; here there was none at all. Would Cookie survive this slow deterioration?

To add to his anxieties, Tim's feet were becoming a real problem. It was the fifth day of the race, and constant moisture from perspiration, combined with the friction of uneven terrain, was a bad combination. The skin on his soles had become deeply macerated and painful, and blisters were beginning to open up and show signs of infection. The men arrived at a flowing stream that had a crossing of a makeshift bridge of thin logs that had sunk to water level. Because there was no snow to melt for water, they filled their bottles in the stream and then sat down to assess the situation. Tim produced what had to be the world's smallest first aid kit — only a miniature knife, one half ounce Neosporin, a glob of Vaseline and a dozen Aleve tablets. After applying some of the precious Neosporin to his blisters, he turned his liner socks inside out to better utilize the "clean" side.

The men fell into a pattern of jogging across frozen swamps and walking the more rolling terrain of the wooded trails. In the late morning, a cyclist named Pat Irwin passed them on the frozen dirt, full of energy and optimism. Since they had passed Rocky on Rainy Pass the previous evening, Tim and Tom had been in first place in the entire race — all of the cyclists, reduced to pushing their bikes by the deep snow, were behind them. Now the trail was dry, more ideal for wheels than sleds, and Pat was surging to take first position. He stopped briefly to chat and eat peanut butter out of a toothpaste-like tube that he squeezed directly into his mouth. After two minutes, he was on his way, and within another minute he had pedaled out of sight.

The trail bypassed a pyramid-shaped formation called Egypt Mountain and entered a long series of frozen lakes and portages through the woods. Each lake crossing was a perilous ballet over the smooth ice. Only shallow scratches where snowmobiles had scraped across the ice indicated any kind of trail. The men stumbled and took their turns tumbling off their feet, until the falls were no longer comical. They knew that a broken wrist or another serious injury in this remote wilderness could be just one more fall away.

One narrow lake meandered interminably, more of a wide stream bed than a lake. The group arrived at the end and discovered there was no trail cut leading into the woods. They pulled out a map, took a compass reading, and determined that the trail didn't traverse this lake at all. After one hour of dangerous ice negotiation, they had no choice but to go back the way they came. Once they returned to the spot where they had deviated, the trail merged into a mostly open plain that was only sparsely vegetated with waist-high spruce trees, and strewn with blackened deadfall. This was the beginning of the Farewell Burn, a region reduced to ash when a massive wildfire swept through in 1978. Twenty-three years later, trees were just beginning to take hold again, and the charred remnants of the burn still littered the landscape and created a tangle of obstacles on the Iditarod Trail.

A light snow began to fall on the barren ground as the men entered the "Burn." Tim considered this a good omen, as a few inches of snow on the trail would make it easier to pull their sleds. Still, the fire-scoured ground did offer a slightly better surface, and they were able to increase their pace to a steady jog. Two more cyclists, Alan Sheldon and Andy Heading from the United Kingdom, passed them as they ran.

Just before 9 p.m., they arrived at Buffalo Camp, a perennial tent camp maintained by buffalo hunters from nearby villages. Lantern light illuminated the canvas tents from the inside, creating a science-fiction-like outpost among the tattered forests of the Burn. Tim's trail notes indicated this landmark was almost exactly halfway between Rohn and the village of Nikolai, their next checkpoint stop. It meant they had traveled forty-five miles in fifteen hours — Tim's fastest pace yet, but one he still felt was unfathomably slow given how hard the trio had been working.

Two buffalo hunters, Alaska Native men in thick canvas clothing with wide smiles, emerged from the doorway and invited the travelers to come inside and get warm. A fire raged in the wood stove, and the inside of the tent felt uncomfortably hot after working up a heavy sweat running through the Burn. The men used the convenience of lantern light to organize food from their duffel bags, but the small tent had little room to spare, and it was clear that the hunters' invitation did not extend to spending the night. Five minutes later, the racers were off again, pressing into the black chill of the night.

The transition between night and day had begun to mean little to Tim. Travel was difficult in the gray daylight, but it was no more difficult in darkness. With only the small beam from his headlamp to guide the way, he was more likely to slip into a comforting autopilot state, expending less mental energy on his aches and the monumental task in front of him. But as the cold of night deepened, Tim became more aware of his deteriorating physical state. In temperatures down to ten below he felt comfortable, and he could suffer to twenty below, but now it was approaching thirty below and he couldn't stop moving for even a few seconds without lapsing into uncontrollable shivering. His best approach was to keep moving and not let his core temperature fall into the danger zone, but this complicated simple chores such as eating, drinking, and adjusting his clothing.

The next landmark on the trail was Sullivan Creek, an open stream spanned by a wooden bridge, about nineteen miles from Buffalo Camp. A water ladle tied to a rope allowed travelers to scoop drinking water directly out of the creek, but Tim was too cold to stop for water. He mumbled an apology to Tom and Roberto, but he would have to press forward. There was no room for waiting, no room for drinking, no room for anything in this oppressive prison of cold.

They were now approaching twenty-four hours without sleep. The hallucinations came back. Tim was so sleepy that he lapsed into dreams while walking, occasionally awakening only when he collapsed face-first into the snow. One time, he awoke to the sounds of himself talking to a tree.

During these sleepwalking hours, one of his mittens fell off undetected. Untold hours of darkness had passed, and still they hadn't seen Salmon Camp, another trail landmark that was only nine miles past Sullivan Creek. Tom pleaded with Tim to stop, pull out their emergency gear, and rest, insisting that none of them had the energy to push all the way into Nikolai without sleeping. The falls, the sleepwalking, the lost gear, and the bad decisions would only get worse. Surely they would freeze to death if they all fell asleep on the trail. Tim didn't disagree, but he didn't stop walking. Roberto did not appear to understand or care. Steel-faced and stoic, he continued trudging along.

At 5:30 a.m. they finally crossed the Salmon River. On the far side of the river was a small cabin with a padlock on the door. There was no way in. Nearby was a square pavilion, an L-shaped shelter with two counters, no walls and no floor. Tim claimed one of the fish-cutting counters for his bed and Tom quickly scrambled to the other. They both pointed to the ground when Roberto lumbered up to the structure. The Italian Moose clearly wasn't happy, but diplomacy was secondary at this point. They were just trying to survive.

The night's cold was so penetrating that Tim closed every zipper and vent to his sleeping bag and bivy sack, shivering and gasping for air as he slipped into sleep out of sheer exhaustion. Two hours later, he awoke with numb hands and a pounding headache from oxygen deprivation. "Rise and shine, boys, it's time to go," he called out from the confines of his mummy sack. He wrestled his way out of the bag and rushed to pack up as quickly as possible, cramming his gear awkwardly inside the duffel bag as a pre-dawn chill wrapped around his body like a snake. If he didn't start moving quickly, this ubiquitous monster would squeeze all the warmth out of him. One minute after leaving his sleeping bag, Tim was already moving down the trail as Tom and Roberto packed their sleds.

There were only twelve miles to the next checkpoint, the three-hundred-mile point of the race in the Athabascan village of Nikolai. Cutting across swamps, sloughs, and lakes, the trail traversed the flat flood plain of the Kuskokwim. The mountains of the Alaska Range were now distant enough that they had passed the edge of the range's "rain shadow," and snow once again covered the tundra. The landscape looked like a white slate stabbed with splintered black toothpicks — the scraggly spruce that populated this region were the only signs of life until Nikolai, itself a remote outpost of human inhabitance. The village was a cluster of homes perched on the edge of a steep river bank. The men pulled their sleds past a gold-domed Russian Orthodox Church and a small cemetery surrounded by a white picket fence, following trail markers to the home of Nikolai's mayor.

The mayor invited the racers to load their wet clothes and sleeping bags into the dryer, and then presented them with breakfast — for the first time in the race thus far, an all-you-can-eat offering. Tim had never been so hungry in all of his life, and threw polite decorum aside to gorge on eggs, toast, leftover lasagna, pancakes, and seconds of everything. Even though Tom and Roberto were both larger men, no one ate more that morning than Tim.

They decided to nap for three hours in Nikolai before continuing on the fifty-mile push to McGrath, but Tim was so tired that he couldn't sleep. Reclining on a couch in the front room, every small noise would jolt him from a half-conscious stupor. Finally, after fifteen minutes, he opted to get up and chat with the mayor and Rocky Reifenstuhl, who had just arrived. He also applied fresh Band-Aids to his blisters, which looked and felt worse than before. Yellow-tinted rings on the skin around the open sores signaled more trouble ahead. After several hours of restlessness, Tim shook Tom and Roberto to announce he was leaving. The group left together with the setting sun.

As soon as the final slivers of sunlight slipped below the horizon, the temperature plunged to thirty below almost immediately. Tim put on all of his clothes, leaving nothing in reserve besides one emergency down jacket. The trail crossed the village and soon dropped onto the riverbed, where it would remain until they reached McGrath. Cold air is denser than warm air and sinks — the river bed was the coldest place to be on an already brutally cold night. Tim was deeply sleep deprived and hobbled by ankle pain and blisters. The men formed a single-file line like bicyclists drafting each other, in an effort to share the workload as they jogged along the river trail at a "fast" four miles per hour. Tim, who could run a marathon at a pace closer to ten miles per hour, smiled at this idea of "fast" on the Iditarod Trail.

Tim's thoughts drifted back to a marathon he had run in Columbus, Ohio, with high winds and temperatures near freezing. Before the race, he wrapped his body in a garbage bag to serve as a temporary wind breaker, planning to shed the layer as soon as the race started. However, as soon as the gun went off, a continued blast of wind coaxed him to keep the plastic bag on as he ran. The plastic blocked the wind, but he only felt more chilled, so he kept it on even longer. After two and a half hours, he finished the race still wearing the garbage bag and shaking incessantly. Race volunteers escorted him to a medical area, and when he tore open the garbage bag, he found it had become packed with ice. The vapor barrier of the plastic had prevented his sweat from escaping, instead freezing to the inside of the bag near his skin. His core temperature had dropped to eighty-six degrees, low enough that the doctor was shocked to see Tim conscious and insisted he be infused with a warm saline IV. Tim refused, choosing a blanket and hot broth instead.

Now he was in Alaska, and felt that same degree of bone-chilling cold. He was low on fuel, with only a few peanut butter sandwiches that he had purchased from the mayor's wife, and hot lemonade that had now become slushy in the subzero temperatures. He hated to waste this source of fuel, but every sip of lemonade slushy would send his body into the same uncontrollable shivering that he experienced in Columbus. Only now there was no hot broth, no blankets, no warmth. There would be no sympathy from a concerned doctor, and his wife would not show up with more clothes. "This is exactly what this race is about," Tim thought. "The true competition is Alaska. Or maybe it's just me."

Tim continued to battle his falling core temperature, knowing that only relentless forward motion could save him out here. Trail landmarks were few and far between, and he wrestled with constant suspicions that they had veered off onto a wrong trail and gotten themselves lost. The trail would meander along the wide Kuskokwim River and cut over bends through dense woods. Finally, a blinking red light entered their sights — an Air Force Radar Station on Tatalino Mountain, about fifteen miles past McGrath. It never seemed to get any closer, but at least it was there as a beacon of direction in a dark wilderness.

After several more hours, the sandwiches purchased in Nikolai were gone. Tim's light began to play tricks on him, casting a deep shadow on the banks of the trail and making it appear like there were high walls on each side. His sleep-deprived mind was also deceiving him, creating dozens of cabins and lurking people where there were none. "Hopefully daylight will come soon and chase away the hallucinations," Tim thought.

The trail became much worse. Apparently most snowmobiles traveling to McGrath used a side route that was shorter, while the official Iditarod Trail continued to meander along the river. The cyclists ahead had taken the shortcut, but Roberto, Tom, and Tim had somehow missed this intersection and continued on the soft and punchy dog sled trail. They discussed turning around, but Tim wouldn't hear of backtracking on any forward progress. The group trudged on, drawn by the feeble dawn light that was the promise of McGrath.

The golden sun rose over another bright, cold morning. The mercury on Tim's thermometer was still buried in its reservoir, meaning it was colder than thirty below. After a short break to munch on hard-frozen chocolate and energy bars, Tim turned his mittens inside out to empty the accumulating flecks of ice caused by perspiration hitting the inside of his glove and freezing. He had again become a human snow-making machine. Fifteen minutes later, he realized he had left the glove sitting on top of his sled. A panic gurgled in his gut — not only at the thought that he might have lost a crucial piece of gear, but also that he'd have to backtrack to look for it, thereby losing ground on his competitors when he was so close to the second mid-way finish. Arriving first on foot in McGrath would mean another win, a hefty purse of prize money, and a sound achievement. But he needed his glove.

Tim unclipped from his sled and started running backward on the trail. As minutes ticked by without sight of the glove, he ran harder. The strenuous effort required more oxygen than the tiny holes in his neoprene face mask could supply, so he pulled down the mask and exposed his face to the sharp air. Sweat streamed down his forehead and his heart pounded, but there was still no sign of the glove. He rounded a bend and then another, before turning around to track Roberto and Tom's position. They, too, were nowhere in sight. McGrath couldn't be more than a few miles away, and they had made a break for it.

That's it, Tim thought. This glove was important, but he had a spare set. He didn't like the idea of continuing to Nome with only one spare glove, but his competitive side burned hotter and he instinctively turned around to catch them. By the time he sprinted back to his sled, he was out of breath. As he reached up to wipe his nose with his gloved hand, he realized the tip was hard. Frozen solid. His nose had no feeling at all, like an inanimate piece of plastic attached to his face.

Tim felt nauseated. How did this happen so quickly? He should have known better than to expose flesh to temperatures below minus thirty, but he had needed to breathe. He quickly pulled the mask back up over his face and let his warm breath hit the frozen skin. Would he lose his nose to frostbite even though it couldn't have been frozen longer than a few minutes? It seemed unlikely, but Tim just didn't know.

As he cinched up his harness and continued marching hard to catch Roberto and Tom, a painful tingling erupted around the tip of his nose, indicating that feeling was returning. High bluffs on either side of the river masked the wider view, but after two bends he caught sight of his competitors. He reeled them in quicker than he had anticipated. Matching their pace would be no problem. He just needed to keep them in sight.

The Kuskokwim River continued on its lazy, serpentine path, carving oxbow bends into the flat landscape of Interior Alaska. Tim couldn't imagine a more infuriatingly indirect way to travel to McGrath, but the river itself was his only navigational tool. The trail was soft, almost indiscernible from the smooth canvas of the river, and progress was slow. An hour passed, then two. Roberto fell off the back of the group, and then Tom struggled for an hour as Roberto slowly caught up. Tim didn't feel the need to sprint ahead, as his one-hour lead back at Flathorn Lake on the first day would be enough to ensure his victory if he finished alongside Tom and Roberto.

Around noon, a row of houses finally appeared behind the interminable woods. They had reached McGrath, only the second village they had seen in seven days. After several minutes of marching cluelessly down the street, a Native man pointed them to the official checkpoint, at the home of a veteran Iditarod dog sled musher named Peter.

Tim checked in at six days, twenty-one hours, and ten minutes — good for another two thousand dollars. Tom was second in six days, twenty-two hours, and one minute, and Roberto was credited for third in six days, twenty-two hours, and forty-seven minutes. They were eighth, ninth, and tenth overall. After unhooking his sled and dragging his duffel bag into the checkpoint, the first thing Tim did was rush to the bathroom to check for skin damage. The skin around his nostrils had blistered, and open sores and purple patches speckled other areas of his face. He smeared the skin with some of the Bag Balm he found in a medicine cabinet and thought that it was good.

No big issue — Nome awaited.

Beyond the Extreme

5

*The world breaks everyone and afterward
many are strong at the broken places.*
~Ernest Hemingway,
"A Farewell to Arms"

After a full night's sleep and more pancakes and moose stew than Tim imagined he'd ever devour in a single day, Tim and Tom left McGrath in the morning under clear skies and subzero cold. Tim's feet were still raw and swollen with infected blisters. With the lingering pain of the sprained ankle, he'd found it difficult to simply hobble around Peter's house in McGrath. It was almost inconceivable to him that they were merely one-third of the way through the race to Nome. Despite this intimidating prospect, the new day brought fresh optimism. He had won the Iditasport Extreme, and now the race was finally over and the journey could begin. The Iditasport Impossible was, well, impossible ... so there was no reason to get worked up over it.

Tim planned to travel with Tom as long as both were still in the race. They set their sights on Takotna, a village about twenty miles west of McGrath. From there it would be another 195 miles to the next inhabited village, so they hoped for one more opportunity to shore up strength before the big push to the Yukon River and the halfway point of the route. Weather forecasts warned of a deep Arctic cold front and temperatures as low as sixty below, so it was only reasonable to seek shelter while it was available.

They marched through the morning up a long climb to a ridge followed by a gradual descent into Takotna, arriving late in the afternoon. A community center served as the Iditarod checkpoint in the village. Four cyclists who left ahead of Tim and Tom had already checked in and out, headed for the ghost town of Ophir, a remote outpost with a single-room cabin about forty miles beyond Takotna. Tim still felt depleted from racing hard to McGrath, and happily took the opportunity to indulge in another eating frenzy provided by the dog sled race volunteers, who comprise most of the community of seventy-five inhabitants.

The volunteers allowed Tim and Tom to sleep in a library next to the community center. The building was warm and Tim found it difficult to sleep. He felt alert and energetic, as though he had managed to catch up on a week of sleep deprivation during their long stay in McGrath. He felt guilty about taking another extended break after only twenty miles. But neither he nor Tom knew what lay ahead, and with Roberto no longer in the picture, conserving energy by sleeping where it was warm and wind-protected was the only logical decision. Tim tossed and turned, dreaming of being back out on the trail.

By morning, Tim felt a renewed freshness that abated his guilt and validated their decision to rest. After leaving Takotna, the trail followed the snow-covered remnants of an old mining road, gradually ascending for nine miles to a divide between the Kuskokwim and Innoko River drainages. It was another clear, cold day, and while the trail was always difficult when traveling uphill, Tim felt a surge of energy at the realization that they were heading into a true wilderness, an untrammeled place unlike any he had ever experienced. Although he never doubted his ability to walk to Nome, this was the first time since the race began that he truly felt ready to go the distance. Excitement replaced exhaustion.

Skeletal birch trees, willow brush, and shabby spruce dominated the rolling landscape. The Iditarod Trail, lined with rusted, bullet-hole-ridden mining equipment and collapsed outbuildings, was still buried in knee-deep snow. The only tracks to follow were from the cyclists ahead, who now numbered three after one had turned around the night before and returned to Takotna with a race-ending ankle injury. Tim and Tom made fast time to Ophir, but upon arrival found only a small cabin with a bush pilot and two older men inside. Tim was happy to see other people, but the men next to the wood stove did not seem to share that opinion, and gave them a less than warm reception. The racers' drop bags remained outside, buried in snow and frozen solid.

Eight miles beyond Ophir, they reached a fork in the trail. The Iditarod Trail splits into two routes for several hundred miles in the middle, creating a Northern Route and a Southern Route. The dog sled race alternates between the two routes every other year, and the human-powered race follows suit. On even years, the trail veers north toward Ruby on a more heavily trafficked village route also used by the Iron Dog snowmobile race. During odd-numbered years, the race veers south toward Anvik on a route created almost solely for the dog sled race. Trail breakers on snowmobiles, paid for by the dog sled race, were responsible for setting the Southern Route trail. Non-race use on this segment was light to nonexistent.

In 2001, the Iditarod races followed the Southern Route through Interior Alaska. The bad news was that Iditarod trail breakers had yet to reach this part of the course when Tim and Tom arrived. What little trail there had been disappeared altogether at the fork — untrammeled snow stretched as far as they could see. The next inhabited village was Shageluk, still one hundred and fifty miles away. The pilot in Ophir laughed heartily when the Tim and Tom asked him about the trail ahead, informing them that the day before he had spotted the cyclists who were in front of them. Although they left Ophir at first light, the pilot said, they'd only traveled fifteen miles in eight hours while pushing their bikes through an unbroken sea of white. "That's the trail," the pilot said of their knee-deep footprints in the snow.

At the Southern Route cutoff, only yellow ribbons tied to spruce branches marked the turn, followed by the distinct tracks of cyclists on foot next to their trench-creating bikes. There was no trail base after the turn; Tim and Tom sank to their hips with every step. The cyclists had wrestled their way through the deep powder, but created little improvement in the trail. All Tim and Tom could do was swim through the fluff as well. Their sleds continually turned over in the V-shaped track created by the bikes. The work was as exhausting as it was futile. They were getting nowhere, and after two hours of almost no forward progress, they decided to hunker down and wait for trail breakers.

Theoretically, the Iditarod trail breakers would pass through twelve to eighteen hours ahead of the first musher. At the rate they were progressing, Tim argued, they would use too much energy and their food would not last through the next village. They pulled into a small stand of black spruce and used their sleds as shovels to dig a trench four feet into the snow. After clearing an area ten feet wide and twenty feet long, they built a fire on one end, fueled by spruce boughs that they were able to break away from the standing timber. As the flames crackled beside their bivy sacks, night fell. Wolves howled and Northern Lights danced in the clear sky. They cooked oatmeal, soup, and hot chocolate on white gas stoves. Tim lay in his sleeping bag, staring at the sky and thinking that finally, he was truly enjoying his Alaska experience. Fear was gone now, but he could not feel fully content because forward progress had been halted. He hoped his calculations on the arrival of the trail breakers were correct.

Early in the morning, Tim and Tom heard the sounds of three cyclists coming back up the trail. Andy Heading from the United Kingdom, Mike Estes from Alaska, and Pat Irwin, a Tennessean who had finished the previous year's race to Nome, reported that they did not have enough food and fuel to make it to Iditarod, and planned to return to Ophir and raid the drop bags of racers who had scratched. They were not sure whether they'd return. The pilot who had reported seeing them fifteen miles down the trail was wrong — they had only made it a half mile beyond Tim and Tom's foxhole before they hunkered down to wait. Two Italian cyclists who had passed Tim and Tom in the night also finally dug in about a quarter mile ahead. The race was at a standstill.

After making another meal of oatmeal and hot chocolate, Tim and Tom decided to continue forward on the route, at least as far as the three cyclists' bivy spot. As they marched through the bottomless powder, they encountered the two Italians, who had turned around after reaching the end of the other cyclists' trail and concluding that they were all going the wrong way. Although the Italians spoke no English, Tim was able to gesture enough to make it clear that they were still most likely going the right way, and were in fact at the front of the race. The Italians broke into an unhindered display of jubilation that, with nearly six hundred miles of unknowns still in front of them, Tim thought was premature. He responded with a shrug. Why deny small pleasures?

The day was beautiful, with moderate temperatures and only a slight breeze. The Italians, along with Tim and Tom, trekked together to the foxholes where the three cyclists had camped. They were still only nine miles from Ophir, a place they'd left one and a half days earlier. The group laughed and made jokes through their language barrier, but anxiety was building. Nobody could afford to be stymied much longer. The Italians offered Parmesan cheese and Tim and Tom prepared freeze-dried meals. They waited, and Tim nervously predicted 4 p.m. for the arrival of the trail breakers, based on the progress of previous years' dog sled races. At 3:30 p.m., they finally heard the faint whine of approaching snowmobiles.

The arriving snowmobile drivers were not, however, race trail breakers. Three red snowmobiles rumbled up, with the lead and rear pulling trailers loaded with fuel canisters and supplies. "Alaskan Outdoor Adventures" was painted on the body panels. The snowmobilers stopped and the drivers removed their helmets. Piloting the middle, unladen machine was a seventy-year-old woman who had commissioned outfitters to take her the length of the Iditarod Trail, ahead of the dog sled race. They too were hoping to soon be passed by the trail breakers, as they were uncertain about the route ahead and bogged down themselves. Tim and Tom were simultaneously relieved and unimpressed.

They waited another half hour for the snow on the newly broken trail to settle in before packing up and setting out again. The Italian bikers still found the trail too soft to ride, and decided to wait for the Iditarod trail breakers. Once again, Tim and Tom were leading the entire race. Strange, Tim thought, for two racers using the slowest mode of travel to overtake everyone this late in a thousand-mile race. Tim knew it would be short-lived and the bikers would come flying past as soon as trail conditions improved. But for now, it was fun to pound their chests and soak in small victories.

Day transitioned almost imperceptibly into night once again. It was too cold to stop, so Tim and Tom marched in silence. A gradual slope rose to eleven hundred feet elevation — above the tree line. Snow cover had diminished to a couple of inches, and bowling-ball-sized tussocks stuck out of a thin carpet of white. Traveling became more technical on the bumpy terrain, and Tim again turned his attention to his injured ankle. Streaks of pain made him hyper-aware that every step needed to be calculated. Focusing became more difficult as sleepiness settled in and hallucinations returned. As the first light of dawn appeared on the horizon, the men finally reached Don's Cabin — the next outpost of shelter on the trail. The small building had no door, and the left wall was devoid of siding. The wood stove had been stolen; only a detached stovepipe remained. The floor was littered with empty fuel canisters. Wind blew straight through what was left of this shell of a cabin. But the men were so spent that exhaustion muted their disappointment. They collapsed on the floor in their sleeping bags.

In what seemed like a few moments, Tim awoke with a throbbing headache and a full bladder. As he wrestled out of his sleeping bag, to his surprise it was a bright sunny day and two and a half hours had passed. Outside, he saw a harnessed dog team resting on evenly spaced beds of straw. Doug Swingley, leader of the dog sled race, was taking a quick break at Don's Cabin to check his dogs' feet and shoulders. As Swingley attended to his dogs, a helicopter hovered overhead, blades chopping through the cold air. The snowmobile trio from Alaskan Adventures pulled up, followed shortly by a duo of Norwegian cross-country skiers who were touring the trail. This was becoming a party.

Tim and Tom prepared breakfast and left first. It was another cloudless, calm morning. The snow cover remained sparse, keeping the footing difficult. After a few hours, Doug Swingley passed with his team. They were approaching Iditarod, once a booming city of ten thousand during the height of the Gold Rush, but now a cluster of abandoned, skeletal buildings whose sidings had been burned for firewood. Still, Iditarod is a famous checkpoint in the dog sled race, and many ski planes stop there. Quonset huts serve as shelter in the eerie ghost town.

Hours passed without any sightings of another dog team, which Tim found strange. Night fell again as they climbed out of the lowlands before dropping into another creek bed, where they wended their way on the frozen stream for miles. Exhaustion clamped down with the darkness, and Tim and Tom dug in for two hours of sleepless rest. Their fatigue was strong and calories were running low. Tim was almost entirely out of food and Tom was down to a quarter pound of fudge. Fast travel to Iditarod, where drop bags awaited, was becoming crucial.

Morning crept into afternoon. Wind had scoured snow from open swamps, and for long segments the tundra was bare. More mushers started passing them, sleds clanking loudly over the barren trail. Frozen tussocks were murder on Tim's feet, and he wondered how bad it must be for the dogs, not to mention the uncomfortable ride for mushers on their rigid sleds. Energy and morale flagged, but each new hilltop yielded no satisfaction. Iditarod was nowhere in sight.

Clouds gathered overhead as the temperature climbed and winds increased in speed, signaling a rapidly approaching storm. Anxiety trickled through Tim's veins; he and Tom couldn't afford to dig in again, now that they had little food and fuel to spare. Snowfall would stymie their progress; there was no way around it. Only the weather would determine how much they suffered, and they had no say in the matter.

Luckily, the storm held off, until the men encountered a filmmaker who was making on documentary about the race and had driven a snowmobile out to meet them. The filmmaker informed them that they were just three miles outside of Iditarod. An hour later, nearly sunset, they finally trudged into the checkpoint. The dilapidated ghost town had transformed into a wilderness race circus. Veterinarians had set up well-stocked medical tents, brightly colored ski planes were parked haphazardly along the river, and a large number of volunteers cheered their arrival. It was odd seeing all of these people after long hours of quiet struggle. But there was no time for culture shock. Tim and Tom found their drop bags and those of racers who had dropped, rifling through them greedily in hope of an unexpected treat.

The men received a cool reception in the crowded veterinarian tent, and volunteers informed them that space was limited. Still, they attempted to cook a hot meal and catch a nap as dog teams arrived and departed, a bonfire blazed on the riverbank, and loud yelling and barking rang through the cold air. So much noise and stimulation was more than Tim's senses could handle, and although he could not have felt more exhausted, sleep just wasn't possible. They repacked and followed a dog team out at midnight, back into the welcome silence. They were halfway to Nome now, Tim thought — the point of no return.

The next section wound through the infamous Shageluk Hills, a series of steep climbs and descents leading to the Yukon River basin. Some mushers claimed there were nine big hills, some said thirteen, and all of the hills climbed at least five hundred feet in elevation on steep grades. Shortly after leaving the checkpoint, Tim could see the unmistakable profile of a mountain blocking the horizon. He was again deeply fatigued, having acquired no rest at Iditarod, but at least he was no longer starving. Tim leaped forward, pulling the rope attached to his sled around his shoulders to put as much weight as he could into the first climb. The men marched up the grueling grade for two hours, launched into a quad-busting descent, and then began another climb anew. The scenery otherwise did not change — as though they were walking on a giant, undulating treadmill.

By 5 a.m. fatigue became overwhelming. They decided to sleep for a few hours, and chose a small stand of tightly woven pines to help block the wind. Tim tore a few branches off the tree as a nest over the fresh powder. He and Tom didn't budge for three hours, until daylight returned in a swirl of snow and wind.

It would be another hard day of marching through deep snow along the windswept spine of a narrow ridge. Passing mushers meandered over the breakable snow crust, and the wind brushed their tracks away within minutes. Tim and Tom mined the blowing powder for evidence of a trail without much luck. Tim could only hold faith that following this ridge was the right way. Anxiety flickered through exhaustion, and daylight surrendered to night once again. Tim felt they were working increasingly hard, but all of the hills made it impossible to gauge progress. Sometimes their speed dropped below one mile per hour.

Around midnight, the final hill dropped into an open basin, as immense and barren as a frozen sea. Without trees or geographical features for visual reference, Tim had the distinct sense that they were marching in place, still stuck on a white treadmill. A few more hours of visual vertigo passed before a dim light appeared over the horizon — a tiny halo heralding the village of Shageluk.

Upon arrival, they were instructed that their drop bags and a place to sleep were located at the local schoolhouse. A dog sled race volunteer called the village teacher even though it wasn't yet 6 a.m., and the teacher came out to open the school for the weary marchers. Trudging into the warm building without the weight of his sled, Tim became acutely aware of the pain in his feet. They throbbed and burned with festering blisters, and it was difficult to bear any weight without cringing. The teacher offered them kitchen facilities and a shower, but Tim only cared about sleep. Beside cramped book shelves in the school library, he tossed and turned for three restless hours. He was exhausted, and agonized as to why he couldn't rest. He wondered if he was becoming a sled dog, far more comfortable outside. Buildings were too hot, too noisy, and the light was distracting. Even stretched out on top of his sleeping bag, he sweat profusely.

In the early afternoon, Tim and Tom each ate several hearty meals, took a heavenly shower, repacked their sleds with new supplies, and then set out to cross the final stretch of tundra before the Yukon River, which was about twenty-five miles away. A fresh pair of running shoes was in Tim's Shageluk drop bag, and he opted to change out his old, worn shoes for this dry pair. At the time, Iditasport race rules allowed for spare clothing to be sent ahead in drop bags, a provision that has since changed. Prevailing running wisdom held that worn-out shoes were a recipe for injury. Ultimately, though, switching shoes mid-race in the Iditasport proved to be a mistake. The new shoes had different pressure points and weren't conformed to his swollen feet. Every step was new agony, but it was too late to turn back now. Still, Tim's spirits were high. The rest, food, and a phone call home had elevated his mood, and he anticipated a straightforward march to Anvik before entering another turning point in the journey, the mighty Yukon.

Ten miles from Anvik, a villager had placed a sign indicating the distance to their next stopping point. The nine-mile marker came a seemingly interminable amount of time later. Darkness had enveloped the white space; it was here that

Tim and Tom met the helpless musher and her lead dog, Louie, in a vortex of wind and snow. After Tim was snagged in Louie's harness and dragged a short distance, the defiant lead dog and his team decided that the extra tug wasn't worth the effort and finally stopped. Tim untangled himself, no worse for the wear, and continued marching into the wind toward the faint glow of Anvik's lights. The village would bring another early-morning arrival to locked doors at the village school, a nap in a hot science room, and a time-consuming treasure hunt for drop bags. It was becoming an all-too-familiar routine — vast hours of nothingness punctured by overwhelming chaos. The wilderness outside, intimidating and uninhabitable as it seemed, was becoming a refuge of peace for Tim.

After packing up again, the men made a quick stop at the Iditarod checkpoint. A volunteer informed them that sixteen different dog teams had left Anvik late the night before, and every one of them had returned to the village because of unmanageable winds. These gales were not normal, and Louie was not alone in his mutinous behavior. On this day, however, the wind seemed to have calmed ever so slightly — although it still sounded like a freight train roaring down the river.

Shortly after leaving the village, the trail dropped off the high banks and onto a slough weaving to its confluence with the Yukon River two miles north. Headwinds blew twenty to thirty miles per hour — strong, but not quite the hurricane force they had experienced the night before. The river itself was an ocean of ice, vast and unending. Snow limited visibility to a mile or less, and they couldn't even see the bank on the far side of the river. It looked like just crossing the river laterally would take an hour. Trail conditions resembled a storm-tossed sea; wind had driven the surface snow into crests and troughs, often three to four feet deep. Pressure ridges created veritable walls sometimes more than ten feet high. Trail markers were sparse, but Tim knew that if he continued to follow the river north, he would find his way. "Just walk into the wind, and you'll be fine," he thought to himself.

The march was brutal, as strenuous as it was slow. Tim thought it would take five hours to travel the next eighteen miles to the village of Grayling, but the duration was closer to twelve. They didn't reach the friendly lights of the village's cluster of houses until nearly 10 p.m., and Tim was already more than ready to rest again. But the checkpoint was bustling with the energy of a half-dozen mushing teams who had passed them on the river. One of the mushers, Mitch Seavey, suggested Tim see a veterinarian about his blisters, which were becoming infected. The vet gave Tim a smelly salve meant for use on dogs' feet. Tim found the odor repugnant, but decided it could be no worse than his own scent after wearing the same clothing for two weeks. He smeared it on his feet liberally.

Tim and Tom made their way to a church for some sleep. The small building had no electricity. A potbelly stove crackled in the corner of the room, but it was cool to the touch, having not been tended to in many hours. The air was cold inside the church; they could see their breath, but it was warmer than outside. Snoring mushers were strewn about on the wooden floor. Tim was asleep in an instant, and when he awoke, most of the mushers were gone. His feet hurt so badly that it was difficult to stand up. The veterinarian's foot salve caused skin to callous — perfect for dogs, but not so great for humans. The hardening skin aggravated the infected area even more.

But as he walked, his feet became more tolerable. He woke Tom, emphasizing the need to start moving. Grayling was not a drop bag checkpoint, and neither was the next stop, sixty-two miles up the Yukon River. Even with a big pasta dinner and a rest, it would be nearly a hundred and fifty miles before their next resupply, and they had no time to waste. Trail notes for the next leg were not reassuring. "It is critically important to stay on the marked trail on the big river," the notes read. "The Yukon is notorious for stretches of open water and thin ice. People run snow machines into the river every winter, and some die. Wind chills on the river can be very low, pushing 100 degrees below zero in the worst cases."

In 1997, a musher wrote, "Eagle Island is so remote that it is actually beyond the edge of the planet … You can rest assured you and your fellow mushers and checkpoint personnel are almost the only living humans in an area larger than many entire states."

As he and Tom walked onto the white expanse, the Yukon River gave Tim the impression of peering into the Grand Canyon — the vastness was indescribable. The western bank towered fifteen hundred feet above the river, with a wooded shelf that looked like an island in the sky. Wide, sweeping bends were followed perpetually by another, and it would take hours to travel to the next curve in their sightline. The trail veered onto the shoreline of an island, and they would walk beside trees for two hours. Enough time would pass to cause Tim to ponder whether they had entered a time warp and somehow bypassed the river section — until they re-entered the frozen plain and realized that the wooded section had simply been an island, nearly four miles long. The Yukon River bore more resemblance to an inland sea.

As the hours passed, Tim stopped counting islands and stopped reviewing his trail notes. He'd get there when he got there; it was as simple as that. His feet hurt terribly, and he suspected the infection would require antibiotics or quickly become worse. His painkillers were gone, his Neosporin was gone, and his socks were puss-stained and filthy, all of them. He continued rotating each pair and turning them inside out, if only to pretend he was actively doing something about his rapidly deteriorating feet. In the Iditarod Trail Dog Sled Race, mushers forego their own sleep and self-care to attend to their dogs' feet. Neglecting any one of the dogs can have disastrous consequences on a whole team. Tim had a sharp and painful understanding about why foot care was so highly emphasized in the race.

As his mind wandered farther from the trail, Tim struggled to stay alert. After hours of nearly dozing off, there was a twinkle of light in the distance. It was too low on the skyline to be the checkpoint, and so small — like a single bulb on a Christmas tree. As he fixated on the light, his leg hit a sudden jolt. Breathtaking pain streaked up from his right shin as his foot and toes began to tingle. A wave of nausea followed, and Tim collapsed into the snow. While focusing on the light, he had planted his foot awkwardly in a small hole in the ice — possibly a hoof print left by a moose. Although Tim had never broken a leg, he was fairly certain that was what had just happened.

Tim knew Eagle Island checkpoint had to be within a mile, but he told Tom he wasn't sure he could make it. As Tom helped him to his feet, Tim found he could put weight on the limb, but the tingling intensified and the pain was almost unbearable. Anxiety and nausea churned in his gut. He appeased himself with thoughts that the injury could possibly just be a tear to a muscle or minor ligament, rather than a fractured bone. As he took a few ginger steps, every undulation in the trail sent a new shock of pain through his leg. Placing his foot down flat and gently seemed to help. Although Tim clung to optimism, certainty remained that he had sustained a fracture to his right tibia. It wasn't a load-bearing bone, and he was able to walk, but not without intense pain. Even as he contemplated the agony and consequences, he couldn't help but wonder if the leg could hold up for another five hundred miles.

It took twenty minutes to reach the checkpoint. A dog sled race volunteer reluctantly shared some of the ramen soup that was "for volunteers only" and pointed the men to a plywood shed fifty feet above the river where they could sleep. The trail to the shed climbed straight up the embankment, nearly as steep as a wall, and getting up there would be a real challenge for Tim on his possibly broken leg. He decided it would be best to crawl up on his hands and knees, moving like a dog. This took most of the pressure off his injury, and he was able to reach the top.

In the barely warm shed, sleep came quickly, but Tim awoke two hours later from the pain in his leg. The tingling sensation shooting into his toes had returned, but so had the almost-forgotten pain from blisters. He could now see light streaming through a sheet of opaque plastic across the doorway; day had returned. Frigid air lingered inside the sled, and Tim quickly donned his down coat to hobble to the outhouse. His feet had become so swollen that he could scarcely pull on his shoes, even with the laces untied. Pushing his feet into the semi-frozen shoes required pressure, which sent unbearable pain shooting through his shin as the open blisters throbbed. "What a mess I am," Tim thought. "How can I possibly survive another five hundred miles?"

Still, there wasn't much he could do about his plight from this remote outpost. As long as he was capable of walking, he thought it best to keep walking. He slid on his butt down the embankment, clutching his right leg to keep it off the ground. Back on the Yukon River, Tim hobbled behind Tom as they marched into the white expanse. From there it would be seventy more miles to Kaltag, a village of two hundred people. After Kaltag, the Iditarod Trail traverses a "portage" between the river and the sea, crossing over Old Woman Pass to the frozen coast of the Norton Sound.

Any time Tim stopped, he faced at least twenty minutes of teeth-grinding pain when he started walking again. After this warm-up interval, the pain would relinquish some of its grip, and he could walk more comfortably at a higher speed. The terrain over the next seventy miles would be very much like the last seventy — a wide expanse surrounded by far-off bluffs and river bends. The sky darkened early, signaling a storm. Soon the wind picked up in ferocity and snow started to fall — vertically at first, and then horizontally. Tom took the lead for most of the day — with his mounting injuries, Tim found it too difficult to maintain a steady pace without lagging. But with Tom leading, he could fall back and then push harder to keep up.

The men exchanged few words during the march, until the headwind became so violent that both men were scarcely moving. They needed rest, and to do so they would have to find cover. The trail was about fifty yards from the east bank, but it was as close to the edge of the river as it had been yet. Tim winced as he tightened the bindings on his snowshoes and trudged up the steep bank.

It took nearly half an hour to reach a protected area of woods on a plateau above the river. Tim pulled his feet out of shoes still strapped inside the snowshoes, and dove into his sleeping bag without building a wind-blocking snow wall. He was asleep before Tom had even finished preparing his sleeping area.

After four hours of sleep and an hour of breakfast-making, snow-melting, and packing, Tim forced his tortured feet back into hard-frozen shoes that were now further constricted by the snowshoe bindings. His shin responded with intense pain that felt too sharp to bear, but after thirty minutes of hobbling, the pain became tolerable again. Barring any awkward turns, walking on the injury seemed sustainable for an indefinite amount of time. Tim's anxiety levels had diminished somewhat as he convinced himself that his injury had stabilized. Tom relented to sharing a handful of antibiotic pills, which Tim hoped would help with his festering feet.

Back on the river, the headwind was still blowing at hurricane force. Visibility was nearly zero, and without goggles Tim couldn't even open his eyes. Any sign of the trail was obliterated by drifted snow. Trail markers still stood in place, but visibility was so bad that they couldn't find their way from one marker to the next. They simply walked in a straight line until the snow was deep enough to indicate they were off trail, and then made increasingly larger circles until they could locate a packed trail base once again.

The going was so slow that Tim was astonished he and Tom were still leading the race. Most of the foot racers had dropped out by that point, but an Alaskan and a Japanese competitor remained a few days back. Closer behind were the two Italian cyclists, as well as Andrew Heading and Mike Estes, who had teamed up after leaving Takotna with new supplies. The headwind was so intense that Tim was certain no one could be moving faster than a mile per hour up the river, no matter their mode of travel. It must have been terribly demoralizing to the cyclists to have a hard, flat surface on which to ride, but winds too intense to turn pedals.

By late afternoon of their fourth day on the Yukon, Tom suggested taking shelter again on the visible east bank. Tim dissented, arguing that they didn't have enough food for more than one day, and they had made very little progress. If they made camp and the weather failed to break for a few more days, they could end up in real trouble. Their progress toward Kaltag was slow, but at least it was progress, Tim reasoned.

A few hours later, the storm abruptly stopped. The blizzard that had been howling in their faces for two days faded within a matter of minutes, as though a switch had been flipped. The sky cleared and although the wind continued to blow, it didn't have nearly the same ferocity as earlier.

As inky darkness once again settled over the sky, a snowmobile came screaming toward them like a jet landing on the river. The driver, an Athabascan Native with a rifle slung across his back, came to an abrupt stop beside them and turned his engine off. "Do you have a gun?" he asked in a gruff voice without any other form of greeting. Tim considered the answer. If he said "yes," would he end up in a gun fight without a gun? And if he said "no," would he still end up in a gun fight without a gun? Either way, he was not going to win. He replied, "No, I don't have anything of value." The man laughed and told a story about a friend who had encountered a wolf on the river near this spot the previous year, and lost his arm in the attack.

"Have you seen any wolves?" the man asked.

"Yes, three days back on the river," Tim answered. "For you, probably only a few hours away."

"Not long," the man agreed. He bragged that his machine could go eighty miles an hour down the river, and Tim believed him. He asked how far it was to Kaltag, and the man said it was twenty-five miles. With that, he revved the engine and continued full-throttle into the darkness.

Tom was furious that Tim had asked about the distance to Kaltag, as he desperately wanted to believe that the village was closer than that. But Tim didn't fully believe his own trail notes, and figured the Native man's odometer could not be far off the real distance. Tom continued to stew as though Tim's question had physically moved the village another ten miles away.

Still, a light haze in the sky announced the village at 3 a.m. As skies cleared, cold, heavy air had again settled over the river, and Tim guessed the temperature was near thirty below. They located the school on the far end of town. The school was occupied by the filmmaker who was still hitchhiking on planes along the course to film the race. The men slept for four hours, after which daylight and pain awoke Tim from dreamless slumber once again. Rising from the gym floor, he could scarcely walk. He gently transferred weight from one grossly swollen foot to his grossly swollen leg as he hobbled to the locker room. In the shower he sat on the floor, as it had become too painful to stand, and cleaned the oozing sores on his feet.

They repacked their sleds with their own supplies and the discarded supplies of scratched racers, and set out at noon. The weather had markedly improved — clear skies, light winds, and temperatures above zero. It looked good for the eighty-mile trek from the Yukon River to the coast across a small range of mountains and tundra. Still, trail notes warned that the terrain was exposed and the weather could change with breathtaking swiftness.

Achieving the Impossible

6

*Life's battles don't always go to the stronger
or faster man. Sooner or later the man who
wins is the man who thinks he can.*

~Vince Lombardi
American Football Coach

After exiting Kaltag, the trail wound through low-lying taiga
— a wooded section of spindly spruce and more deeply accumulated snow. The
thin ribbon of trail was rippled with moguls, which snowmobiles created as drivers accelerated to blast through the powder. The uneven surface was taxing, and
Tim had to pay extra attention not to set his broken leg down in a bad position.
Again, the pain slowly diminished as he walked. A rhythm returned, and he and
Tom began to climb until the sparse trees gave way to barren tundra.

Above the tree line, the wind had become ferocious once again, and visibility
dropped in a swirl of blowing snow. Tim's eyelids began to freeze together, so he
reached into his sled to pull out his goggles, impatiently breaking the strap in the
process. He was in no spot to stop and fix them, so he'd just have to do without.
He couldn't see much better with his eyes opened than closed, anyway. The men
groped around for log tripods that marked the trail, which was entirely drifted
over with snow. Finally they reached a crest on the ridge and began to descend
back into the relative protection of the trees.

Fifteen miles past the summit, Tim's trail notes indicated an area of pot-
hole lakes where the trail wound through snow-covered sand dunes. Shortly
after that, they would reach a gently sloping area known as Tripod Flats, where

a BLM cabin stood just off the trail. Exhaustion had become so severe that Tim desperately willed the cabin to appear around ever new bend, and it just wouldn't. A spur trail off the Iditarod dead-ended in fifty yards, revealing nothing. They were death marching now, barely moving. Two in the morning came and went, and then 4 a.m., and then 6 a.m. There wasn't any tree shelter in this place, and still enough wind to make the thought of setting up camp more daunting than continuing to march toward the cabin. At 8 a.m., the men finally arrived at the base of a larger mountain, and just beneath it, a small building. The dilapidated cabin had no door, broken walls, and had been badly ransacked. A sign over the door read "Old Woman's Cabin" — Tim never even considered the possibility that they'd bypassed Tripod Flats, but in reality they'd traveled close to sixty miles since leaving Kaltag.

Luckily, the trail notes indicated a new cabin had been built a short distance past the original, with an outhouse, a large wood stove, two bunks, and a picnic table. Five-star accommodations, Tim thought. Mushers had left quite a bit of food piled up in the cabin — myth speculates that the ghost of an old woman haunts the cabin, and if travelers do not leave an offering for her, bad luck will accompany them to Nome.

As Tim and Tom chowed happily on the old woman's bounty, a snowmobile engine approached from outside. Two teenagers from Unalakleet stepped into the cabin, enjoying an extended weekend outing for spring break. They were astonished that the men had walked all the way from Anchorage, having never ventured that far from home themselves. One of the boys, a high school freshman, regaled the men with stories about the days when he was a "kid." The sea ice was much thicker then, he said, and he would accompany his grandparents onto the Norton Sound to club seals.

"How different this place is from my hometown, where kids play golf and tennis," Tim thought.

The teenagers continued down the trail, and Tim and Tom caught two more hours of sleep before continuing over smaller hills toward the coastal village. The tundra was wind-scoured and barren. Daylight seemed to slip away in a trance, and night arrived in a cloak of disorienting darkness over a landscape almost devoid of snow. As they marched, new depths of pain cut into Tim's broken leg. Snowmobile tracks now feathered out in all directions, and after several miles without spotting a marker, Tim knew they had wandered off course. Still, he could see a red light blinking in the distance, indicating the Unalakleet air strip, and felt confident that if they kept moving in that direction, they would find the village. The snowmobile track they were following veered off a small river, and the pain in Tim's leg had become so pronounced that he couldn't even climb the short bank. Gingerly, he dropped to his hands and knees and crawled.

They finally reached Unalakleet at 3 a.m., locating the school, which, inevitably, was on the far edge of town. A visiting high school basketball team was asleep on the floor of one of the classrooms, and Tim and Tom staked out their own sliver of space beside them. They were awakened several hours later by scampering feet, and Tim noticed a torn piece of paper next to his bag. "Alas, we meet again ... The Bikers," the note read. Tim felt a surge of disappointment but he knew this had been coming. It was unfathomable, actually, that two walkers could still be leading more than seven hundred miles into the race. Tim and Tom got up, enjoyed a meal at a hospitality suite set up for the basketball players, and went to an inn to meet the cyclists and the filmmaker. "The Bikers" were down to two — the Brit, Andy, and the Alaskan, Mike. Apparently the Italians could not push through the storm on the Yukon and opted to return to Eagle Island. They eventually were picked up by a snowmobiler, who took them to Kaltag, where they scratched from the race and flew back to Anchorage. The other two walkers had dropped as well — now only four remained in the Iditasport Impossible, 271 miles from the finish.

Tim purchased more painkillers at the village store, as his regime had increased to double the recommended dose. The bikers said they planned to leave in the afternoon, but Tim and Tom decided to try to grab some more rest and set out after dark. Tim slept fitfully; there was too much commotion at the school because of the basketball tournament. Realistically, he knew he simply couldn't obtain quality rest in villages, but the draw of warmth, kindness, and civilization was too enticing to pass up. Even without sleep, and even with the substantial increase in pain once he stepped out of his routine, these village stops were crucial to rejuvenate his and Tom's spirits. Still, by nightfall Tim was again exhausted, and it was time to pack up and leave.

After their twenty-hour stop in Unalakleet, the outside air felt dreadfully cold. It was twenty below zero — at this point a moderate temperature for Tim — but the wind was blowing and he felt a sharp urge to slip back into the warmth of the school and wait until morning. "The indoors softened me," Tim thought. "No wonder sled dogs prefer to sleep outside." His leg ached fiercely and now, with the cyclists in front of them, his race mentality had faded. There were only four competitors left, and when he and Tom weren't in the front of the race, they were in the back. Still, Tim felt strongly that he needed to finish this journey within his projected timeline.

Outside of the village, the winds were so strong that a swirl of snow obscured visibility close to the ground. They groped around on the outskirts of town for nearly an hour, searching for the trail. Tim felt exhausted and anxious. They shouldn't have puttered around all day, he thought. They should have traveled when it was warm and light, and rested through the icy darkness. Shadows flickered and disappeared. He had a nervous sense that his alertness was slipping, that his mind couldn't be trusted. But with his mounting physical shortcomings — broken bones, swollen limbs, festering blisters, exhaustion, and weight loss — he realized that doubt in his cognitive abilities was one anxiety he could not afford.

The trail began to veer away from the coast, turning inland toward the Blueberry Hills. Tom led as Tim struggled to keep up. During every restart, his leg pain persisted longer than it had the previous day. Tom complained their pace was too slow, and Tim insisted he was moving as fast as he could. At first light, six hours after leaving Unalakleet, they had traveled twelve miles. Even Tim was incredulous about the pace — trail conditions seemed to be good, but they were barely moving. He had been certain they'd been climbing all night, and yet the trail remained at sea level. Daylight left no question — they stood on a small creek with the frozen coast still in sight. Still, with the numbing effects of hours of marching, his leg pain improved, and renewed daylight stripped away some of his sleepiness.

In the late afternoon, a silhouette of the village of Shaktoolik appeared against the setting sun. A perfect row of dilapidated buildings was perched on a bluff above the edge of the sea. This was Old Shaktoolik, abandoned years ago. The populated village was just beyond the ghost strip, nearly identical to the old village, except that the buildings had windows and doors. On the inland side of the village was a twenty-foot wooden barricade. This was Shaktoolik's wind-blocking snow fence, without which the village would undoubtedly blow into the sea.

This day's weather was nearly perfect — only moderately cold with light wind — and Tim disliked the prospect of stopping in such conditions when the weather could turn on a dime. Still, he had obtained too little rest in Unalakleet, and the next section of trail included a forty-mile crossing on sea ice over the Norton Sound, with no protection from the elements and no possibility of stopping. They decided to eat and sleep for a few hours and leave at 4 a.m.

As it turned out, cyclists Andy and Mike had left Unalakleet after Tim and Tom, and arrived in Shaktoolik two hours later. The four racers divided up the bounty from the drop bags of racers who had dropped out of the Iditasport. Andy found a small plastic water bottle full of clear liquid, and was about to guzzle it when Mike screamed at him to stop. Andy had no sense of smell or taste as a result of a car crash that had killed his training partner a year earlier. The bottle was full of white gas — fuel for a stove — and Andy had come precariously close to drinking it. Tim could only shake his head at all of the ways a person could be killed in a race like this.

Tim and Tom set out in the pre-dawn darkness but failed twice to locate the trail beyond the barricade. After returning to the school a second time and receiving no better directions, they opted to grab two more hours of sleep and leave at daylight. Tim's ankles were so swollen that they protruded out of his shoes like rising bread dough. Ice shards scraped folds of flesh whenever his feet broke through the snow crust. The morning sky was red, and he could taste moisture in the air — not a good sign. He had learned to smell bad weather.

Tim knew they needed to do everything they could to beat the weather across the Norton Sound. Out on the sea ice, wind and snow would quickly swirl into a white out, and they'd be as good as blind. Tim's trail notes cautioned to set a compass bearing to 340 degrees and follow it in a straight line in the event of a white out. Open water churned against the pack ice to the southwest, so they'd better be certain they were headed north.

A number of fissure cracks rippled across the surface of the sea ice — the openings were as much as six inches wide, and dropped directly into the sea. The ice was so thick that water did not gurgle through, but Tim had to be wary of where he placed his feet. Snow covering the ice had been polished to a hard crust, and travel on the surface was flat and fast. Winds remained in the twenty mile-per-hour range — light for the Norton Sound — but dark clouds were building to the West.

Nightfall brought the snow; heavy accumulation hid evidence of snowmobile tracks, and darkness cloaked the spruce trunk tripods that marked the trail. By Tim's calculations, they were only four or five miles from the coast, and he felt sick with anxiety that they'd come so close only to get lost here. He'd heard too many stories about mushers going off course in a storm and arriving at open water dozens of miles from land. But with careful attention, he continued to spot tripods. A trapper passed on a snowmobile and informed them that they were six or eight miles from Koyuk.

Sure enough, the village appeared around 2 a.m. They always seemed to arrive at their destinations in the middle of the night. They located the school, which was unlocked and occupied by the bikers. They had caught them again. Tim placed a chair sideways on the floor to prop up his legs; pain was manageable on the trail, but came roaring back with compound interest every time he stopped. Despite the throbbing agony, Tim was asleep within seconds.

They left with the bikers at first light. The sky was clear but winds had increased to forty miles per hour, rushing in from the northeast. Leaving Koyuk, the trail returned to the sea ice and headed west along the coast, far enough off shore to avoid the icebergs that littered the shoreline. As expected, his leg was nearly unbearable for the first hour, despite a recklessly generous regime of Advil. In addition to leg pain, Tim's back was beginning to ache due to the misaligned body position he maintained to compensate for his weak and painful limb. Tim remained certain that his tibia was partially fractured, and wondered what would happen if it broke all the way through. Nome was still a hundred and fifty miles away; could he possibly make it before he crumbled to pieces?

The trail cut inland again, following a series of low hills and taiga forests so scrawny that the men could almost peer over treetops. They descended back to the sea along a wide river valley that was famous for funneling cold Arctic winds toward the Bering Sea. These air streams were referred to as "blow holes" — wind currents that rip like white tornadoes down the canyon. Blow holes have been known to pick up entire dog teams and toss snowmobiles across the ice like toy cars. The weather was uncharacteristically friendly on this day, however, and the winds seemed no worse there than anywhere else along the coast.

After a brief stop at a shelter cabin that marked the halfway point between Koyuk and the next village, Elim, Tim and Tom returned to the ice with the setting sun. The trail again left the beach and made slow uphill progress into wooded bluffs. Winds quieted with the darkness, and the night was extremely cold. If Tim stopped moving, even momentarily, his body would become wracked with uncontrollable shivering. His toes felt wet, and Tim took this as a sign that they were freezing. He needed to push harder to warm up, even as his leg protested the hard marching. Tim walked with a pronounced limp. A compensating swing in his left arm had also become more prominent, and he curved his back to shift weight off his injured leg. Tom teased him about leaning to the left, and Tim denied this — claiming that even as an independent voter, he has always leaned to the right.

At 2:30 a.m., village lights appeared again. The school was open, complete with bikers and drop bags. Tim was incredulous that they'd caught the cyclists once more. Again they were up at dawn, completing their chores and out the door with the bright, heatless sun and fierce wind. The trail followed the coast just off shore, next to a wall of jumbled ice.

After eight miles, they veered inland toward a steep climb up a mountain called Little McKinley. The temperature had warmed some, and the hard work of towing his sled uphill necessitated a stop to remove clothing. The view over the frozen ocean was surreal — a relief pattern set in scarcely discernible shades of white, bright and glittering and gorgeous. The barren mountain was windswept to a hard sheen, so smooth it looked like water. A herd of caribou congregated on the ridge just above the saddle. Tim wondered what these animals possibly had to eat; he saw nothing but snow and ice in all directions.

A three-mile descent led to Golovin Bay, with the village of Golovin just beyond another five-mile sea ice crossing. The downgrade hurt nearly as much as the climb, but at least gravity pulled his sled. With thoughts fixed firmly on Nome, Tim and Tom didn't even slow down as they marched through a row of houses lining a thin peninsula. Darkness descended with its breathtaking cold, and the miles to White Mountain lagged. From that village, there would only be eighty more miles to the finish. Like the fresh moisture of an approaching storm, Tim could smell it.

They reached the village of White Mountain just after midnight and located the school, again on the far side of town. This building's doors were locked, and the bikers, if they were still there, did not hear the men knocking nor their cries. Tim's thermometer mercury was buried in its bulb; it was well below minus twenty. Even running in small circles did not generate enough heat to stay warm. Standing in place, Tim was a mess of shivering within seconds. For nearly ninety minutes, Tim and Tom circled the area, pounding on the doors of adjacent buildings, before they finally awakened the principal, who grumpily handed them the keys to the school. The bikers were no longer there, having checked out at 7 p.m. Tim no longer cared. He struggled to walk down the stairs, and it was becoming an effort to stifle urges to scream out in pain. As he clung to the railing, his eyes teared up with each step. Eighty more miles, he thought. Just eighty more miles.

The cook at the school cafeteria prepared piles of French toast for the men in the morning. She warned Tim and Tom that grizzlies would be coming out of hibernation soon, and heading straight for the sea to eat dead seals. Tim wasn't concerned. If a bear saw an opportunity, at least it would end swiftly because Tim wasn't in any condition to put up a fight. Outside, a wisp of a cloud hung on top of Little McKinley, as though it had been snagged while crossing the mountain. This was a good sign for the weather that day — a high pressure system promised more clear skies, and the day's high temperature was forecast at fifteen below.

Their plan was to march to Nome without stopping. It was 11 a.m. on the twenty-fifth day. If they could reach Nome before 3 p.m. the following afternoon, they would meet Tim's prediction of twenty-six days and set a new record. In addition, Tim could catch his scheduled flight home. Through all of the pain, fatigue, calls of the wild, and primal sensibilities, punctuality remained important to him.

Between White Mountain and Nome, the thinning taiga faded altogether. They were beyond the tree line, even at sea level, and depth perception faltered in a sea of white. The trail was hard-packed; snowmobilers often traveled between White Mountain and the "city" to the northwest. It cut a faint white line through the steep, rolling hills along the coast. The sun shone bright and the air felt almost warm; Tim couldn't believe that the temperature was still below zero. He felt oddly comfortable, although his broken leg throbbed with pain. Even the pain itself was becoming part of his routine and there were occasional blissful hours when he hardly noticed it, similar to the way one might become accustomed to the roar of trains after enough time living near tracks. This — the pain, the blinding whiteness, the cold, the faint glow of a village in the middle of the night, the howls of wolves, all of this — was Tim's world out here.

Ski planes buzzed overhead throughout the day, spreading echoes of a civilization Tim could scarcely remember. The trail undulated into progressively longer climbs and descents. Some were almost unworkably steep. The nearness of Nome gave him vigor, but his leg seemed to answer with intensifying shocks of pain.

They climbed another steep mountain, Topkok Head, which also serves as a funnel for hurricane-force blow holes. From the thousand-foot summit, Tim could see for dozens of miles in all directions. Skies were clear, signaling a safe window for travel. The ground was a simple relief of white and shadow. There were ripples of larger mountains to the north, and a glimmer of dark ocean just over the horizon to the south. Amid the colorless background, the top of this mountain appeared to kiss the sea.

The sun again sank into the southern horizon. The men descended to a shelter cabin, where they planned to eat supper and melt snow for drinking water before continuing to Nome. Inside the small building was a stove, which Tim stuffed to the brim with driftwood in an effort to expedite the heating process. It proved to be too much — the stove rapidly heated to metal-glowing temperatures, and the temperature inside the cabin rose to sauna levels. Tom was angry that Tim had over-fueled the fire, but they couldn't take burning wood out of the stove. To cope, they both stripped to their tights, leaving their clothes to dry pieces of chain-link fence suspended above the stove.

As Tim and Tom sat side by side on a section of log without shirts or socks, a snowmobile engine came roaring up to the cabin. Seconds later a man and a woman opened the door. The couple looked at the skimpily clad men, and without a word turned around, shut the door, fired up their snowmobile, and drove away.

Tim and Tom finished cooking and set out again just before dusk. The saturated orange and red streaks over the horizon were nothing short of incredible — Tim viewed this as a good omen. There were twenty-five more miles of potential blowhole dangers before they reached the final, now abandoned Iditarod checkpoint on the route — appropriately named Safety. If they could cross this section of trail with good visibility and weather, the remaining twenty-two miles would be a flat victory lap to Nome.

The trail ventured back out on the sea ice, so wind-scoured that the surface was smooth and slippery. One surprise blast of crosswind would surely sweep them out to sea, but for now it was relatively calm. "The winds along this stretch are not an empty threat to make the race look more dangerous for publicity purposes," the trail notes read. "In 1994 a musher inadvertently headed out onto the ice. She finally got her team stopped only a few hundred yards from open water. The winds were so bad, searchers could not find her until the next morning, and by then she had badly frostbitten her hands in the minus 130-degree wind chill and had to scratch."

Two years earlier, a local musher was caught in a blowhole and could not make his way back to the shelter cabin in time. His body was packed in snow by the time he was found the following morning. Nome was close enough to feel, and yet Tim's anxieties made it seem impossibly far away.

As night deepened, green waves of aurora filled the sky. The temperature was about twenty-five below, and the air was blissfully calm. The trail followed a narrow spit of land and the driftwood line was prominent — less than a quarter mile past that line was open water. Tim knew the weather could turn without warning. He wouldn't take anything for granted, but for now their passage was gentle, almost easy, and he kept his sights fixed on small goals: the shelter cabin six miles from Topkok, followed by the Solomon River where a lagoon drained into the sea — site of the Solomon Blowhole, the most notorious of all. If he could just reach that point, he was as good as in Nome. As they walked, the light breeze strengthened. Tim's heart raced.

The harder the breeze blew, the harder Tim pulled. His trail notes indicated the route would join an unplowed road twelve miles from Safety. Amid his nervousness Tim didn't even realize they had reached the road, until he noticed a mile marker sticking out of the snow. They were close! Finally, Tim could gaze up and enjoy the latest episode of the Northern Lights Show. Cold air wrapped around him like a wet rag. His hands were going numb despite a fist-clenching routine. Daylight was still many hours away, but his anxieties were weakening.

At about 3 a.m., Tim noticed a tall sign constructed with white plastic standing next to the trail. Suspended from this frame, about fifteen feet off the ground, were three multicolored flags with strange symbols, probably a Native language. Fifteen minutes later, a similar sign appeared — this one even larger, with three similarly strange flags. As Tim wondered about these flags, he came to a cyclone fence blocking the entrance to a large concrete building. A yellow sign on the fence read "Caution, High Voltage — Stay Out."

Tim thought it must be a nuclear power plant — but what was such a plant doing way out here, almost thirty miles from what was already a very small city? Maybe it was some other kind of industrial facility? A water treatment plant? The outer walls were painted white. "Tom, what do you think this place is?" he called out.

Tom turned around with a confused look on his face. "What are you talking about?"

"That building of course."

Tom looked blankly toward the direction Tim was pointing and said, "What building?" When Tim turned to look again, the entire complex had vanished without a trace.

The hallucination was so detailed, so vivid, that its lack of existence frightened Tim even more than if it had been real. Something in his mind had conjured this scenario that was as real to him as the trail on which he walked, or the stars in the sky. How was he to say now what was real and what was not? He understood how some people simply walked into the sea without explanation. Perhaps they, too, saw something that no one else saw.

Two hours later, he saw another building in the dark. This log structure had no lights and looked abandoned. Draped over the side was a banner welcoming Iditarod mushers to Safety. This building was real. Safety, population zero, had been attained. The buildings were locked. Nothing to do now but walk.

More than a hundred years earlier, cabins lined this entire stretch along the route to Nome. The "Gold Coast" was peppered with nuggets, and thousands of people sought fortunes on the wind-swept beaches. Federal laws prevented claims to the beach, so all comers were and still are welcome to try their luck. Nome's population, once over thirty thousand, has dwindled over the century to fewer than three thousand. But even in modern times, tourists still fly to Nome during the summer months to scratch around on the beach in an ongoing search for fortune. In the winter, the only signs of civilization are occasional empty fishing shacks. Tim was grateful that the trail seemed well-traveled. With Safety behind them and undiscovered gold buried beneath the ice, only one goal remained.

A cold crosswind kicked up from the south, stinging the left side of Tim's face for a change. His toes lost all feeling, and ice built up thickly on his face mask, freezing to the skin on his cheeks and clamping his eyelashes shut. Cold and pain pushed against forward progress as hard as it had yet, but Tim was as serene as a monk; little things could no longer bother him. Night finally surrendered to dawn for the last time as the men approached Cape Nome, a seven hundred foot hill. The road circled its base, requiring no climbing.

At 8 a.m., amid the soft glow of morning light, the bungee cord securing Tim's sled to his harness snapped. It was unbelievable, Tim thought, that after a thousand miles this cord had to fail with a mere twelve miles remaining in the journey. It was too cold to re-secure the sled to the auxiliary ring in his harness, so he simply tied the broken bungee around his hip belt. Surely that would hold up for another few hours.

After rounding the Cape, Tim gazed ahead at another rock formation at the base of a distant hill. As the sun rose behind him, he saw a glistening reflection and realized that what he was looking at wasn't a rock outcropping at all — it was Nome! The reflection came from a glass window on a large building, and other structures were beginning to take form. A floodgate of emotions rushed through Tim's body and his eyes welled up with tears that instantly froze. He called out to Tom, who was already aware that they were looking at their final destination. Tim was enchanted, as though they were approaching the Emerald City of Oz.

The final two miles of the route headed straight down the tarmac of Front Street, the first cleared road Tim had seen since the race started twenty-six days earlier. As they approached the edge of town, they saw Andy, who had finished with Mike at 8:07 the previous evening. Although Mike had caught the early flight to Anchorage, Andy lingered in town, waiting for Tim and Tom. He snapped photos and giggled like a child, seemingly as happy as Tim felt. Locals rolled down the windows of their vehicles and cheered. A musher whom the men had leapfrogged on the Yukon waved from the porch of a two-story building above Front Street. Terry, an Iditarod checker from Rohn, was there, as was the school cafeteria dishwasher from White Mountain.

At 11:46 a.m., the famed burled arch finally came into view — a thousand miles, twenty-six days, and an emotional lifetime after leaving Knik. Tim and Tom finished side by side, together shaving fourteen days from the previous foot record. Tim's heart boiled over with emotions, and he couldn't help but burst out into cries of joy and victory.

"Who will they send against me now?" he called out beyond the small crowd of spectators, into the emptiness beyond.

And yet, it was only the beginning. Three years later, he would begin to understand just what "they" were capable of sending against him.

A New Challenge

7

We are what we repeatedly do. Excellence,
then, is not an act, but a habit.

~Aristotle

After the 2001 Iditasport, Tim spent most of the year rehabilitating
from his broken leg. A post-race hospital visit revealed that his right tibia was
fractured three-quarters of the way through. Any number of missteps could have
splintered the bone entirely, rendering him incapable of walking. That the bone
held together was a small miracle, and added to the impressiveness of such unlikely success. When a filmmaker interviewed Tim in Nome shortly after the
finish, Tim announced that he was happy to have accomplished such a grand
adventure, and was even happier that he never had to do it again. Famous last
words, as they say.

Shortly after the 2001 event wrapped up, the Iditasport organization began
to unravel. In the two years since he had launched the thousand-mile Impossible race to Nome, race director Dan Bull faced compounding complaints about
misplaced drop bags, alleged safety violations, and checkpoint disputes. Tim had
not been alone in his experience of arriving at a checkpoint or village and being
unable to locate drop bags. Other participants claimed that the race director's
negligence in delivering supplies and promised services forced them to withdraw
from the race. Bull cited financial strain as a source of the problems, claiming
Iditasport made no money due to expensive promotions and prize purses. The

race's unpaid board of directors pressed for changes to improve the safety and profitability of the race, but Bull remained stubbornly defiant of their suggestions. The resulting clash led to an implosion of the Iditasport. The board of directors quit, volunteers pulled out, and sponsors withdrew their support. A tentatively planned race in 2002 never materialized. Shortly thereafter, Dan Bull left Alaska, taking the Iditasport trademark with him.

One of the members of Iditasport's board of directors was a wily Alaskan named Bill Merchant, who had completed the previous four runnings of the 350-mile Iditasport Extreme. When veteran racers approached him about continuing the human-powered Iditarod race, Merchant stepped in with an idea for a "no-frills, nonprofit race put on by racers for racers." With just two distances — the 350-mile race to McGrath and the thousand-mile race to Nome — no prize money, and definitely no frills, the newly formed Iditarod Trail Invitational launched in 2002. Merchant emphasized the need for wilderness experience and self-reliance over athletic achievements. He scaled back drop bag deliveries, cut all but a handful of rules, and kept the marketing surrounding his race to a minimum. While the Iditasport sometimes garnered international attention and a small media circus, the Invitational fell off the radar almost entirely. Once again, almost nobody knew about the crazy athletes who set out into the Alaska wilderness without the assistance of planes or snowmobiles or even dogs. Still, everything that was important — the beauty of the Alaska backcountry and the allure of an ultimate challenge — remained. Twenty-seven athletes signed up for the 2002 event.

Despite a difficult recovery from his injuries, Tim considered joining the inaugural Iditarod Trail Invitational. Like the dog sled race, the Invitational would follow the Northern Route that year. Tim's adventurous side yearned for this new experience, and his competitive drive was intrigued by reports that trail conditions were typically much better and travel was faster on this middle third of the Iditarod Trail. Plus, he had experience now, and despite sleep deprivation and mind-clouding pain, his memory had acutely recorded all the nuances of the trail. The walk to Nome had been one of the most intense experiences of his life, and the desire to relive such an experience was just as strong. By February 2002, however, Tim was nowhere nearly recovered enough, mentally or physically, to take on such an arduous journey again. He waited patiently until 2004, the next Northern Route year. Tom, his fellow 2001 finisher and friend, also wanted in on the action.

Ninety miles and two days into the 2004 event, Tom quit the race at Skwentna Roadhouse. There was no forewarning; his heart just wasn't in it this year. Tim pressed forward knowing he would likely remain alone for the rest of the journey. He felt some reservations about traveling solo, but he also had more confidence in his experience and abilities. This time around, he opted for shoes one size larger to help with swelling in his feet. He also brought antibiotics in case of blister infection or respiratory illness. He had a sled custom made long enough for his body, so he could leave his sleeping system unrolled and crawl into the sled for a quick nap. Although the ease of access was an advantage, Tim discovered the longer sled also caused more drag on soft snow.

Similar to his previous journey, Tim slept very little in the first days of the race. By the third night he was so sleepy that he dove into his sleeping bag head first so that he wouldn't be required to take off his shoes. Tim left Rainy Pass Lodge in the midst of a howling windstorm that buried the trail in loose, sandy powder. Although he'd started up the climb to Rainy Pass several hours behind a group of British cyclists, he caught up to them within two hours, proving he was moving at least twice their rate of speed. Blowing snow masked the trail and the cyclists groped around, uncertain which direction to proceed. Tim felt for the trail with his feet — beneath the shin-deep powder was a hard base that would give way to waist-deep fluff whenever he stepped off the trail. Still, movement was blind and thus slow. Tim and the cyclists opted to work together, consulting their maps and scouting for the occasional trail-marking tripod.

Once they dropped off a ridge line toward the recognizable topography of Pass Creek, Tim felt more confident in his navigation and opted to press ahead, hoping to crest Rainy Pass before dark. Near the pass, Tim came to a sinkhole with fast-flowing water churning underneath. It was an open eddy of Pass Creek, and the unstable snow bridge over the water had collapsed. Although it was only a small hole, Tim suspected the thin snow crust on either side was just as unstable, and he didn't know how or where he would find more stable snow on which to cross the creek. He opted to take the known, packed trail that had been broken by the sinkhole, even though another collapse could potentially drop him ten feet into open water. But he saw no alternative route.

Tim unhooked his sled and dropped to his hands and knees, trying to spread his weight over unstable snow as he crawled across the fragile bridge. He could hear cold water gurgling beneath his knees as he nudged the sled forward in front of him. At the halfway point, the snow shelf began to collapse behind him. Panic gripped his gut and Tim lunged on top of his duffel bag, pushing the sled forward on his stomach as though he were bodysurfing a breaking wave. He made butterfly-stroke motions with his arms to continue propelling himself forward, flailing his warms wildly as the rear end of the sled tipped downward into the hole. The motion swirled up a cloud of snow, and he blindly groped at the white space in front of him until he grabbed onto something hard. Leverage from the unknown object allowed him to anchor his sled as he propelled it forward, beyond the collapsing shelf. Water churned in the newly formed sinkhole just inches away from his feet, but his sled had made it to solid ground. With a pounding heart, Tim looked toward the unseen object he was grasping and realized it was the windshield of a plane, apparently broken loose in a bush plane mishap. Some pilot's misfortune had turned out to be Tim's saving grace. Later,

Tim would learn that the bikers managed to cross the creek further up the slope without incident.

Beyond the crest of the pass, the trail was less drifted, prompting a swift descent of Dalzell Gorge. Just a few hours after they avoided the collapsing snow bridges of Pass Creek, one of the British cyclists, Carl Hutchings, crashed his bike into a rock outcropping and sustained a massive head wound. Blood was pouring from his forehead and his skull was exposed when he arrived in Rohn. Reluctant to drop out of the race, Hutchings made arrangements to fly back to Anchorage, have his wound surgically repaired, and fly back to Rohn so he could proceed with the race. He lost fewer than 24 hours in the process.

Warm weather and soft, new snow gave way to wind and bitter cold, with daytime highs south of twenty below. Battered and exhausted by the arduous conditions through the Farewell Burn, all of the cyclists who had signed up to continue onto Nome decided to abandon the race at the 350-mile finish. Although he left the checkpoint before all of the competitors had arrived, Tim suspected that the slow progress to McGrath combined with the draining effect of the cold would lead all others to end the race there as well. He left the last outpost of civilization for hundreds of miles knowing there was a good chance he would be alone on the trail for the remainder of the race.

In Takotna, only eighteen miles beyond McGrath, the packed trail abruptly ended. Tim circled the village in an effort to locate the tracks set by the Iron Dog Snowmachine race, which was held nearly a month earlier. All visible traces were swept beneath a soft carpet of new snow. Now Tim felt truly alone, without even the Iditarod Trail to keep him company. He located an unplowed road bed leading toward Ophir, with several inches of snow on top of the road base. After several miles of blazing his own path toward the abandoned mining town, a large bull moose thrashed through a willow bush and landed on the trail less than ten feet in front of him. Tim froze as the moose regarded him suspiciously, clouds of vapor streaming from its flared nostrils. After several tense seconds, the moose turned and cautiously walked away. Tim had likely spooked the moose out of the brush, and he was extremely fortunate that the moose decided this small, lumbering creature wasn't a threat. In the winter, Alaska moose are usually grumpy, but also hungry. Late-season fatigue is sometimes the only thing that saves humans and dogs from being stomped to death.

The cold deepened, and the trail continued to be sporadic and difficult to locate. Iditarod checkers in Ophir informed Tim that the leaders of the dog sled race were about two days out, and the trail breakers would be through soon. Temperatures had dropped to forty below overnight, they told him, and it was likely to be even colder the following night. As the Iditarod Trail wound through taiga and wind-scoured tundra beyond Ophir, the faint hints of tracked path seemed too circuitous, as though the trail had been established before the waterways froze. The meandering route frustrated Tim, and the trail was so scarcely broken that it was hardly helpful, but he was too anxious about getting lost to blaze a more direct path.

As hours passed, Tim's toes and fingers began to go numb. No matter how fast he moved, he couldn't coax them to warm up. Icy numbness was also beginning to trickle toward his larger extremities. "Best to sleep through the coldest part of the night," he thought as he crawled into the sleeping bag already spread out in his sled. Once he had the drawstring closed, he began to shiver violently, working up a weak barrier of warmth in the down bag. His balaclava was frozen to his head, and even after several minutes inside the bag he could not pull it off. Sleep came in spurts and fits, and Tim awoke after two hours, still shivering, with an almost desperate urge to pee. His balaclava was still frozen to his head. He moved to crawl out of the bag, but the zipper was frozen in place. He grabbed his shoes from the foot of the bag, but they too were ice-hard with the openings frozen together. He couldn't leave the bag if he couldn't put his feet in his shoes, so he pressed them against the skin on his stomach. The frozen footwear burned the skin on his abdomen as he drank the rest of the warm water in his Nalgene bottle, then used it as a urinal.

It took another hour of shivering softly in his bag before his shoes had softened enough to squeeze his feet inside. He wrestled with the frozen zipper until he could pry it open, and emerged into the clear pre-dawn darkness. All of the residual perspiration on his body and around his head quickly froze, until his whole body was encased in flecked white ice. Tim thought he must look like an abominable snowman, lumbering stiffly in the dark — but there was no one around to comment on his appearance.

The next village was still two hundred miles away. When temperatures drop below minus forty in the Alaska wilderness, most movement effectively ceases. Air becomes breathlessly still, as though even oxygen could freeze in these temperatures. Ice crystals cling to surfaces, machinery stops working, and humans retreat to shelter. Even animals hunker down and try to conserve energy amid the strength-robbing chill. For three days Tim pressed on into the outer-space-like cold, alone in Interior Alaska, without seeing a breath of movement or human presence. No snowmobiles passed and no bush planes buzzed overhead. It was as though the frigid air had frozen time, and only he continued walking while everything else stood still.

The Iditarod Trail Invitational race organizer had dropped a bag of Tim's supplies at a place called Wolf Kill Slough. Tim did not know exactly where this place was or what it might look like. He had been cutting his own track across the faint trail base for three days. The trail was often completely obscured by new snow, and at one point he walked in a spiraling circle over the wide-open tundra for nearly six hours just to locate the lost path. If too much time passed without seeing a reflective marker, Tim would retreat back to the last known trail sign, knowing that the wind-drifted snow would obscure his tracks within minutes, and then he would be truly lost. Although he was developing a distinct fear that the world had ended without him knowing and he was now the last person on Earth — intellectually, Tim knew the first Iditarod dog teams would have to pass through here soon. His progress on snowshoes was interminably slow, and he gained little by pressing forward. Although he was running low enough on food to be concerned, Tim opted to stop and set up camp, and sleep until the trail breakers arrived.

Seven snowmobiles roared up to his camp two hours later, at about 11 p.m. The drivers were shocked to find a human in a sleeping bag. They informed him that they thought Wolf Kill Slough was just a few miles away. Encouraged by this news, Tim got up and followed their newly broken trail into the night.

Wolf Kill Slough, however, was many more than a few miles away. Tim didn't arrive until eleven hours later, at 10 a.m. By that point, he had been out of food for sixteen hours. Sitting next to the trail was a large burlap sack with all the contents of Tim's and all of the other scratched racers' drop bags. Tim rifled through a king's ransom of goodies and pulled out his stove to cook a feast of freeze-dried meals and soup. As he ate, the snowmobile driver who had guessed at Wolf Kill Slough's distance drove back down the trail, searching for Tim. The driver said that he was very upset that he had misrepresented the distance, and wanted to make sure that Tim had reached his drop bag. Tim said he appreciated his concern, but he needn't have worried. Still, it was nice to have company, even briefly.

Along the lonely Northern Route, miles blurred together like water in a stream. After many days by himself, the anxiety of being alone faded, and Tim felt empowered by his ability to make his own decisions and set his own schedule. He made good time traveling downriver on the mighty Yukon. In what seemed like both a wisp of time and a small eternity, Tim completed the unknown section of trail and returned to villages he recognized. The familiar buildings sparked fond and vivid memories, like a time machine into the near past.

"This is so much better without a broken leg," he thought.

The Iditarod Trail seemed to accept him as well, and instead of the compounding misfortunes of his rookie year, this journey brought waves of serendipitous luck. Just when his lips began to crack, after he had used up all of his lip balm in the incessant winds, Tim found a Ziploc bag with a new stick of lip moisturizer and breath-freshening gum on the trail. He had opted not to pack a toothbrush to save weight, and after deciding this was a mistake, Tim found a disposable toothbrush in one of the British cyclists' drop bag. The overland trek into Unalakleet forced him to fight an icy headwind, and wearing all of his clothing, he had to lean forward just to make progress. He thought that a pair of trekking poles might help to maintain momentum, and found a couple of longer trail stakes that did the job well. A while later, after crossing the Norton Sound and turning west toward the setting sun, Tim thought it would be nice to have a hat with a brim. Almost as soon as he started thinking about it, he found a Russian-style polar fleece hat complete with a brim and ear flaps, just lying in the middle of the trail.

"The Iditarod Trail provides," Tim thought.

As he traveled along the coast from Koyuk to Elim, heavy snow fell and visibility deteriorated in the blowing wind. Trail markers became difficult to spot, so Tim switched his smaller headlamp for a larger one with three LED lights — two small side lights and a large, spotlight-throwing headlight in the center. The headlight picked up reflective markers from a farther distance, but consumed power faster than Tim could afford with his dwindling battery supply. The trail turned away from the sea ice and cut into the woods. Tim figured he had twelve miles left to travel to Elim, so to conserve battery life he turned off the center headlight, leaving only the two side LEDs illuminated.

Around midnight, two snowmobiles approached from behind. A blizzard was still raging and visibility was bad enough that even their bright headlights blurred in the swirling snow. Tim faced the drivers and shook his head, hoping the motions of his own headlight would catch their attention so they wouldn't run him over. Once they were about thirty yards away, both snowmobiles stopped on the trail. Tim waved his hands to acknowledge he saw them and would wait for them to pass. Instead of slowly proceeding on the trail as drivers typically did, one snowmobile pulled off the main trail and circled back toward Tim, again stopping about thirty yards away. The second snowmobile driver turned his engine off. Tim didn't understand what was happening, so he shook his head a few more times to indicate that he was standing there and wouldn't move until they passed.

As the snowmobiles idled in place, Tim felt the hairs bristling on the back of his neck. His muscles tensed, but he couldn't determine why he instinctively sensed a threat. A long minute passed, and then the snowmobile driver who had driven off trail turned the engine back on and accelerated toward Tim, cutting the throttle just as he dipped back onto the trail. The man was fully armored in a cold-weather snowmobile suit, hood, and goggles, with a rifle slung across his back. The man was imposing, Tim thought, but not threatening. Still, his muscles remained tense.

The man chuckled at some unknown joke and then explained that when Tim shook his headlamp, he assumed the separated LED lights were the eyes of an Arctic Fox. He and his friend were out hunting wolves, but a fox was a fine trophy as well. After driving his snowmobile to a strategic spot, the man pulled out his rifle and had the crosshairs in the scope fixed directly on the lights of Tim's headlamp. He was fractions of a second away from pulling the trigger when Tim moved in a way that made the man realize he was not an Arctic Fox, but a human. He would have fired a shot directly from the trail earlier, he said, but opted for an easy-kill direct shot when Tim did not immediately dart away.

Tim had encountered many dangers on the trail, but the prospect of being shot in the head by a local who mistook him for fox was a danger he had never suspected. He did not use that headlamp again.

Tim reached Nome twenty-three days after starting, the first person to complete both the Southern and Northern Iditarod routes on foot. His Southern Route record of twenty-six days held, but the overall record had since been broken by "Italian Moose" Roberto Ghidoni at approximately twenty-two days and seven hours, on the Northern Route in 2002. Tim had missed that record by one day because of unbroken trail and slow progress during his loneliest days after leaving Ophir. He was certain that the walk to Nome could be completed in less than twenty days, and knew that he'd be back to try again, one more time.

Setback

8

All you can do is hope that all the rest of it goes well for you.

~ Susan Butcher,
Four-time winner
of the Iditarod Sled Dog Race

As Tim mulled over his ambitions to run the Iditarod Trail in fewer than twenty days, an even more outlandish dream began to take shape — continuing along the western coast and crossing the frozen Bering Strait, all the way to Russia. Even with aspirations to break the overall record, the enormity of traveling from Knik to Nome had lessened in Tim's mind. He'd already done it twice, so clearly he'd have to up the ante in order to truly increase the challenge. Poring over maps, he determined a viable route. He could continue northeast from Nome on a snowmobile trail connecting the village of Teller, and from there use GPS headings to cross a bay another seventy or eighty miles to Wales, the westernmost point of Alaska. From there, he could cross the unpredictable and often treacherously unstable sea ice to the Diomede Islands, and then Siberia.

A few weeks before the race, the principal of the village school on Little Diomede Island warned Tim that the winter had been stormy and temperatures warmer than usual. The ice hadn't even fully taken hold in the churning waters of the Bering Sea, and conditions were likely to be volatile. She reported an abundance of polar bears in the area and laughed out loud when she realized Tim was serious about his ambitions to walk to Siberia. Undaunted by the principal's concerns, Tim filed for a Russian visa. He knew the Bering Strait could be crossed because it had been done before. Native lore was filled with elders who had traveled between continents on the sea ice, and Tim knew of at least one documented crossing where a father-son team successfully reached land after drifting nearly three hundred miles off course on the shifting ice. The year before, two people attempting the crossing called in a helicopter rescue. Tim had no idea whether the ice would set up in time to even attempt the journey, but he proceeded with plans as though it would happen.

In the midst of focused preparations, Tim neglected to get a flu shot as he had done before the 2004 Iditarod Trail Invitational. Even though that shot had been his first, and he hadn't had the flu in years, he was downed by debilitating sickness within a week of the race start. Three days before the race, Tim was still feverish and wracked with coughing and sneezing as he drove to the airport with another ticket from Pennsylvania to Anchorage. Tom Jarding was there as well, on board to take another crack at the Northern Route to Nome. However, Tom made it clear that Nome was his only objective — he wanted no part of the Bering Sea crossing to Siberia. By the time they boarded their plane, Tom wanted no part of Tim at all, refusing to sit next to him as Tim continued to cough and groan.

Once in Anchorage, Tim lay in bed at a friend's house, scarcely moving until a few hours before the race start. He had started a round of antibiotics that he had preemptively acquired for respiratory infections, and the drug regime seemed to improve his condition. Although still coughing and feverish, he could at least get out of bed without feeling dizzy. Maybe after a day on the trail, he would be back to full health. Optimism reigns when there are no other options.

The race started at two on a cloudy Sunday afternoon. Tim aimed to keep up with the lead foot racers out of the gate, but their starting pace seemed exceptionally fast. He wasn't sure if it felt this way because he had been weakened by sickness, or because Steve Reifenstuhl, an Alaskan who had established a new 350-mile foot record the previous year, was setting the pace. Sweat poured from Tim's body, soaking his clothes, and his head spun. He was dizzy and feverish, still, and the pace was much too intense. He sensed that he should back off, but refused to relinquish the lead so soon in the race. His alertness began to falter, and at mile ten he took a hard fall, spraining one of his ankles in the process. Tim realized that if he did not slow down, he would be forced to stop.

The weather, which had been exceptionally mild all winter, chose that night to introduce the cold. In fact, it was the coldest night of the year thus far in Anchorage, and by the time they reached Flathorn Lake at mile twenty-five, the temperature had plummeted well below zero. While this would seem mild to Tim if it were later in the race and he were more acclimated, the cold air cut straight through his soaked clothing and feverish skin, chilling him to the core.

Red Bull representatives had set up a bonfire on the lake, which Tim took advantage of to change out of his wet clothing and chug a couple of body-heat-generating energy drinks. Tim and Tom pried themselves from the warmth of the fire after midnight, and Tim felt utterly exhausted. He attempted to persuade Tom to stop short of the Susitna River in a place called the Dismal Swamp to sleep. Steve Reifenstuhl was now somewhere far ahead, but despite his competitive drive, Tim had no energy to give chase. Tom was reluctant to stop so early, and after several minutes of discussion, he convinced Tim that they should continue on to the first checkpoint, about twenty-five miles up the river.

Tim's lungs were so congested that he could not attain enough oxygen as long as his face mask covered his mouth. The temperature had fallen to twenty below zero; frigid, dry air infuriated his pulmonary system. High-pitched wheezing noises, which sounded to Tim like bird songs, whistled in his lungs. Even when he pulled his face mask down until the skin on his nose began to freeze, he felt like he was breathing through a thin straw.

They continued to follow Steve's tracks upriver, but something seemed off. The surrounding bluffs had an unfamiliar feel, and the river seemed to be moving away from distant mountains. Although he was reluctant to stop in the cold, Tim suggested they check his GPS device for their location. Sure enough, the arrow pointed to a hard left behind them, indicating that they had traveled too far up the Susitna River rather than turning at the confluence of the Yentna River. The bicycle tracks they were following, as well as Steve's footprints, were headed in the wrong direction. They turned around and found a snowmobile trail leading up the correct river. They lost a couple of hours, but by the early morning, they finally made their way to Luce's Lodge at mile fifty-two. The temperature was close to thirty below.

At the lodge, Tim was too sick to even eat one helping of spaghetti. Every joint in his body ached, and although the temperature in the cabin was only one degree below sweltering, his body trembled with chill. Tim and Tom snagged two hours of sleep on the floor, then pushed on just as dawn's light was reaching across the river. Most of the lost cyclists had found their way to the checkpoint, but Steve was still unaccounted for. They would later learn that he had dropped out of the race, apparently disheartened by his early misstep.

Ten miles up the river they passed Yentna Lodge, which was bustling with activity early in the morning. The Iditarod Trail passed right by the runway, so they stopped in for a cup of coffee. Although Tim typically would have no interest in stopping after such a short time on the trail, he welcomed more rest. The congestion in his lungs gurgled loudly with every breath, and he was now harboring doubts about his ability to even finish the race to McGrath. Still, his head was feeling more grounded than it had the night before, and daylight definitely helped. He assured himself that with his antibiotic regimen he was getting healthier by the hour, hoping that simply believing it would make it true. He knew all too well that his only hope was to harness the power of positive thinking.

"If you think you can do something, you're right. And if you think you can't do something, you're also right," he repeated to himself. Tim desperately wanted to believe he could do this, but his body demanded rest with such intensity that exhaustion knocked down even the highest walls of optimism.

The day was beautiful with no wind, although still very cold. Tom set the pace and Tim followed, frequently falling behind and pushing to catch up. Finally Tom pulled away, and Tim arrived at the mile ninety checkpoint, Skwentna Roadhouse, twenty minutes behind Tom. They ate and slept until 2 a.m., then headed out. Tim was now lapsing into full-blown coughing fits, but it seemed his fever had broken.

Within a couple of miles of leaving Skwentna, the trail split. Tim saw fresh bike tracks veering to the right and followed them, pushing through the darkness toward a climb that Tim assumed would traverse the Shell Hills. After two hours, they arrived at a large lake. Tim couldn't remember a lake this large appearing before the descent to Shell Lake. After a few more minutes, Tim saw cabins on the shoreline of the lake and was certain he didn't recognize this spot at all. They had clearly taken a wrong turn. The GPS showed the waypoint of Shell Lake Lodge about eight miles away as the crow flies, but the trail dead-ended at the edge of the lake with no apparent path going in the direction of Shell Lake.

Seeing a small light at the other end of the lake, Tim and Tom decided to veer across the ice and ask someone in the building for directions. It took a half hour to cut through the unbroken snow, and another ten minutes to struggle up the steep embankment to the cabin. Inside the building was a running power generator. A stack of cut lumber indicated an ongoing construction project. But the people working on the building were nowhere to be found. With no other direction, Tim and Tom had to confront the reality of returning to Skwentna, knowing they had veered off trail hours earlier. The backtracking journey seemed to move in slow motion, with the men knowing that they were simply unraveling hours of hard work. At the trail intersection, Tim noted that the bike tracks they'd followed were simply short-cutting the Y-shaped split before veering left onto the correct trail. Later, he learned that the destination that had cost them six or seven hours was called Hewitt Lake. Clearly, Tim thought, he had been unconsciously drawn to the place.

Plodding along on the now-correct trail to Shell Lake, Tim was unable to maintain Tom's pace. He'd race to keep up, but often had to stop altogether to catch his breath. They arrived at the lodge by mid-afternoon, had a cup of coffee, and set out toward Finger Lake, twenty-five miles away. Tim's shortness of breath persisted, and eventually he told Tom that he was no longer going to try to hold this pace. Oxygen became more readily available at a slower pace, but Tim's lungs continued to make bird noises and his head was becoming cloudy again. As the night wore on, the wind picked up, stealing away what little strength his lungs had left. His breath was so short that he felt lightheaded, and decided that he had no choice but to bed down. In sleep, he thought, he would be able to process more oxygen and hopefully recover enough to continue.

But as he lay down in his sleeping bag, his airways sealed off completely; he couldn't breathe at all. Engulfed in panic, he wrestled with the closed zipper of his bivy sack. Even sitting up, his breathing was so labored that he wondered if he was having an asthma attack. He calmed enough to convince himself he just needed rest, only to experience the same consequences when he lay down again. Unable to recline in his sleeping bag, cold air seeped in from the outside and chilled his sweat-drenched skin. There were two choices — continue walking until he reached Finger Lake or … he didn't like to ponder the other option.

The weather mounted a biblical battle. Hurricane-force winds blasted his face with stinging snow, filling his lungs with a furnace blast of cold as he gasped for air through his face mask. Even with ski goggles, visibility was near zero and seeing the trail was impossible. Snowdrifts buried the surface, sometimes several feet high. Tim stopped to check his GPS frequently.

He finally reached the checkpoint at 2 a.m., a couple of hours after Tom, who was sound asleep in a wall tent. Tim still could not lie down, so he propped himself up against a canvas wall and eventually drifted to sleep in a sitting position. His sleep was frequently interrupted in episodes of coughing and choking, sputtering until his airway opened up enough to breathe again. Tim knew he was in real danger. He hated the thought of abandoning all of his grand plans just a hundred and thirty miles into the race, but he saw no other option. Tom got up to leave and Tim couldn't even muster the energy to say goodbye.

By morning, several other racers had gathered in the tent with intentions to scratch. One had frozen fingers that needed medical attention, and a few others had simply come to their senses. They headed up to Finger Lake Lodge only to learn that high winds and blowing snow would prevent ski planes from landing on the lake. A physician's assistant happened to be staying at the lodge. He placed his ear against Tim's back and diagnosed him with a severe case of bronchitis, cautioning that by no means should he continue with the race. The physician's assistant did advise Tim about common asthma medications that might alleviate some of the symptoms. As it so happened, Tim found an asthmatic worker at the lodge who was willing to part with leftover steroid pills, and the physician's assistant conceded that those might help. But he cautioned that side effects included rapid heart rate and sleep interruption, two issues Tim was already struggling with as a participant in an extremely difficult adventure race. Tim disregarded the side effects and ingested a piece of one of the pills. The drug did seem to improve his shortness of breath. Seeing as how the queue for the next plane out of Finger Lake was already full, Tim decided to push on to Puntilla Lake Lodge, thirty miles down the trail.

Tim felt better on the climb toward Puntilla, but the exertion did take its toll. As he rested at the lodge on the edge of the Alaska Range, the shortness of breath returned. He knew the condition had persisted too long and become too serious to expect an immediate recovery, and would likely only continue to deteriorate amid heavy exertion and gasping breaths of frigid air. His conscience was practically screaming in his ear as he packed up to set out over Rainy Pass, begging him to quit and save his own life. He knew he was being foolish and the odds were stacked greatly against him. But Tim is a stubborn man. If he was inclined toward reasonability, he would have never ended up in Alaska in the first place. And he told himself that he would push on, fight the odds to recover, and catch up to Tom before reaching Nome.

Beyond Puntilla Lake was the point of no return. Within minutes of stepping out of the warm air in the lodge, the rasping and chirping sounds began echoing inside Tim's balaclava. He planned to proceed at a steady pace but not push to the point of respiratory distress. As Tim marched toward the craggy mountains, a strange white mass draped over the lower slopes like a curtain. Tim removed his goggles, suspecting that ice had frozen to the corners of the lenses. But even without goggles the white curtain remained, roiling across the wide valley. His worst suspicion was confirmed — just ahead was a ground blizzard that was sure to be accompanied by hurricane-force winds. Bile filled Tim's stomach as his anxiety poured over. What now? He was completely exposed on the high tundra, with no choice but to either press directly into this terrifying storm, or retreat. And after all the willpower he had summoned to leave Puntilla, retreat was not an option Tim was willing to entertain.

The headwind steadily grew stronger as Tim climbed. Blowing powder had carved elaborate patterns across the surface of the snow, cresting like petrified waves in a white ocean. The distinct shape of shoe prints were elevated above the scoured surface where compressed snow stuck while loose snow blew away. Tim knew these were Tom's tracks, placed within the past twenty-four hours. In all of his miles of racing in Alaska, Tim had never seen inverted footprints before, and he was mesmerized by the sculpted shapes. As he neared the white wall of the ground blizzard, he zipped up his outer coat and adjusted his balaclava to ensure no skin was exposed. He could see the tops of the mountains still above the storm, and calculated that it might take eight hours to reach Rainy Pass, which was likely beyond the blizzard. Eight hours of misery, he thought. But determination overruled all else, and he put his head down and marched.

Within a half hour of making this final decision, he was enveloped in a furnace blast of frigid wind and opaque snow. Visibility fell to less than a hundred yards, and even then it was heavily obscured by the blizzard. Still, there were flickers of movement in the distance, and Tim became convinced he could see two dark figures making their way toward him. Just when he assured himself it was just an optical illusion, two people pushing bikes appeared through the swirling snow. The race director, Bill Merchant, and his wife, Kathi, had left Puntilla Lake a day earlier and holed up in a shelter cabin during the storm.

After waiting for most of the day, they decided to return to Puntilla Lake rather than push forward in the storm. Through the roaring wind, Tim could only hear half of the words they shouted, and they kept the conversation short. They told Tim that the shelter cabin was just off the trail a mile ahead, and advised him to seek shelter there.

Tim suspected he would never find the cabin, but about an hour later the faint tracks of footprints and bike tires veered off the trail. Inside the small log shelter was another cyclist who was surprised to see Tim. A stream of snow had blown through the doorway across the floor of the cabin, where it remained even though the cyclist had been there with a fire burning for more than a day. He offered Tim some heated grape Kool-Aid that had been left behind during a previous Iditarod race. After forty-five minutes of rest, Tim stood and announced he was heading out and planned to press on toward the pass. The cyclist appeared eager to join him, but then hemmed and hawed, admitting that he regretted not returning to Puntilla with Bill and Kathi. After several more minutes of deliberation, he agreed to follow Tim. The two suited up and headed out. Tim put on his snowshoes and leaned into headwind, assuming that the cyclist was following close behind. But when Tim turned around to ask how the cyclist was doing, he realized no one was behind him. The cabin was still just a few yards away, and Tim could only surmise that the cyclist stepped out the front door and instantly turned back toward Puntilla without so much as a goodbye.

The misery was all-encompassing, but a mere two hours later, Tim broke through the storm. Just as quickly as he had walked into the whiteout, he emerged into the clear violet sky of late afternoon, like climbing out of a swimming pool. He was delighted with the sudden change of weather, but right on cue with the diminishing survival threat, rasping breaths returned. Tim crested Rainy Pass and started down the Dalzell Gorge. The broken trail wasn't readily apparent, and he drifted too high on a canyon slope while looking for the path. The detour necessitated a steep slide into the gorge.

As Tim inched down a near-vertical snow wall, he thought about the Iditarod snowmobiler who had been killed in an avalanche near this spot just a week earlier. Minutes later, he arrived at an area of disturbed snow near an overhanging rock. Steel rods were punched into jumbled blocks of snow, and to the left there was a deep indentation where something large had been extracted. On the edge of this hole was a crude wooden cross made of willow branches. The wind had almost ceased and the night was eerily quiet and dark. But Tim had no emotional space left for the sadness of loss or the unease that crept around the edges of his resolve. He muttered a short prayer and moved on.

He took another broken piece of the steroid pills he was carrying, but his breathing problems were only getting worse. Even on the downhill slope, he needed to stop every few minutes to catch his breath. The night deepened and the trail seemed to go endlessly downhill, yet visible forward progress was elusive. Hallucinations started to press through the darkness like waking night-mares; Tim feared the pills were impacting his presence of mind, which was even worse than the lack of oxygen. In a desperate move he took the remaining pills and tossed them into the snow. He ached for the rest that he needed to think clearly, but knew he couldn't rest until he reached the next checkpoint, where he could prop up his body against a wall to sleep.

A strange combination of panic and exhaustion churned in his gut, but exhaustion was winning. Alertness was fading. Suddenly, an invisible force yanked his feet out from underneath his body. His back slammed onto the glare ice of a frozen stream, and his skull knocked against the hard surface. He had stepped into a deep embankment, which should have been obvious, without even realizing it. Even as he lay on the hard ice with a throbbing headache, he could feel himself dozing off. Whether under the influence of the medication or the sickness, he was losing control. He needed to sleep, but laying down he could not breathe. There were no other options but to press toward Rohn. If it took all night, so be it, but he simply had to proceed at whatever pace he was able to sustain.

Torturous hours followed. A thin tunnel of awareness fixated directly on maintaining labored breaths. Tim had to concentrate on putting one foot in front of the other, using his trekking poles to propel his heavy body forward — first out of the narrow gorge, then across the smooth ice of the Tatina River.

While Tim shuffled along, a sharp pain erupted through his Achilles tendon as though it had been slashed through with a knife. A burning sensation followed, and Tim suspected he had torn something near his heel. The injury was not disabling, but between his incessant coughing, weakened muscles, and labored breathing, it seemed like the obstacles between him and Rohn were becoming insurmountable. Marching on nothing more than a will to live, Tim finally reached the spartan checkpoint with its cluster of unheated tents. He stumbled to the tent set up for Iditarod Trail Invitational racers and propped his back against the canvas wall, feeling sorry for himself. He was no longer interested in catching Tom, and he no longer cared about breaking the Northern Route record or crossing the Bering Sea. His only concern was whether he could get out of Rohn alive.

There were no planes scheduled to arrive in Rohn for nearly a week, and no way to get ahold of a pilot before then. Tim also held a strong conviction that if he was able to walk, he should be able to walk himself out of this wilderness outpost rather than rely on emergency evacuation services to extract him. After eating and sleeping while sitting upright for a few hours, he was again able to breathe without stress. If he could somehow make it to McGrath, he could at least end this experience with dignity and some modicum of success because, after all, that was the finish of the 350-mile race. With the Alaska Range behind him, the significant climbs were over, and none of the remaining terrain would be too physically taxing if he continued to take it slow. With renewed rigor, Tim set out toward Nikolai at 10 a.m.

While previous days had given him several hours of morning reprieve from his more difficult breathing problems, on this day he was wheezing by noon. Wind raged around the toothpick-like spruce that comprised the forests on the far side of the Alaska Range, and Tim required frequent rests just to breathe at all. Nightfall arrived with renewed feverishness and more severe respiratory distress. After a few hours in the rasping darkness, Tim needed rest with a desperation that eclipsed even that of the night before. He climbed into his sleeping bag and tried to prop himself up against a snow bank. As he dozed off, he would roll over and wake up moments later gasping for air. Several failed attempts made him realize that, like the approach to Rohn, he had no choice but to keep moving until he reached Bison Camp, a tent encampment that was ten to fifteen miles away.

Finally, at 3 a.m., Tim reached the cluster of three small canvas tents. Each one was filled from wall to wall with snoring bison hunters. By the time he checked the third tent, Tim no longer cared how many people occupied it — he was going to wedge himself inside.

A bison hunter from Anchorage and his Native guide were sleeping on the spruce-bough-lined floor. Tim crawled into the tent, trying to be quiet but stymied by uncontrollable coughing fits and labored breathing. The guide, a big man from a nearby village, stirred awake and came to Tim's aid, grabbing a log and setting it next to the little wood stove so Tim could sit down. Tim was convulsing too much to remove his outer clothing, and the switch from cold air to warm air exacerbated his coughs. He tried to slow his breathing enough to answer the guide's questions, and it took Tim several minutes to utter a few words.

"You're in trouble," the guide told him. He explained that his forty-year-old friend had the same symptoms a year earlier and sounded exactly as Tim did. His friend was diagnosed with advanced pneumonia, and Tim surmised the diagnosis matched his own condition. He asked the guide how long his friend sounded this bad. "Just until he died," the guide replied.

Tim found that piece of information unsettling, but said he was still able to breathe as long as he remained upright. "That's exactly what my friend said," the guide replied. "When they found him, he was dead sitting upright." The guide explained that he had a satellite phone, and he was going to call someone in Nikolai. Without putting up any more resistance, Tim agreed. He could no longer doze off for even a minute without waking up with incessant coughing and sputtering. Bill and Kathi arrived at the bison hunters' tents later that night, and Bill said he had never heard anything quite like Tim's respiratory distress.

"I heard a death rattle," Bill told him. "I didn't think you'd leave that tent alive."

By mid-morning, two snowmobiles arrived to take Tim to Nikolai, where he caught a chartered flight to McGrath and a commercial flight back to Anchorage the following day. At the hospital, doctors diagnosed Tim with severe bronchitis, triggering asthma.

Tim realized that he had made risky decisions and was lucky to survive, but felt hollow about failing even to reach McGrath. Still, Tim felt inclined to blame planning — he should have gotten that flu shot before starting the race. The mystery of the Alaska wilderness still held him like a net, pulling him to greater depths of intrigue and ambition.

An Adventure Shared

*Deep in the forest a call was sounding, and
as often as he heard this call, mysteriously
thrilling and luring, he felt compelled to
turn his back upon the fire and the beaten
earth around it, and to plunge into the
forest, and on and on, he knew not where or
why; nor did he wonder where or why, the
call sounding imperiously, deep in the forest.*
                                  ~ Jack London
                          "The Call of the Wild"

After the 2006 evacuation, Tim asked his wife, Loreen, to forbid him
from ever going back to attempt the Iditarod again. His desire might be strong,
but if his wife said no and stood firm regardless of his rationalizations, he could
resist the temptation. Had it not been for her own conflicting aspirations, Loreen may have given in to this request. However, she had her own fascinations
about winter racing and Alaska, with a curiosity that expanded each time her
husband returned from another adventure. She ran the hundred-mile Iditasport
and performed well in 2000, and longed to attempt the 350-mile race to Mc-
Grath herself.

Tim agreed to accompany Loreen in the race to McGrath, but a monkey on
his back after his failed 2006 effort persuaded him to sign up for the full distance
to Nome. Since he was planning to serve as something of a guide for Loreen, he
invited two friends from Pennsylvania to sign up as well. Rick Brickley, a fellow
adventurer who had climbed Mount Whitney in California with the couple
two years earlier, and Rick Freeman, an ultra runner who co-directed the Laurel
Highlands seventy-mile race in Pennsylvania with Tim, were both on board.
Tom Jarding, who had abandoned his two previous attempts to reach Nome —
in 2006, Tom stopped in McGrath — also was back for the 2008 event. Tim,
Loreen, and the Ricks planned to travel as a group, and Tim figured he'd catch
up with Tom after leaving McGrath.

Weather at the Knik starting line was perfect — temperature around fifteen degrees, no wind, and a compacted trail that helped the sleds glide almost effortlessly on flat terrain. It was a good rookie start for his wife and friends. Still, Tim knew all too well the challenges that begin when one forces their body to pull a sled up and down hills for days on end. By the end of the first day, everything is sore. Knees creak, hips ache, quads and calves burn, fingers and ankles swell, and backs stiffen. Headaches clamp down and muscles will rebel against the relentless sustained effort level with an onslaught of cramps and twitches. Cold seeps into the body's core and exacerbates stiffness and fatigue.

Instead of viewing early physical discomfort as an insurmountable setback, Tim had come to understand it as a period of adjustment — a difficult transition, but only a transition nonetheless. Eventually his body would acclimatize to the temperatures, and he'd become stronger and more conditioned to the workload. The early days of suffering were the price he paid for this strength. He knew this, and hoped Loreen and the Ricks understood as well.

The first night was clear and cold, with temperatures dropping to minus ten beneath a wash of stars over the Yentna River. The group reached the first checkpoint at sunrise and decided to take advantage of relative warmth and daylight to continue toward the second checkpoint. At mile ninety, they finally rested before setting out into the predawn darkness toward Shell Lake. As they marched, Rick Brickley continued to fall behind. Tim suspected his sled was too heavy, and his taller height — six-foot-two — meant the five-foot plastic poles attached to his sled pulled at his back from a more acute angle. He required frequent breaks to rest his aching back. Tim, Loreen, and Rick Freeman pressed ahead toward the lodge at Finger Lake, figuring they would wait for him there. Rick Brickley arrived several hours behind them, complaining that back pain was radiating numbness into his limbs and slowing him down substantially. But he had worked hard to reach this point, and was determined to continue. He told his friends he would rest and head out in a few hours.

Tim was excited to show his wife and friend the famous Happy River Steps, a series of steep descents into the Happy River Gorge. Although he had told them stories about the steps, he knew no description could substitute for the experience of actually being there. Even after four years on the trail, the steps still caught Tim off guard. They spent hours winding through a dense spruce forest, when suddenly the trail disappeared into a descent that looked as sheer as a cliff. As they edged closer to the point of no return, an angled slope came into view, plunging precipitously into the ravine.

"No big deal," Tim announced. He unhooked his hip belt and let the sled slide independently down the trail, which was cut like a trough into the snow. Then he sat down himself and followed suit, careening down the drop with his legs and arms spread out for traction. It's impossible to complete this maneuver without a combination of screaming and laughing, thereby putting on a grand show for the others in the group. Loreen and Rick Freeman followed suit, wide-eyed and giggling as they took a load off on the frozen slide. Tim lamented that Rick Brickley wasn't there to share it with them.

Of course, these steep descents into the gorge are logically followed by a series of steep ascents out of the gorge — sometimes so steep that Tim had to kick steps into the trail to keep traction under his feet. Tim relished in these challenges — mini-adventures that would make the resulting memories that much sweeter. The climb required several breather stops, but eventually the trail emerged in a rolling valley. Jagged white peaks framed a snow-frosted forest in a scene that was as idyllic as a Christmas card.

As night set in, Loreen slowed down, overcome with fatigue. The day's hard work and insufficient calorie intake after two nights of limited sleep seemed to be taking more of a toll on her than the men. They stopped for a nap and dinner before continuing a few hours later, but Loreen's distress was becoming progressively worse. At times she would stop every hundred meters to rest her hands on her knees and gasp for oxygen. Finally, by late afternoon, they arrived at Puntilla Lake Lodge, on the shores of a frozen lake surrounded by the towering peaks of the Alaska Range.

Asleep in the bunk cabin was Anne Ver Hoef, an Alaskan who was also competing in the 350-mile race on foot. She had arrived a few hours ahead of the Pennsylvanians and planned to leave by 2 a.m. Both Anne and Loreen were ahead of course record pace, and Tim could sense that Anne was fiercely competitive. She was traveling so light that Tim had noticed her sled bouncing on the hard trail while she was moving. Anne's sled had a flat cover, while their sleds were heaping with sleeping gear, extra clothes, and food. Tim suspected she packed minimal supplies in a bid to move light and fast. As Loreen organized her gear in the cabin, Anne openly stated that she was feeling some pressure and would advance her departure to midnight.

Rick Brickley arrived several hours later and announced that his back pain had become crippling and he had lost sensation in much of his leg. Puntilla would be the end of the line for him. Tom Jarding also admitted he planned to abandon there, concerned that he had a stress fracture. The Pennsylvania contingent was reduced to three.

As they geared up for their 2 a.m. departure, Tim felt sadness about leaving Rick Brickley behind. He enjoyed showing off this slice of Alaska backcountry to his family and friends, and remembered with fondness the contours of Rainy Pass, the white peaks and glacier-carved valleys. Everything about it defied written and spoken descriptions, and had to be experienced to be truly appreciated. The early morning was fiercely dark, as the moon hid below the horizon and towering mountain walls blocked out ambient light. A thick vapor of frozen breath swirled in their headlamps, collecting in droplets of ice around their faces. The world appeared in sinister shadows, but there was a welcoming ambiance as well, as the familiar subzero air wrapped itself around Tim like an old friend.

An hour later, Tim turned back to check on Loreen and Rick, and discovered they had a stalker — someone with a headlamp, clearly also walking, about a hundred meters back. Tim was confused because while there had been a few other racers at the lodge, none of them were on foot. Perhaps this was a rookie cyclist, letting the group lead the way over the pass. Either way, even when they slowed, the person with the headlamp would slow too, and when they stopped, the light stopped. Were they actually being stalked? Isolation is deep in the Alaska wilderness, and it breeds a creeping paranoia. Tim was glad there were three of them against one unknown stalker.

By 7 a.m., darkness still reigned but the group had slowed considerably. Tim suggested a short, refreshing nap, to which everyone agreed. As Tim snuggled into his sleeping bag, he heard the footsteps of their stalker finally approach and pass them without a word. They slept an hour and awoke at first light, when Loreen and Rick caught their first glimpse of the mountains bathed in pink light. During the blindness of night, they had climbed above the tree line into the heart of the Alaska Range. For Tim, it was always a breathtaking surprise to wake up in the morning and find himself surrounded by a fortress of white peaks.

They were up and moving within minutes, and passed a red bivy sack spread out next to a bicycle, no more than a hundred meters down the trail — their stalker. Tim wondered if he should wake the mystery cyclist, who was clearly trying to travel near the group, but decided that without a wake-up request, he had no authority to do so.

The day was clear and not too cold, with only a light wind — an enviable condition, and a day custom made for photography. The trail serpentined through the narrow canyon, rising over one bend to meet another. With clear markings and tracks, the route to Rainy Pass was easy to follow this year; all they had to do was occasionally glance down to gain their bearings. But mostly, they looked up.

At the summit, the group stopped to cook some lunch. While firing up their stoves, their stalking biker finally arrived. It was Christian, a British rookie who had broken one of the pedals on his bike. Unable to turn the crank any longer, Christian was determined to finish by walking his bicycle the remainder of the distance. He admitted he was nervous about the unknown wilderness and purposefully following the group, but did not want to interfere. He continued pushing his bike toward the steep ravine of the Dalzell Gorge, and the group packed up a few minutes later.

The rich aroma of wood smoke greeted the group in Rohn just before dark. The checker there, Rob, waited for them in a canvas tent outfitted with a small wood stove, where he heated river water with flip-top cans of Progresso soup submerged inside. Both the water and the soup was lukewarm, but a welcome change from the frozen snack foods they had been gnawing on all day. They made their way to the official race accommodations, an unheated nylon tent where Rick and a couple of Italian racers had already claimed most of the floor space. Tim had a miserable sleep in Rohn. The tent seemed colder than outside, and the closeness to other racers made sleep nearly impossible. Again, he reminded himself that comfort is found in the woods.

They packed up and left at 2 a.m., making their way to the confluence of the Tatina and Kuskokwim Rivers. Winds always scoured this section; river rocks were visible below the clear ice, and frozen sand bars provided short breathers between hair-raising skates across the ice. Eventually the trail veered into the woods and traversed a series of rolling hills, each one steeper than Tim remembered. There was far less snow cover on the dry side of the Alaska Range, and their sleds dragged heavily over frozen tussocks and gravel. As winds increased and temperatures plummeted, Loreen couldn't hide her frustration. Tim had led her to believe the trail would be flatter and easier beyond Rohn, and it was anything but.

Still, Tim was optimistic that the Post River Glacier would provide some much-needed comic relief. He could always count on the wide, frozen waterfall to mix things up. Without crampons, the climb on glare ice is often sketchy, with sheer cliffs on both sides and no way to go around without veering off trail for a quarter mile through deep snow. With each step, the consequences of falling become more severe. Although not so steep as to precipitate a free fall, any slip will initiate a swift slide down the two-hundred-meter slope, where rocks and small trees protrude from the ice. For Tim, this was supreme entertainment. They skittered up the most exposed part of the ice, until a river bend allowed them to skirt the edge on a snowy embankment. The vegetation along the bank was too thick to drag their sleds, so they unhooked their harnesses and led them sideways along the edge of the ice, the sleds bucking and pulling like disobedient pets. After twenty yards, more cliffs forced the trio to return to the ice, and they slid from one protruding rock to the next.

The next ice obstacle was the Farewell Lakes. Near-constant winds tear through the valley and blow the lakes free of snow, leaving a shimmering, blue ice surface. From the shoreline, it's nearly impossible to discern where the trail returns to the woods on the far side of the lake. If they were lucky, they'd find faint scratches in the ice where snowmobiles drove across, but otherwise the trail had no visible cues. A fierce side wind blew as the group skittered onto the surface, and their sleds acted like rudders, pulling them off course. Loreen and Rick appeared to be engaged in an awkward dance with their sleds, shuffling and swiveling their hips as the sleds skirted back and forth. Tim enjoyed watching their reactions, knowing this was a first experience for them. The dance of the wind still thrilled him after all these years, but there was nothing like the first time.

As the day wore on, Loreen once again began to stumble through growing exhaustion. Staying warm in extreme cold while pulling sleds up and down hills caused a deepening calorie deficit. Loreen didn't have the muscle mass or stored fat to keep up with the sustained effort, and weakened more quickly than Tim and Rick. At dusk, they stopped at Bison Camp, the cluster of wall tents where Tim had evacuated during his last attempt. Rick started a roaring fire in the wood stove, and they made a plan to get going at 2 a.m. The wind howled outside, violently shaking the canvas walls as they drifted to sleep. Bison Camp was nestled in the last small valley in the rolling hills of the Farewell Lakes area. Just beyond the next ridge, the terrain flattened as the trail traversed the Kuskokwim River Valley through the sparsely vegetated Farewell Burn. Out there, they would be much more exposed to a quartering north wind, and Tim knew they would all need strength to fight these gales. When the watch alarm went off at 2 a.m., it was surprisingly Tim who suggested they grab two more hours of sleep. When they rose at four, they all felt much more refreshed, and the wind seemed to be subsiding somewhat.

Later, they learned that Anne had pressed on through the night into those winds and frozen the corneas of her eyes. Apparently almost blinded, she was staggering down the trail when an Italian cyclist caught up to her. Anne did not have a warm enough sleeping bag in her sled to consider stopping, and was trying to reach Nikolai in the midst of hurricane-force winds. The cyclist, Alessandro, tried to guide Anne by having her hold on to the back of his bike, but Anne was too distraught to maintain a grip. Alessandro tucked her into his own sleeping bag and rode into Nikolai to seek help. A local drove out on a snowmobile to rescue her, and she chartered a flight to Anchorage the following day. At the hospital, she was treated for severe frostbite to her eyes and face. She would eventually make a full recovery after a prolonged treatment period.

With the return of daylight, the group caught sight of their stalker, Christian, pushing his broken bike a half mile ahead. With the flatter terrain and only sparse tree cover, the winds were unimpeded and the trail was almost entirely buried in drifted snow. This made for difficult marching for the Pennsylvanians, and brutal pushing for Christian, whom they quickly caught. Temperatures were in the minus twenties and the wind continued to rage. Even on flatter terrain, Loreen was struggling, and a sink of frigid air descended with nightfall. Tim tried to encourage her to eat and drink to provide the fuel her body needed to produce heat in this extreme cold. But her body was shutting down and she couldn't hold down food for long. For the first time, Tim was scared about his wife's condition. Was it a mistake for her to be out here? Very few women compete in the 350-mile race to McGrath, and only two had finished the race on foot. Maybe there was a good reason for this.

The group stopped for several minutes so Loreen could lie on her sled to rest, but just for a few minutes. Any longer, and her core temperature would plummet, which she might not be able to recover given her diminished strength and energy. She drank a few sips of water and ate a candy bar. The break rejuvenated her for a short time, but with the deepening night their pace all but stalled. Tim knew Nikolai was just too far away under these circumstances. They would have to climb into their bags for a more prolonged sleep.

Tim awoke after an hour, shivering. He shouted to Rick and Loreen, and they reluctantly rose to start moving again. The wind had calmed, and the air was so deathly still and cold that it didn't take a stretch of imagination to envision outer space. After several more hours of marching in the pre-dawn emptiness, they finally arrived at the village checkpoint. As they removed layers in the house entryway, Tim was startled by Loreen's appearance. Her face was so swollen that she was scarcely recognizable. Was she in serious medical trouble? Was this some kind of thermal injury? Had her kidneys stopped functioning? Tim could see from Rick's reaction that his concerns were valid.

Loreen announced she felt tired but otherwise healthy, and saw no reason to consider stopping. They decided to eat and sleep a few more hours before reevaluating. Over mild objections from Rick, they slept for five hours. But upon leaving the checkpoint, Loreen's face still bore no resemblance to the woman Tim had married. She was probably carrying an extra ten to fifteen pounds of water, her swollen knees and ankles bulging. She was a hollowed-out shell, cracking around the edges, but a fierce determination still burned in her eyes.

The air was cold, still well below zero, but spirits were high because McGrath now seemed real. It was still fifty miles away, but it was the next point on the map, and there were no easy opportunities to quit before the finish. Several hours after leaving Nikolai, they came to a fork in the trail, and two bike tracks veering to the left. Tim knew the Iditarod trail continued to follow the river on the right, but he also knew of the existence of a trapper's trail that supposedly led to a thirteen-mile road into McGrath, which would likely be packed down and easier to walk on than the wind-drifted trail. They were now accompanied by Christian, the walking cyclist, and the group unanimously decided to take a gamble on the unknown.

An hour later, all evidence of the bike tracks disappeared. Either they had blown in, or the tracks actually represented one biker who tried this route and turned around, which would have made the tracks appear like they belonged to two bicycles. But across the river was a fresh set of snowmobile tracks, accompanied by droplets of blood — apparently from a trapped animal — and the smell of fresh campfire smoke. Surely this track would lead to the road? Where else was there for a snowmobile to go?

They decided to take a lunch break and mull over the situation. If they backtracked now, it would cost them two hours. Christian announced he would turn around. But Tim and Loreen knew that the women's foot record was still in reach, and backtracking would jeopardize her shot at breaking the record. If they were in fact on an alternate trail, they'd be in better position to break the record.

But even if they weren't, there was a still a better-than-not chance that this track led to town. They decided to press forward.

The trail was punchy, a collapsible crust over a layer of sugar snow. It was slow going and exhausting, and doubts crept closer to the surface. A GPS check showed that since their lunch stop, they were no closer to McGrath — in fact, they were heading ninety degrees away from the correct course, directly west into the setting sun when they should be going north. Nonetheless, they found the occasional trail-marking tripod, usually after crossing a frozen lake. With each step, Tim felt increasingly more lost, and yet turning around became increasingly more unacceptable. Another hour passed with no change in trail conditions or the GPS reading. As the raven flies, they were still twenty-two miles away and getting no closer. After another hour, their course began to veer toward McGrath, but they were still twenty-two miles away. It was as though they were circumnavigating the village in a giant arc.

"In for a penny, in for a pound," Tim thought. The sun slipped below the horizon, and Loreen was fading with it. After dark, they closed the GPS distance to seventeen miles, and were now moving more or less directly toward McGrath. By 10 p.m., there was still no sign of the road. They had slowed and needed rest. After some discussion, it was decided they would sleep for an hour and make the final push to McGrath without stops. As they settled into their sleeping bags, Tim heard small footsteps milling around their camp. He thought it was likely a curious wolf, but he was too tired to investigate. No one set an alarm. They would wake up when they were ready.

After an hour everyone was stirring, and they were quickly back on the trail feeling somewhat refreshed. When it was close to midnight, they emerged from the woods onto what appeared to be a road, but it wasn't packed and the snowmobile tracks here were no better than the makeshift trail through the woods. Worse yet, Tim had no idea which direction to go. GPS didn't make it immediately clear, so he picked left. After a half mile, the road veered in the general direction of McGrath. As they ticked off GPS increments, Tim noted their pace had finally climbed to more than two miles per hour. McGrath was slightly over twelve miles away, and they had six hours to set a new women's record.

Again, Loreen was fading. The relief of finding the road took the edge off all of their anxiety levels, and exhaustion was settling in. Nighttime always did this, and Tim encouraged Loreen to keep pushing. She was upset, with frustration seeping through her shattered expectations. The trail was still soft and punchy, and they were certain now that following the overland route had been a mistake. But there was no way to correct that at this point. Tim's encouragement only angered Loreen, and he decided it was best to let her move at her pace and take the record off the table. Rick, too, was hobbling on painful legs, and the pre-dawn air was exceedingly cold. The only bright spot in the black hole of a night was a fantastic display of Northern Lights dancing overhead.

Loreen's pace had slowed to nearly a crawl. Tim decided they had nothing to lose at this point, and suggested sleeping another forty-five minutes. Loreen didn't even take off her shoes to get in her bag. Tim surprised himself by dozing off as well, and after forty-three minutes he was startled awake again. "Time to go!" he shouted. Loreen shot out of her bag, stuffed it haphazardly in her sled, and was off like a rocket, marching down the trail before Tim had time to put on his shoes. He took his time because he expected to catch her quickly, but nearly an hour passed before he was walking beside her again. The trail over the road continued to improve. Loreen was stoic, with every part of her being focused on forward momentum. Frustration had turned to anger, because she believed that the record had slipped away.

Rick finally caught up as well, and they marched together in silence at a pace that topped four miles per hour. With three miles to go, they reached the plowed segment of the road. Tim looked at his watch and realized it was still just 4 a.m. — Loreen had two and a half hours to finish the easiest three miles in the race. He was so proud of her, but Loreen had no idea she was still on record pace. She was in no mood to talk and simply wanted to get this over with. Tim mistook her resolve as pacing for the record, when in fact she was pushing herself as punishment.

When they arrived at the finish line one hour and twenty minutes ahead of the old record, Loreen was in disbelief. She thought she had missed the record by at least an hour, but they had covered eight miles in just two hours. Before they stopped, they had averaged one mile per hour. Tim was in awe of his wife's spirit, her ability to drive her body to do something that seemed impossible to her. And they had made it, together.

For Tim, the party was over but the task would go on — to make a bid at a third trek to Nome, thereby becoming the first person to travel to Nome under their own power three times. He would miss his wife and his friend, and it was difficult to push himself out the door. The days ahead provided equal measures of beauty, sleep deprivation, and terror. The sea ice brought its biggest adventure yet, blizzard conditions and a wind chill approaching one hundred below zero. In these temperatures, old-timers would say, you could watch spit bounce and crap crystallize before you can even pull your pants up. But after twenty-three days, he again found himself under the burled arch in Nome, finish line of the Last Great Race.

Whiteout

10

*We go into the Alaskan backcountry to look
for cracks in ourselves. We go back a year
later to see if we have done anything about
them.*

~ Bill Merchant
Iditarod Trail Invitational race director

One might expect that, given enough repeat excursions, even a
thousand-mile route across deep-frozen Alaska wilderness would start to become
routine. But the Iditarod Trail isn't your typical trail, carved in dirt and rock.
The ethereal nature of ice and snow prompts dramatic changes from year to
year, and even minute to minute. No one will ever see the same trail twice, and
each year presents a fresh slate of unknown conditions and learning potential.
Tim had been irrevocably hooked into the allure of a singular but ever-changing
adventure — a chance to leverage accumulated experience into new discoveries.

In 2009, Tim had enticed lots of familiar company to his annual pilgrimage.
The contingent from Pennsylvania was back, minus Loreen, but another friend,
Chuck Struble, was along to give the Ricks some company. Tom Jarding had
returned to toe the line as well. Among the ultra-running community, much
of the pre-race chatter revolved around a rising star in the sport named Geoff
Roes. While Geoff was fairly new on the scene, he had recently broken a course
record in the hundred-mile Alaska winter race, and kept a detailed online log of
his training. It was clear Geoff was planning to move fast and light in the 350-
mile race.

Tim considered how effectively he could race Geoff to McGrath when he was still committed to the full distance to Nome. Through his years on the trail, Tim spent a lot of time pondering whether it was better to work hard, move fast, and rest for a longer period of time, or to go slowly and steadily with less rest. After experimenting both ways, he concluded that the human body is nothing more than a machine that will burn whatever stored energy it has, and then it must be rested and refueled. The faster a person moves, the quicker they expend their energy, and the more the body breaks down. But if he managed to find a sustainable pace with a regulated body temperature and steady heart rate, Tim could refuel on the move and only had to deal with the discomfort of sleep deprivation. The perfect balance supported near-constant motion and recovery on the go, but the sleep monster still needed to be fed.

At the start of the race, Geoff took off fast and hard, and Tim wondered if the talented runner could sustain this pace with a sled for multiple days. After wrestling with his competitive instinct, Tim decided to let Geoff go. He moved steadily along the early miles of the trail as nighttime temperatures plummeted to twenty below, and then thirty below. After wandering off trail, Tim reconnected with Tom and fretted about his position in the race. As it turned out, Geoff had a bad case of bronchitis and the cold night had done a number on his health. He arrived first at Yentna Station but, unable to recover, decided to bail out at the first checkpoint, just fifty-seven miles into the race. Unaware that Geoff had dropped out, Tim and Tom took their places at the lead of the foot race, leaving Yentna at first light.

The nights remained clear and cold with waves of Northern Lights. When Tim learned Geoff was out, he turned his focus inward again. The trail was softer than usual, and travel seemed slower, but much about this section had become familiar, comfortable even. In many ways, the early river-based miles felt like a warm up to the journey, which didn't begin until mile 135, when the trail began the long climb into the Alaska Range. After leaving Finger Lake, the men pushed through the night to gain ground on several cyclists, arriving in Puntilla at 8:30 in the morning. The clear and cold night gave way to cloud cover and an approaching storm.

In the early afternoon, Tim and Tom exited Puntilla beneath a swirl of blowing snow. It had been snowing all morning, and several inches of fresh powder covered their sleds. The storm intensified as they ascended the steep slope above the tree line, and the trail became indiscernible from the rest of the open tundra — just a petrified sea of sastrugi waves and a raging tide of windblown powder. The cloud ceiling was hundreds of feet below them, and they had to grope blindly through the vertigo-inducing whiteout, feeling for the invisible trail base with their snowshoe-clad feet.

They arrived at a log tripod at the end of a plateau, with the slope dropping off to seemingly all sides. Tim remembered this spot from previous years, and the trail from here was often a mystery. Tim and Tom decided to split up and make circles in search of a trail base, which Tim knew should drop toward a frozen creek in the valley below. After floundering around for twenty minutes before returning back to the tripod with no leads, they saw a snowmobile headlight moving toward them from the lower valley. The light was inching forward, and every so often moving in reverse. "That guy must be as lost as we are," Tim thought.

The snowmobile continued its back-and-forth pattern, edging slowly closer. The driver was Rich Crane, a volunteer for the Iditarod Trail Invitational. He explained that he and the race director, Bill Merchant, were able to break the trail as far as Rainy Pass, but beyond that the snow was too deep and visibility was too poor to continue. There was a shelter cabin near the pass with a blown-off roof, Crane said, and Merchant was holed up there with all of the bikers who were in front of Tim and Tom. Crane had been sent back to tell anyone making their way up the pass not to proceed until the trail was broken.

But this was Tim he was talking to, and turning around was not an option. Crane pointed the men in the direction he had come, stopping at a narrow creek crossing where his snowmobile had crashed through the ice. Tim and Tom made the volatile crossing on their hands and knees, straddling their sleds, and reached the other side without incident. From there they waded through knee-deep snow, looking for Crane's faint snowmobile track. Tim continuously veered off course, so Tom, who had an inexplicable extra sense for locating the invisible trail base, took over leading.

Concentration on the task was all-encompassing, and hours passed quickly. Almost imperceptibly, a derelict cabin appeared out of the raging featureless gray. The roof was missing and the rest of the structure was buried beneath ten feet of snow. Tim had never noticed this cabin before; it was well off the main Iditarod trail. This year, the faint trail went directly there because Merchant and Crane were the only humans to attempt the crossing so far this year; unlike every past year, no one had ventured over Rainy Pass before the race. A snowmobile was parked nearby and several bicycles were propped against the outside walls, but inside it was quiet and dark. A blue tarp hung from the ceiling, providing a meager canopy for a row of bunks. Each bunk was taken by a sleeping racer; even the floor was carpeted with down cocoons. Tim complained loudly that no one left a light on for them, awakening Merchant, who was shocked that anyone pressed through the storm to reach the cabin.

There was no room left even to sit down on the lower level, so Tim and Tom climbed into the loft, where they pushed aside piles of snow and huddled under the remaining chunk of roof. The storm raged overhead but the cabin provided acceptable wind shelter, even if it was the same temperature inside as outside.

In the pre-dawn hours, the downstairs crowd began to stir. A few of the cyclists had left hours earlier, breaking trail toward the pass by pushing their bikes through the bottomless snow. With no tracks of any kind to follow, only veteran racers stood a chance of locating the route. GPS coordinates help with navigation, but maps would be useless with no visibility. Tim's tiny Garmin Gecko GPS only had waypoints, mainly village locations, but no maps or trail locations. Tim and Tom cooked breakfast and set out a half hour after the final cyclists left the cabin, hoping to take advantage of the bikers' trail breaking. Within a half mile, they caught up to the line of hunched people, who were wallowing next to their bikes in the waist-deep snow. Despite only being able to maintain a glacial pace themselves, with snowshoes and without bikes, Tim and Tom were able to pass the cyclists as though the entire line was standing still. The runners traded trail-breaking duties as they attained the pass and began thrashing their way through willow and alder thickets.

They stuck close to the narrow stream bed that Tim knew would lead to the Dalzell Gorge. As the slope steepened they found it more difficult to maintain even footing. He and Tom frequently lunged forward after stalling in a deep drift, and tumbled sideways down embankments. Tim thought this would be a fine comedy to watch from a helicopter — two sled-dragging humans throwing themselves down a canyon like drunken river otters. They tip-toed across thin snow crusts and swam through chest-deep drifts spread unevenly over glare ice. After several hours of this, two snowmobiles finally approached from below. Two checkpoint volunteers were attempting to break a trail through the canyon, and intersected the racers about ten miles outside of Rohn. Tim wanted to wrap his arms in a big bear hug around one of the volunteers, but a subtle "thank you" is usually better received in the Alaska wilderness.

One of the volunteers, Terry the self-proclaimed "deputy" of Rohn, said they had been working all day to reach that point. They managed to travel ten miles in the equivalent number of hours by hacking their way through alder thickets with a chainsaw. They also had to construct bridges over open leads in the creek, which they did by felling branches and small trees, throwing them over the water, and covering the stick piles in snow as the water gurgled over and froze the bridge to solid ice. They'd constructed more than a dozen bridges like this — it was slow and difficult labor, and the afternoon was growing late. It takes a lot of man hours and labor to maintain the Iditarod Trail, even if it sometimes seems like nothing more than a faint track through an expanse of snow.

In Rohn, Tim and Tom crowded into the checkpoint tent with the lead group of cyclists, who were moving together in a pack of four. The cyclists were up and out within an hour, and Tim and Tom left after midnight. On this side of the pass, the storm had quieted, but the sky was still overcast and the air was deathly still. As the night lumbered along, Tim continuously caught hints of wood smoke wafting through the air. He was certain they'd come upon a camp of buffalo hunters, but each new curve in the trail revealed more stillness and quiet. Later, Tim would learn that a wildfire had raged through the area the previous summer, and the aroma of scorched spruce still lingered amid the deep freeze.

After Tim and Tom climbed the frozen waterfall known as the Post River Glacier, trail conditions shifted from deep powder to a thick ice crust over six inches of granulated powder. The collapsible layer cake was impossible to read. Sometimes they broke through the crust all the way to the ground, and sometimes they skirted over the top like tiny birds on a snow bank. Most often, they would punch only partway through the crust and then slip on the sandy snow surrounding their snowshoe-clad feet, gaining almost no traction with the fallen foot as they stepped onto the crust with their forward foot. It was almost more difficult walking on this surface than it had been breaking trail over Rainy Pass.

Too add to the difficulty, the wind picked up again as they approached the Farewell Lakes. The lake ice had been blown clear of snow, and traction remained elusive as they searched for trail markers across the shimmering surface. Despite the difficulties, they made relatively quick progress to Bison Camp. No one occupied the camp, and the tents were empty and cold. The men started a fire in the wood stove, which soon warmed the canvas-walled room enough to dry clothing and melt snow. After a short nap, they were back on the trail just as darkness settled over the uniform spruce forest of the Farewell Burn. It would be a long, cold, sleepy night. The darkness and cold didn't scare Tim as much as sleepiness.

As expected, hallucinations started to appear after midnight. There are two kinds of hallucinations that occur in the minds of the extremely sleep deprived. The first type can happen in daylight or at night, when the mind takes real images and fills in the empty space with stories. A stump may become an animal, a shadow a horse. Trees often turn into people, and dark spots in the snow look like speeding trains. The second type of hallucination only appears after dark, when sleep consumes the mind even as forward motion continues, and dreams begin to overtake waking thoughts. Entirely new worlds will form in the dark space between consciousness and unconsciousness, haunted by monsters and ghosts. Type-two hallucinations were always the most bizarre, and unsettling. Although on some level Tim understood that these visions were creations of his mind, they were as real to him as the trees and frozen swamps. Sometimes a pervasive fear of his mind's own creations was the only force that kept him from collapsing into the snow.

Tim and Tom arrived in Nikolai early in the morning, and opted to take only a short break and push on toward McGrath while there was still daylight and relative warmth. The snow surface was still soft, but with snowshoes they were able to maintain a three-mile-per-hour pace to McGrath, arriving in the middle of the night, as is Tim's custom. Peter, the resident who hosted racers at his home every year, woke up to cook the men the customary finisher's feast. Of course for them, the journey was only beginning. They would be back up and out the door by early morning.

With deep, new snow still obscuring any hints of the trail, it was a tough restart from McGrath. Iditarod volunteers had set a base a week prior, and Tim was grateful that at least there was a trail in place. Snowshoes were becoming another piece of gear they donned first thing in the morning and kept on all day, as primary as shirts and shoes.

In Ophir, dog sled race checkers offered Tim and Tom a beer that turned into two beers, and they left the checkpoint wobbly from alcohol-enhanced exhaustion. The night felt twice as cold as it had going in, but they wanted to find the junction that split the Northern and Southern routes before they slept. The trail would travel the Southern Route again this year — although this route had been Tim's first experience with the trek to Nome, he hadn't traveled it since 2001. After locating the crossed path marking the trail junction, Tim and Tom retreated a short distance to a thickly wooded patch where they bedded down for a few hours' sleep. Tom stomped around off trail to make a flat sleeping platform, but Tim knew only one trail breaker had even bothered to access this spot in weeks, and no one would make the journey that late at night. He spread out his sleeping bag on the edge of the trail and was snoring before Tom got into his bag.

Wind-drifted snow had all but obliterated the track beyond the junction. Tim and Tom marched single file in their snowshoes, alternating the lead every half hour. As it had in past years, Tim's body was absorbing the shock of the first week and settling into a comfortable rhythm. His feet were healing and his muscles were evening out the soreness and sharp pains. Anticipation of the next checkpoint and excitement about reaching McGrath were over, and now it was time for the heavy lifting to begin.

As they approached Don's Cabin, the Iditarod trail breakers finally passed. The group of seven machines dragging sledges traveled with such efficiency that barely a tip of a helmet was offered as they passed the men, who hadn't seen another human in days. A few hours later, two Bureau of Land Management workers who were touring the trail on snowmobiles passed and stopped to chat. "You must be Merchant's Marines," a man named Kevin Keeler addressed them, referring to race director Bill Merchant. "The guys from Pennsylvania."

Don's cabin, a dilapidated shelter with no door, arrived ten miles later. The BLM duo left the choice lower bunks open for Tim and Tom. When they arrived it was well after midnight, but Tim's stove had been acting up, and he wanted to fix the problem as soon as possible. Something was causing the stove to sputter as though it had no fuel, making snow-melting a long and sometimes nail-biting process. Tim feared that the stove — his only reliable source of drinking water — was on the verge of failing. When he pumped the fuel intake, there was too much resistance. As he lay in his sleeping bag, he used a Swiss Army knife to loosen a nylon screw in the valve. The fuel pump was still stiff, so he pushed the plunger down violently, which responded with a sickening pop. In slow motion, he watched the white screw shoot through the air and out the nonexistent door of Don's Cab. He felt as though he'd just watched someone plunge their fist into his chest and rip out his heart before he could react.

Now what could he do? He needed his stove to survive. He could take water from villages, but those were sometimes as many as four days apart, and he couldn't prevent a large amount of water from freezing for that long. He might be able to find water in open streams and overflow, but the opportunities were random at best and certainly not reliable all the way to Nome. He could borrow Tom's stove, but he couldn't rely on staying with Tom until the finish. He needed to find that needle in a haystack, a white screw in the snow. Using his headlight like a precision tool, he cast tight beams of light across every square inch of hay on the frozen floor, then through the snow outside the doorway. But it was useless; that screw was never going to be found. Shivering gripped him as he crawled back into his sleeping bag, attempting to comfort himself with thoughts of finding a new stove to purchase in Shageluk, or building a fire to melt snow if all else failed.

In the morning, he heard one of the BLM employees, Bruce, talking loudly from a tent he'd set up outside. Kevin was still in his bunk, and Tom was in the cabin as well. Tim wondered whether cabin fever had claimed another victim when he realized that Bruce was talking on a satellite phone. A way out! Tim asked to borrow the phone for few minutes so he call his wife, who agreed to mail a new pump to the next village, Shageluk. Tim could walk a little easier knowing a lifeline was on its way.

The men passed the trail breakers again in the ghost town checkpoint of Iditarod. The group was paused for the time being, waiting for a part to arrive for a broken snowmobile. It was early in the morning. Tim and Tom received a cool reception from the Iditarod volunteers, who hinted that the tired walkers were not welcome to loiter in the checkpoint tents. Tim was anxious to keep moving anyway, so they resupplied their sleds with food from their drop bags, supplemented with food from dropped racer's bags, and set out to haul the heavy loads over the slow-motion roller coaster of the Shageluk Hills.

Progress was slow ahead of the trail breakers, but it was a clear day and Tim enjoyed the expansive views of spruce-dotted hillsides rippling over the horizon. The BLM duo passed them again after Tim and Tom had pulled off the trail for a break and to boil water, reclining barefoot on their sleds as wet shoes and socks billowed with steam next to the hot stove. Although the sun was out, temperatures were well below zero; Kevin and Bruce howled with laughter at the sight of two guys sunbathing around boiling pots of water in the Alaska wilderness. Tim offered up some ostrich jerky and donuts he'd collected from drop bags in Iditarod, feeling generous with his newfound bounty.

The good fortune and occasional hopscotching with Kevin and Bruce continued until the men reached the Yukon River. After that, their BLM friends raced up the river ahead of a storm front that ushered in gale-force winds and piercing cold. Granulated snow swept across the trail, and the tracks of mushers who had left Grayling less than an hour earlier were barely visible. Few other mushers passed the men on the river — apparently most were holed up in Grayling, waiting out the storm. It was too cold to stop moving, and the river bank was too far off the faint trail base to access any protection from the wind.

As darkness settled in, they were both thirsty and pining for a hot meal and water. To the left, they noticed the distinct outline of a small structure on the bank. Tim couldn't tell whether it was a functioning cabin, but even if it was a ruin, it would at least provide some protection from the wind. They strapped on snowshoes and veered off trail. As they waded through the powder, it became more obvious that they had misjudged the distance of the structure, as well as its size. What had looked like a tall cabin morphed into a squat, square frame that appeared crudely constructed out of twigs. Tim guessed this had once been a temporary fish camp, cobbled together from thin spruce trunks that had been stripped of their branches. At one time there may have been bark siding, but that had long blown away and they could see straight through the building in all directions. The roof was a similarly gaping row of sticks. The interior was entirely filled with snow. Still, it was located on the leeward side of a river bend, and the crosshatching of logs provided additional wind protection. It also stood thirty feet above the river, just above the roiling wind tunnel.

From this vantage point on the bank, the Yukon River appeared to be alive. Wind stirred up a torrent of snow, which rushed downriver with the swirling violence of Class Five whitewater. The river valley acted like a straw, sucking Arctic air toward the sea, and deep cold kept the winds low and localized. When Tim and Tom plunged back into it, they might as well be swimming upstream — such was the force of the current they were fighting. But there, just a few feet above the river, was a relatively quiet bank where they could rest, eat, sleep, and hope the winds would soon subside.

Tim awakened after two hours with a startle, utterly disoriented. In the dark cocoon of his sleeping bag, all time and space was lost to him, and it took several seconds to reconnect the origin of a deafening roar and remember exactly where he was — in one of the most remote corners of Alaska, pinned down by a storm. They were in a relatively protected area and the wind was as loud as it had been on the river, if that was possible. He drifted off for another two hours and awoke to the sound of a freight train streaming past just inches from his head. As he sat up, he could feel wind pressing like a barricade against his body, making it difficult to move at all. "What do you think?" he yelled toward Tom.

"Are you kidding me? Let's wait." Tim was not a hard sell.

For several more hours, and well into the next day, this process repeated. Tim thrashed around restlessly, wondering if they had entered some kind of time-sucking vortex. The wind wasn't just bad, it was likely impassable. If they ventured onto the exposed river ice and got into any trouble, stopping would not be an option. The temperature was well below zero and wind chills had to be off the charts. They hadn't heard or seen a dog musher pass since early the day before. Later Tim would learn that one musher's dog had frozen to death during the night and the dog sled race had come to a standstill. Other mushers had retreated to the prior checkpoint to escape the Arctic blast.

Twenty-two hours after arriving at the skeletal fish camp, they saw three dog sled teams caravaning up the river. "If the dogs can make it, conditions must be improving," Tim said, trying to convince himself as much as his friend. The white hurricane continued to roil, but Tim could no longer contain his frustrations. He owed all of his success to a relentless drive toward forward progress, no matter how difficult or how minuscule. Tom, also feeling restless, did not put up any resistance to Tim's suggestion that they stage an escape.

They packed up and descended back into the frigid tempest. It was difficult to tell whether conditions had actually improved or whether they were just fresh after nearly twenty-four hours of rest; ground blizzards still raged around them, but the headwind did feel more manageable. After a couple of hours, Tim's goggles were coated in thick ice. His only line of sight was a tiny patch in each lens, as though he were locked in a dark tunnel that ended in a white-out. Tim considered it a victory that he could see at all; goggles were not optional no matter how much they obscured his vision. Without them, his eyes would freeze, and he couldn't risk removing them for a second without breaking the air seals and causing them to ice over entirely.

It was 2 a.m. and the howling wind made it impossible for him and Tom to hear each other, even shouting, so they marched in silence. Through his tunnel vision Tim could see a small light that he thought was approaching from a great distance, but within a few seconds they came upon a musher standing a few feet off the trail. The musher's dogsled was flipped on its side, offering a protective wall against the wind. As Tim turned his own light toward the encampment, dozens of dog eyes lit up.

"Are you okay?" Tim shouted at the top of his lungs. "What happened to the other mushers?"

"We are all here," the man shouted back, barely audible even standing just a few feet away. "We have four teams buried here. We couldn't make it any further in the wind. You guys are studs." The mushers had dug holes down to the ice in an effort to hunker below the wind tunnel, and the dogs had buried themselves in snow. Beyond those meager barriers, they had no protection. Tim couldn't imagine stopping in such conditions.

They slogged on and on. Tim's goggles became so iced up that he could only see shadows and forms, and a deepening sleepiness caused him to cut a serpentine track over the drifted snow. By mid-morning, all of Tim's water was frozen and progress had slowed to a near-standstill. They tried to dig in for a nap, but their efforts to hide from the relentless wind proved futile. They shivered awake in their sleeping bags for forty-five minutes until drifted snow completely packed their two-foot-deep trenches. Their choices were either to dig out, or abandon the dream of rest and push on toward Eagle Island. They chose the latter.

A few miles before the checkpoint, the dog teams they'd encountered on the Yukon began to pass them again. Now widely spaced out, the third musher informed them that one of the teams was in trouble and help would have to be sent back for them. It would still be a few more hours for the walkers, but finally, after nearly three days of isolation and wind-driven whiteout, Tim caught sight of four yellow tents huddled on the edge of the river bank. Supplies were stacked with ramps of drifted snow, and a kitchen area had been constructed from snow blocks cut with shelves. It looked like the base camp of a mountain climbing expedition, a far-away outpost with no permanent structures or telephones.

Although the checkpoint was crowded with volunteers and the mushers who had arrived before them, Tim and Tom were welcomed inside and sent to the veterinarian tent. The canvas structure had a small oil-burning heater with a thin smokestack. The base was covered in a sheet of AstroTurf, and the only free floor space was in a sinkhole next to the stove. The men were advised that sick dogs took priority over them, and if any arrived they would have to leave. They cooked, ate, and managed a night of sleep without interruption before they heard dog teams preparing to head back out on the river. The wind had diminished slightly by morning, but a penetrating cold remained.

The trail surface worsened as windswept drifts hardened to concrete-like moguls. Tim and Tom either had to break trail through thigh-deep snow to go around the obstacles, or hoist their sleds over the top. Both options were difficult, ankle-twisting work. Even with improving weather, the uneven footing kept forward progress to a minimum. Tom was beginning to falter, having developed a bad case of diarrhea that required frequent stops. Heavy air hung over the river and the temperature was well below minus thirty; Tim couldn't linger even for a few seconds before shivering set in. They were only twelve miles from the village of Kaltag, but Tim suggested they stop and sleep rather than force a pace that was already too slow for Tim and too arduous for Tom. Tom was too sick to even cook, so Tim melted snow and cooked freeze-dried meals as Tom suffered with shivering bouts in his sleeping bag between nature calls.

Tim woke up with a startle thinking he had not slept at all, but bright sunlight streamed through the tiny opening in his sleeping bag. Tom bounced up and announced he was feeling much better, and the men commenced their morning ritual of pulling on frozen shoes and packing their sleds. Tom seemed eager to prove his vigor had returned, and pushed hard for three hours to Kaltag. Once there, he was adamant they find the school and rest again. Since they had slept most of the night and it was early morning of another clear, relatively calm day, Tim requested they push on toward the next shelter cabin that was twenty-five miles ahead. Tom wouldn't budge. Their partnership was beneficial so Tim relented, but worried that the foot racer behind them, an Italian named Marco Berni, might be fast catching up.

Tim tossed and turned at the checkpoint for a few hours, but did not sleep. Always loathe to waste time, he eventually got up to look for Tom, who was just returning from the bathroom in the Iditarod Dogsled Race checkpoint building when Tim intercepted him. Pale-faced and nearly in tears, Tom admitted that the diarrhea had returned and he was feeling extremely weak and dizzy. Almost simultaneously with this pronouncement, he hunched over and vomited everything he'd tried to refuel with at the checkpoint. "I can't go on," Tom whimpered.

Tim demanded that under no circumstance should Tom quit. They'd come too far, and worked too hard to reach this point, Tim argued, and anyway Tom already had "too many quits" in the Iditarod Trail Invitational. Since the mail plane had already taken off, he would not be able to leave until the next day, so Tim advised him to go to the village school and sleep until morning. If Marco caught up in the meantime, Tom could travel with him and finish the journey to Nome. Tom agreed to this plan, but Tim had a hunch he wouldn't see his friend on the trail after Kaltag. Shortly after Tim departed this final village on the Yukon River, where the Iditarod Trail turns overland toward the coast, Tom called race headquarters to let them know he was scratching. Tim was alone again.

The Blow

11

*Generally speaking, a howling wilderness
does not howl. It is the imagination of the
traveler that does the howling.*
~ Henry David Thoreau
"The Maine Woods"

Between the Yukon River storm and Tom's sickness, Tim felt
he had wasted too much time. With so many unknowns in the equation it was
impossible to calculate whether a record was in reach; it seemed unlikely, but a
little luck and a lot of determination could get him there.

After leaving Kaltag, he marched swiftly in silence, reaching Tripod Flats
cabin sometime after midnight. As his mind drifted through shadows and
waking dreams, a bright orange light came streaking across the night sky. The
hot-glowing mass tore through the darkness directly over Tim's head, so close he
could almost hear it — a spinning fireball seemingly aimed right at him. Tim
was so startled that he screamed and dove head-first into the snow. By then it
was dark again. Fully awake, he started to run down the trail as another meteor
streaked across the night sky. The shooting stars were so bright that distances
were impossible to judge, but Tim was certain that he stood at the target center
of their collision course with Earth. He ran faster.

The adrenaline rush boosted Tim's pace, and he made good time to Unalakleet amid deteriorating weather. His largest concern now was whether Tom's
apparent virus would snare him as well. Although he felt woozy and sometimes
nauseated, Tim couldn't tell how much of this was real and how much was conjured by a paranoid mind. He slept only a few hours in the village, reasoning
that his best bet would be to march hard while he was still feeling relatively
healthy in case the illness clamped down before he reached Nome.

As he descended the Blueberry Hills, the stiff north wind strengthened and ground blizzards swirled through the frigid air. The final thirteen miles to Shaktoolik crossed an exposed spit, and Tim shivered violently as he removed his mittens to wrestle his feet into his snowshoes. A man on a snowmobile appeared out of the blow, shouting as though this was a dire emergency. The driver frantically motioned to Tim to get on the machine, and Tim screamed back that he was okay and out in the storm under his own volition.

"Compared to being dead, I'm okay," Tim thought silently. Compared to any higher standard, the term "okay" was questionable. The man shouted that the weather was bad all the way to Shaktoolik and likely going to get worse, but Tim knew from past experience that the weather wouldn't stop him unless he let it stop him, and so he just kept walking.

The village at least provided a brief respite. Shaktoolik's school principal had returned to New England to visit family for spring break, but her husband Bud was happy to have some company and offered to cook spaghetti for Tim. He showered and slept in the school. The wind was still howling in the morning. Bud made breakfast with a side of sympathy, and continuously questioned the wisdom of going out in the storm. Tim was resolute. He stuffed his pockets with candy, gel, and a couple of cellophane-wrapped mystery items from a scratched racer's drop bag before heading back into the tempest.

As it tore along the coast, the wind was every bit as fierce as the Yukon blow, but without the respite of even a distant river bluff. The next fifty miles would traverse open tundra before cutting a hard line across the frozen Norton Sound. Just before the sea ice crossing, about twelve miles from Shaktoolik, there was a shelter cabin at a rise of land called Little Mountain. Setting the cabin as his next destination made the white-out gale seem more manageable, and Tim pressed into the storm.

His goggles froze quickly and he struggled to locate trail markers in the swirling snow. On open tundra, wooden lath were always placed in a straight line. In theory he should have been able to continue looking forward to locate the next one, but the ground blizzard was disorienting and the wind nudged him sideways, constantly throwing him off the path. The waves of drifting snow did not align with the trail, which also funneled Tim off course. The wind had scoured the surface of the sea ice to a hard sheen, creating the possibility of wandering for miles in any direction without ever realizing he had left the trail. He couldn't lose track of those stakes. Whenever he failed to locate the next one, he would pull down his goggles and squint into the vortex until something, anything, stood out in the confusion. Occasionally that something would be a booty thrown by a dog and filled with snow as it froze to the trail surface. Wind would then swirl around that object, making it stand out from the otherwise two-dimensional white slate.

Tim worked this way for six hours, and still hadn't come across Little Mountain cabin. Another hour passed, and just when he convinced himself he had somehow missed it in the storm, the rock promontory that guarded the structure appeared like a ghost in the mist. Tim's heart dropped, because he had managed to convince himself he was hours ahead of where he was. Not only was he more than thirty-five miles from Koyuk, but he was progressing at a rate of less than two miles per hour. It felt too early for rest, but he needed to eat. He had plenty of water and had already decided that cooking or building a fire would be a waste of time and energy — energy he needed to save for the fight across the sea ice.

He would duck into the cabin only for long enough to eat a snack. Sitting on a cold bench, he unwrapped some jerky and the unmarked cellophane wrappers he'd taken from the dropped racer's bag. To his surprise, the wrappers contained Dove ice cream bars, still frozen after being shuttled to Shaktoolik from Anchorage, stored in Bud's freezer, and hauled across the sea ice in Tim's coat pockets. Tim devoured the ice cream greedily and gave a silent thanks to the racer who left them for recharging his spirits.

Tim dreaded going back out into the blow. He knew that once he started across the exposed sea ice, there would be no more stopping until he reached Koyuk. He paused momentarily at the doorway, held his breath, and plunged into the whiteout, resigned but also empowered by the knowledge that the crossing was going to take as long as it took, and that was that.

As Tim marched, a dog team approached in the swirl. The musher yelled to Tim that the storm was unnavigable and he was returning to Shaktoolik. Tim refused to believe that the gales could get any worse, and he was still moving just fine, so he continued forward. After several hours, wind speeds actually fell to about thirty miles per hour, and a clearing appeared to the south. Tim was absolutely exhausted from the strenuous physical and mental effort, and decided to take advantage of the lull to steal some rest. After clearing a small area, Tim stabbed several trail stakes into the crust and propped his sled against them to create a low wind barrier. With his head next to the upturned sled, he felt reasonably protected and was asleep within minutes.

Upon waking a couple of hours later, visibility was still good, but the weather quickly deteriorated again as he marched toward Koyuk. Tim was grateful that he'd had the presence of mind to take advantage of the brief rest window, because now he felt recharged and ready to fight again. Distant lights from the village flickered in and out of view, obscured by the blowing snow. Still, the brief cloud breaks provided visual proof that he was making forward progress, which was comforting.

When he was about three miles from the village, a snowmobile raced toward him. The driver had spotted Tim out on the ice and became convinced that he was a person in distress, possibly one whose own snowmobile had broken down and forced a life-threatening struggle to reach the village. Again, Tim had to assure his would-be rescuer that he was in fact intentionally out there and okay. This driver was unpersuaded even after several minutes of conversation, but eventually he gave in to Tim's stubbornness and returned to the village without him.

Crossing the sea ice had been even more difficult than the Yukon River. It was the hardest thing he'd ever done. A Native boy looked at Tim and asked if he was "the Devil." After assuring the boy that he had crossed the sea ice with legitimate intentions and assuredly was not "the Devil," Tim caught a glimpse of himself in the mirror. Both of his eyes had broken blood vessels, giving him bright red eyes and validity to the boy's concerns. Tim thought with some amusement that this race actually seemed to only get harder, not easier, the more experience he accumulated. Yet, now he was in Koyuk, and approaching the home stretch. Amid his deepening exhaustion was a growing sense of strength, invincibility even. If he could cross the sea ice in a hurricane-force gale, he could do anything else.

That night Tim traveled all the way to a cabin past the village of Elim, where he planned to take a short rest while shelter was available and then continue his hard drive to Nome. Not wanting to stop long, he built a small fire in the wood stove and zipped himself snug into his bag, hoping the weak heat would be just enough to simply dry some clothing. He was awakened an hour later by a loud roar and bright light shining through the Plexiglas window. The door slammed open and a large, visibly drunk Native man charged into the room, equally surprised to find the shelter cabin occupied. It was after midnight. The Native stomped across the room and shined a flashlight directly into Tim's face, shouting a rapid fire of questions: "Are you walking to Nome? Why don't you build a bigger fire? It's cold in here. Do you want some whiskey?" And without giving Tim a chance to answer, shouted, "My name is Arno, like the river in Italy."

Tim stammered a bit, explaining that yes, he was walking to Nome, and he did not start a larger fire because he didn't want to burn too much wood in case someone else needed it more than him.

"Burn the wood!" Arno commanded. "You need your calories to get to Nome and shouldn't use them up staying warm." Arno explained that he lived in the village of Elim. He and others stocked this safety cabin with wood precisely for travelers like Tim, and so Tim was obligated to "Burn the wood!"

A woman stepped in the door behind Arno and removed her helmet. The two rubbed noses, surprising Tim with the notion that Eskimo kisses were a real thing. Arno explained that he was not from Italy and had never been outside Alaska, nor had his parents — but they read the name of the river in a book and liked it, and so he was named Arno. He and his companion finished the whiskey after a final offer to Tim, which was again politely declined. "Well, we better let you get some rest," Arno said, commanding Tim one last time to "Burn the wood!" The cabin was as hot as a sauna by the time the locals left.

Just beyond Elim, high winds had already torn most of the ice away from the coast, and open water forced a reroute of the Iditarod Trail over an inland mail route. The trail rose along the narrow spine of a ridge that fell steeply on both sides. Tim carefully led his sled along the knife edge of the mountain, concerned that if Cookie tracked off the trail, the momentum would send them both tumbling into the white abyss. Trees and vegetation were absent in this region, and depth perception became a guessing game. Undulations in the trail could be a few inches high, or they could be thigh-deep drifts with a precipitous drop off the other side. Tim genuinely could not tell, so he moved with caution.

After sunset, the relentless wind didn't die down as Tim hoped it would. As he stumbled over one petrified drift into the pocket of another, he realized that he might no longer be on the trail. Although he could see lights from the village of Golovin ahead, experience reminded him that the village was still more than a dozen miles away, with the trail rising over another small hill before crossing five miles of ice on Golovin Bay. This wasn't the time to blaze trails overland. Tim decided to backtrack, turning straight up the steep incline, as experience reminded him that gravity and subconscious preference can cause one to stray too far downhill. After a hundred yards, when he was certain he could not have drifted that far off the trail, he caught a glint from reflective tape on top of a trail marker. It was still another hundred yards up the slope. He was being as careful as possible to hold a straight line, and still managed to drift two hundred yards off course in less than a quarter mile. Sleepiness clawed at his eyes, but he would need to maintain forceful and constant vigilance.

The wind persisted as Tim traveled through the villages of Golovin and White Mountain, and on to the final seventy-seven-mile stretch to Nome. This segment was stark and treeless, utterly exposed to the north wind. Although he could almost smell the finish, Tim understood how vulnerable he was in this landscape. Darkness settled in, and Tim hoped night would bring a respite from the wind, as it often did. He put his head down and pressed through the howling tunnel. With almost nothing in the way of landscape features to offset the whiteout, he could no longer see the thickness of the blowing snow or gauge visibility. The storm obscured all of his senses; he smelled and tasted only the moistened ice of his face mask, heard only the ceaseless howl of the wind, felt only the hard shove from the north, and saw only a single dark shade of gray. It was almost impossible to perceive whether wind speeds or ground blizzards were worsening, but there were clues.

First, he began to trip himself with his trekking poles, which the wind blew sideways every time he lifted them out of the snow. Occasionally, a strong gust would slam into his body, forcing him to hunch to the ground to reduce his profile. Even with goggles and a face mask, wind pierced through the foam seals until Tim's eyes burned, forcing him to hold up one of his mittened hands to shield the side of his face. With his headlight focused on the front of his feet, he studied the snow for signs of the trail. He felt like a detective scanning the scene of a crime for the most subtle details. Unless he stood within two feet of a trail marker, there was no way to see one through the storm. He was so close to the finish, just fifty more miles to Nome, walking straight into the jaws of an Arctic blow. It was as though the Iditarod Trail was putting up one last, great resistance — the lion at the end of a gladiator's obstacle course. If Tim wanted to win, if he wanted to survive, he would have to fight.

"Cookie, stay with me!" Tim screamed to his sled. "We are going to make it, but we have to work together!" Cookie was tracking hard to the left, tugging on Tim's body with a force almost stronger than his ability to resist, as though his sled was consciously trying to drag him out to sea. It was after 3 a.m., but adrenaline surged through Tim's blood and drove him to march as hard as he could. Then, in a heart-stopping instant, everything went dark. Tim was pressed into a wall — invisible, and yet so solid that he couldn't step forward. He was the proverbial unstoppable force against an immovable object, pushing desperately in place as wind raged in his face. He braced himself against the backward-shoving wall and reached up to remove his headlamp, thinking its batteries had died in the storm. But as he held the light in his mitten, the beam was still shining. "That's odd," he thought. When he pulled the light back onto his head, the beam went dark again. The ground blizzard was so thick that blowing snow blocked the headlight beam. Not even light could penetrate this black hole of a storm.

Tim couldn't move forward, so he would have to retreat. He couldn't pause any longer; his core temperature was already dropping, and his fingers were going numb. As he turned away, his headlight once again cast a beam into the blowing snow, reflecting off a trail marker just a few feet away. The stake was ninety degrees from where Tim knew it should be; now he had no idea which direction was correct. Was he moving forward or backward on the trail? Uncertainty gripped him, but he had to make a decision now. There was no time to think.

As Tim stumbled toward the trail marker, he realized that the wind was again grabbing his sled, which was now pulling his body to the right. Confusion swirled through the blizzard. He had to act, but he had to figure this out, first. He tucked his trekking poles under his arm and removed an outer mitten, unzipping his parka just enough to reach into the chest pocket, pull out his GPS device and turn it on. In slow motion, the liquid crystal screen flickered to life and showed traces of an arrow pointing to Nome. With his head down, he picked a direction and marched, keeping his eyes on the screen until the line moved one hundredth of a mile in the right direction. Within a few minutes, he caught sight of another trail marker. As he puzzled over his disorientation amid the snow wall, he realized that his sled must be acting like the tail of a kite, pulling his body straight into the wind without Tim even realizing he had made a ninety-degree turn. He hadn't been able to move forward because it was not humanly possible to walk directly into the wind. The force of the blizzard was so strong that not even visible light could escape through the blasting snow. Even walking with the wind at his side, just staying upright demanded all of Tim's strength.

He thought he must be about five miles from the next safety cabin. The crosswind roared, but Tim understood now that it was within his physical ability to fight it. If he met another unmovable wall, he now knew to turn ninety degrees to his left. He worked his way up and down a series of low-lying hills. With no sight lines, he could only guess his location. At the summits of each hill the wind swirled, collecting snow in circular drifts that camouflaged the trail without an apparent orientation. Tim continued to search for feedback that the wind wasn't moving his body out of line again — a frozen edge from a dogsled runner or even stained ice from dog feces was good enough. Trail markers were cause for celebration.

As he descended, the hillsides created a funnel that once again directed the wind with nearly immovable force, right at his side. At one point, he made the brief mistake of turning to face it. A gust ripped his goggles right off his head, and in an instant they disappeared into the gray expanse. Now he was blind, but he could not panic. Turning away from the wind, Tim pulled his balaclava up to the bottom of his eyelids, closed the draw strings of his hood below his eyebrows, and shifted his neck gaiter up over his eyes. With his right mitten against his face to seal out wind, he could see through the small slit in his clothing, but was limited to looking down and to the left.

After a half mile of squinting toward the flickering beam of white light at his feet, his headlight finally picked up reflectors from the safety cabin. He fell through the doorway, exhausted. There were things he needed: fire to melt snow for water, driftwood to build a fire, some dinner, and a place to hang his clothing to dry. But for minutes, he just sat on a cold bench and stared blankly at the plywood graffiti-stained wall. The appearance of the darkened shelter had calmed the last of his adrenaline, and his energy was extinguished. Eventually he roused himself to gather snow and make stew, then crawled into his sleeping bag.

Like clockwork, his bladder awakened him two hours later. There were still two hours before sunrise, and wind continued to rattle the stovepipe, which emitted an eerie whistling sound. Handwritten notes on the walls recapped the experiences of others who remained holed up in this cabin for days, waiting for the wind to die down. To Tim, the thought of remaining at the cabin this long was unacceptable. He was so close, only forty-five miles from Nome. Within five miles, he would pass another shelter cabin and the edge of the infamous Salomon Blowhole.

Tim packed up his sled and headed out once again into the raging darkness. The wind hadn't given a single inch of ground; if anything, it was blowing harder. Cookie continuously flipped over; every twenty feet, Tim would have to stop and right his sled. He considered repacking the load to maintain a lower profile, but then he remembered the fate of his goggles. If he unhooked from his sled, there was a good chance he'd never see it again.

He put his head down, repeating his mantra that relentless forward progress would eventually release him from the blowhole. The wind's roar seemed to be subsiding; either he was becoming accustomed to the deafening noise, or the storm was actually quieting. In the same instant he formed that hopeful thought, a tornado blast picked up his sled, spinning his hip belt around his body. Tim leaned back into the wind. Cookie flapped like a kite in front of him, remaining suspended in the wind above Tim's waistline as he planted one foot deep into a drift to anchor his body. He grabbed the connecting poles, sending the sled and its contents into a spin before it slammed back into the snow, jamming the poles into Tim's ribcage. He could barely breathe as he frantically unclipped his hip belt and pounced on the poles. Grasping one pole, he crawled toward his bucking sled and spread his body weight over the duffel bag. Tim retained this awkward reclined position as he shifted the contents of the bag to lower the profile, and futilely tried to brush away the fine sandy snow that had accumulated at the bottom of the sled.

Despite the effort, Cookie continued to tip over in the wind, often elevating off the ground for several milliseconds before flipping over like an angry walrus. Tim hooked his hip belt around his left elbow, which allowed him to hunch over and hold the nose of the sled down in an effort to keep wind from sweeping underneath the platform. This position appeared to work, but now he was forced to limp like a hunchback across the ice, dragging an overburdened left arm behind him. The storm seemed to be pulling out all the stops, and in his exhausted state, Tim felt acutely hurt by this. Why was Nome pushing him away?

And then, his body added insult to insult. A pressing need to relieve himself would wait no longer. He'd made a valiant effort to hold off until he reached the next shelter, but his bowels were quivering now, and he knew it was coming whether he stopped or not. Twice before, in conditions less dire than this, even short bio breaks had proved nearly fatal. Tim had become an expert on the science of a quick dump, but this would have to be a record-breaking effort. Otherwise, his frozen corpse would tell an ugly story.

Briefly removing his mittens and pants, he managed to complete the task in seconds with a one-swipe wipe of toilet paper. He quickly bundled back up and immediately started running down the trail. The pause in motion had not been long, but his fingers had already curled into a petrified fist, and the feeling was gone in his feet and hands. For a half hour, Tim ran to the limit of his ability, heart thumping and lungs searing, until blood circulation returned to his extremities. He'd never felt so close to the tipping point of freezing to death, and he had only stopped for a moment. He had no choice but to keep moving. There would be no more stopping in this storm, no matter what.

Anxiety gurgled in his gut and he began to hyperventilate. "Hold it together, just hold it together," Tim scolded himself. During his bathroom stop, he had removed his liner gloves and stuffed them in his shell pocket. As he pulled them out of the coat to put them back on, they were entirely filled with snow — as solid as the icy hand of a dead person. Blowing snow was packed into every crevice of his clothing and sled, and he felt disconcertingly like a full-body ice cast himself. Tim had always taken pride in his ability to stay calm when conditions warranted panic, and now was not the time to give in to blinding fear. He had to focus. One foot in front of the other. Flip the sled back over. More steps. Right the sled again. Keeping walking. The storm raged at him with blow after knockout blow, and his only hope for survival was to stay upright. If he hit the deck and started sliding, that was it.

Eventually, Cookie only flipped over every few minutes rather than every few steps. Then a half hour passed without needing to right his sled. The outline of Cape Nome, the final major geographical landmark before the finish, appeared on the horizon. Tim knew this 800-foot-high hill still had to be about twenty miles away, and this meant visibility was improving. Then another landmark he recognized, Bonanza Bridge, appeared out of the white-washed landscape like a mirage. It wavered in the blowing snow, and Tim questioned its existence. But sure enough its outline reappeared several times, each new view clearer than the last. This marked the western edge of the blowhole boundaries, and the beginning of a thirty-two-mile roadbed that would lead him into Nome. The next milestone would be Safety, a dog sled checkpoint with a vacant bar surrounded by small fishing and gold mining camps. The checkpoint would be closed because the last musher had already passed, but its vacancy didn't bother Tim. Safety was named as such for a reason. Nome was twenty-two miles ahead.

After a long night of listening to nothing but the relentless roar of wind, Tim heard the distinct whine of a snowmobile. The driver was Phil Hofstetter, an Iditarod cyclist who lived in Nome. Phil was incredulous. How had Tim possibly survived this blow? Phil had been tracking a weather station based at Tommy John's Cabin, which indicated sustained winds of sixty to seventy miles per hour, and gusts over one hundred miles per hour. Hurricane force. Phil said the conditions were as bad as he'd ever seen after ten years in Nome, and he couldn't believe that Tim had chosen to leave the shelter cabin in the middle of the storm.

"It's going to continue to suck until you get to Nome," Phil explained, "but this is certainly better than that." Tim reached over to give Phil a big bear hug, elated. Now he knew that not only would he survive, but he was also going to finish the race. The rush of emotions was too much, and he started to sob.

In a few more hours, Tim marched victoriously down Front Street in Nome and arrived under the Burled Arch. Despite the relentless barrage of obstacles the trail had thrown this year, Tim had taken a day and a half off his Southern Route record.

Number four was in the books.

Record

12

*Courage doesn't always roar. Sometimes
courage is the little voice at the end of the
day that says I'll try again tomorrow.*
~ Mary Anne Radmacher
American Author

In 2010, Loreen returned to defend her foot record to McGrath,
and Tim was determined to finally capture the overall record that had eluded
him in two previous finishes on the Northern Route. Also back for another
try, with his own quiet ambitions to vie for the record, was Tim's friend and
potential rival, Tom Jarding. The race to McGrath would be a barn burner this
year, with several men pushing hard up front. Their fast pace was a source of
both competitive drive and conflict for Tim, who struggled with the prospect of
leaving his wife alone.

Loreen insisted she was experienced enough to travel on her own; Tim knew
she was competent, but still couldn't shake his concerns. After Finger Lake, he
raced ahead to catch the lead pack of three, reeling in their nearly six-hour lead
by the time they reached Rohn. There the checker, Rob, informed Tim that
Loreen had left Finger Lake with their friend Rick Brickley, and it was likely
they were traveling together. Still, Tim was wracked with guilt. He left Rohn
with Tom, but after a few hours Tim knew he would not rest until he was sure
that his wife had safely crossed the Alaska Range. Tom said he understood and
offered to wait for Tim in McGrath, as he'd not yet traveled the Northern Route

and hoped to team up again.

Assured that the race would be back on after they reached McGrath, Tim retraced his steps to Rohn. Not in a hurry to make fast backtracking miles, he took the opportunity to go easy on an ankle he'd turned while trekking over Rainy Pass. But he felt too anxious to just wait at the checkpoint, so he continued marching back up the winding corridor through the Dalzell Gorge, hoping to see his wife and friend around the next bend. Every turn that yielded no sightings increased his anxiety, but he finally relented to sleeping when he reached a point where deeper snow overtaxed his hurt ankle. Several hours later, he was awakened by a surprised voice: "What are you doing?" Loreen and Tim were reunited, and he did not leave her alone again until they arrived in McGrath.

As his wife and Rick celebrated their 350-mile finishes, Tim learned that Tom had left McGrath nearly two days earlier. He felt betrayed. Why did Tom say he'd wait if he had no intention of doing so? Why not just be honest about his desire to keep racing? At first Tim wondered if Tom had grown restless waiting for him, but he had left McGrath almost immediately after arriving. No, Tom was taking advantage of Tim's backtracking to build an insurmountable lead. At best, his promise to Tim outside Rohn had been insincere.

Tim felt angry at Tom for not being honest, and angry with himself for being vulnerable. Whatever the reasons, it no longer mattered. He was just going to have to double his efforts to catch Tom. He knew in good conditions, a two-day lead would be almost impossible to close. Tom was a strong walker with a longer stride than Tim; when they traveled together at Tim's comfortable walking pace, Tom could easily pull away. But Tim was a better runner, and when Tim engaged a "power walk" mixture of jogging and hiking to push the pace, Tom could not keep up. If Tim could maintain an occasional running pace, he could slowly reel in Tom. He also knew he excelled in adverse weather, and storms or bad trail conditions would likely help him close the gap.

But the snow and the wind didn't arrive. On the Northern Route, the trail base was solid and conditions were conducive to a fast pace. Deep in the Interior, Tim would be out of communication for nearly two hundred miles, so there was no way to gauge his progress on Tom's pace. When a challenging condition finally did arrive, it was deep cold.

The night sky was so clear that all the stars melded together, shining through bright green bands of the Aurora Borealis. The air was so calm that Tim's breath froze before it drifted away, enshrouding his head in thick vapor. The first dog team passed shortly before the Iditarod dog sled race checkpoint of Cripple, with barely a wave from the musher. About two hours later, Tim saw a headlamp flickering in the woods; the light was moving toward him. At first he thought it was a musher, but the gait and speed indicated a human walking. It couldn't possibly be Tom, but who else could it be? Maybe Tom was lost or hurt.

Tim kept walking until his headlamp caught the source of the other light; it was John Baker, the lead musher who had passed Tim earlier. John seemed disoriented, and Tim asked where he had left his dogs. John said he'd anchored his team up the trail a short distance, and headed back to study the markers because he was convinced his team had somehow veered off the Iditarod Trail. "What is this trail?" John asked.

Tim replied that it was definitely the Iditarod Trail. He'd been passed by the trail-breaking caravan the night before and he hadn't left their tracks since.

"No, this isn't the Iditarod," John insisted. "It has the wrong trail markers."

Tim pointed to a permanent reflector affixed to a tree as proof, but John remained unconvinced. Tim announced that this was his fifth trek to Nome and he was certain they were on the right trail. John retorted that it was his fifteenth Iditarod race, and he was certain they were not. Tim started to lecture John about leaving his dogs unattended in the Alaska wilderness, but John only wanted to debate evidence of an incorrect trail. Tim pulled out his GPS; the device was so cold that the screen was almost black, but he was able to discern a waypoint for the Ruby-Poorman Road, which was on the route and fifteen miles directly ahead. No sale. Tim was a successful lawyer in Pennsylvania, but he couldn't manage to convince a longtime musher that they were on the Iditarod Trail.

As the argument became more heated, Tim noticed the vapor swirling around his mouth was turning to frozen flakes. Every time either man spoke, snow would fall out of their mouths. Tim had never seen this happen before, which meant this was the deepest cold he'd ever experienced. Several minutes of snowy conversation had left his core deeply chilled, and Tim began to shiver. He couldn't stand still any longer, not for any reason. He told John he was just going to have to decide for himself, but Tim was done with the debate.

John continued walking in the opposite direction. Tim passed John's dog team a quarter mile later. Each husky looked up at him dolefully from their anchor in the snow. Tim apologized for the stupidity of humans, and the sparkle in their eyes indicated that they already knew the score. Later, he learned John hooked his team back up and mushed backward on the trail for an hour until he encountered another musher, a young man named Dallas Seavey, whose progress persuaded John to turn around. Dallas went on to beat John to the Cripple checkpoint by eleven minutes, claiming a $3,000 purse that went to the first musher to reach the halfway point. The strange confusion cost John a robust lead, and eventually the race. After his encounter with Tim, which was reported in the Anchorage Daily News, the Iditarod Dog Sled Race committee voted to change its rule on GPS use, allowing mushers to carry the previously prohibited devices.

When Tim arrived in Cripple, the temperature was fifty-two below zero. Volunteers informed him that temperatures had warmed since his overnight encounter with John.

Besides the lowest temperatures he had ever experienced, Tim encountered no major obstacles as he raced toward Nome. Trail conditions didn't deteriorate, no new snow fell, and the winds were never impenetrable. He stayed true to his pace plan, moving efficiently and continuously, but without adverse weather he never harnessed enough of an advantage to catch Tom. Although Tim arrived in Nome in twenty-two days and four hours — two hours ahead of the Northern Route record set by Roberto "The Italian Moose" Ghidoni in 2002 — he was still a day and a half behind Tom. Tom fought hard to hold onto his lead, forgoing checkpoint stops and pushing through the interior for nearly three days without sleep, and arrived in Nome after twenty days and fourteen hours. Although Tim still felt the cold sting of a knife in his back and told Tom as much, he had to admire his rival's fierce effort.

Still, the fact that Tom had taken advantage of Tim's chivalry and then captured the elusive Nome record for himself left a bad taste in Tim's mouth. After five successful finishes, he had little left to prove — but he knew he could walk to Nome in twenty days or less. If he had to harness the volatile unknowns of the longer Southern Route to do it, so be it.

* * * * *

By 2011, the Iditarod Trail Invitational was becoming popular — in relative terms, of course. But in ultra-racing circles, the race across Alaska had become a coveted achievement. Despite a strong desire for vindication that sparked the moment Tim finished the 2010 race, the 2011 roster filled before he had a chance to sign up again. Even the wait list was overflowing, but race director Bill Merchant assured Tim that no one could complain about squeezing in the only person to have completed five human-powered journeys to Nome. Loreen would return as well. Tom Jarding was resting on his laurels and wouldn't join the fun this year. As finicky as the Southern Route could be, Tim had amassed an impressive depth of experience over the past decade. He felt confident that he could move forward effectively and efficiently regardless of trail and weather conditions. Five successful journeys had taught him the most important skill of all — how to push through mental barriers that accumulate with bad trail, sleep deprivation, cold, wind, and physical exhaustion.

Tim now viewed the Iditarod Trail as a challenge rather than a threat. The Southern Route, with its unpredictability and difficult trail conditions, was the measuring stick of performance. Pre-race preparations in Anchorage proceeded as usual — too little sleep, too much breakfast, and steady Gatorade ingestion. During the bus ride to Knik, Tim and Loreen listened as a rookie cyclist from Colorado explained his race strategy to another participant. He emphasized the importance of eating every twenty minutes, and had a watch set to ensure he would stay on schedule. Tim could only smile at the humbling shakeups this rookie would undoubtedly experience. Nothing ever goes as planned on the Iditarod Trail.

As the field nervously counted down the final seconds to the race start, Tim thought about the famous mantra of "A journey of a thousand miles begins with a single step." A race director yelled "go," and every other runner launched across the lake at a dead sprint. This fast start amused him but didn't make any sense — the journey of a thousand miles doesn't happen at hundred-meter pace. Still, he supposed racers needed to burn off their nervous energy — energy that would be nice to have back at 3 a.m. when jet lag, sleep deprivation, and pre-race anxiety all coalesce in a spectacular energy crash.

Tim and Loreen traveled together through the night, arriving at Yentna Station just before dawn. The overheated cabin had the look and feel of a zombie apocalypse — clothing strung everywhere as gray-faced racers and volunteers walked stiffly amid a haze of exhaustion. As usual, the first checkpoint was no place to hang out. Tim and Loreen ordered breakfast and refilled their hydration bladders. They would be back out on the river within the hour, pushing to make it to Skwentna Roadhouse before darkness set in.

The following night, they set up their bivy sacks just off the trail in the foothills of the Alaska Range. Stars splattered the indigo sky with infinite depth, and Tim had the familiar yet exhilarating sense that they were hurtling through space rather than standing on Earth. Tim thought about how preferable it was to sleep in the Alaska wilderness rather than crammed into a stuffy checkpoint. They were free of race drama and others' excess energy. Through a fist-sized opening in his bag, Tim could watch the Aurora Borealis dancing amid the treetops, speckled in stars. He was grateful to have Loreen nearby to share these moments of unfathomable beauty.

As they approached Rainy Pass, fierce winds brought a bone-chilling cold. This was typical, of course, but Loreen was succumbing to exhaustion, becoming more depleted and hypothermic. When she began shivering, Tim suggested they hunker down in a small bowl near the pass, take a nap, and eat something. They propped their sleds against their trekking poles as a wind barrier and slept for an hour. This seemed to do the trick, but just beyond the pass, they were both stumbling sleepily and needed to stop again. They awoke to blazing daylight, and Tim had a guilty sense that they'd wasted too much time. But it's difficult to limit sleep when exhausted, and he accepted it as a necessity.

Tim and Loreen continued this pattern through Nikolai, and Tim was surprised when they left the checkpoint before the man who had been leading the foot race, Eric Johnson. Tim's natural race instincts sparked back to life, and after some discussion Loreen agreed that they should split up so that Tim could challenge Eric for the 350-mile crown. Tim always felt uneasy about leaving Loreen behind, and he scolded himself for spending extra energy on being the first to arrive in McGrath when it was just a waypoint for him. Still, competitive instincts die hard, and Tim broke into a run along the meandering corridor of the Kuskokwim River.

Within a few miles, Tim looked over his shoulder to see Eric charging toward him as fast as he'd seen another foot racer move in the Iditarod. Tim wasn't in the mood to engage in a neck-to-neck race for fifty miles, but it was clear Eric was intent on catching him. When Eric closed the gap to a hundred yards back, Tim stopped to wait for him. He proposed traveling together and Eric agreed, and they continued moving at an aggressive pace while alternating running and walking. One of the soles separated from Eric's shoe, and Tim stopped to help him make repairs, first with duct tape, and then by pulling a large wool sock over the shoe to hold the pieces together.

As they ran, Tim and Eric passed a cyclist who was stopped on the river just off the trail, hovering over his lit stove. It was the rookie from Colorado — the one who had appeared so confident about his plan before the race. They were less than fifteen miles from McGrath, and Tim wanted to suggest that if he were to travel just one more mile down the trail, he would be able to climb to a higher bluff where wind would be lighter and temperatures substantially warmer. From the cyclist's reserved demeanor, Tim got the sense that he was probably not pleased to be passed by two runners, and well-meaning advice might not be well-received. Tim felt the urge to ask how the cyclist's twenty-minute-interval calorie intake plan was working out, but refrained. Every rookie in this race must learn their own way; this is both the beauty and the terror of the Iditarod Trail.

The McGrath tower came into view, indicating that they were about five miles from the finish. Tim told Eric he needed to relieve himself, and when Tim stopped, Eric began running again. Although Tim was loathe to overstrain himself at this point, he felt guilty for leaving Loreen behind and decided that he should at least try to make up for it by winning the race to McGrath. Tim broke into a similarly determined run, towing a sled that was considerably heavier than Eric's, who had foregone some survival gear in the interest of racing 350 miles fast and light. Tim couldn't afford the same risks on the thousand-mile trek to Nome, and the additional clothing and sleeping bag weighed him down. But determination can trump handicaps, and he employed a stealth strategy by turning off his headlamp as he raced to catch his opponent. Within three miles of McGrath, Tim startled Eric as he ran up beside him. Eric looked as exhausted as Tim felt. They negotiated a truce and arrived in McGrath together.

Loreen arrived ten hours later, setting a new women's foot record of six days, twenty-three hours. "Not bad for a 54-year-old," Tim thought of his wife, now a three-time finisher in McGrath.

Tim was alone again, with no agenda but to arrive in Nome as quickly as possible. Although he'd enjoyed the exciting battle with Eric to McGrath, he knew that keeping a sustained pace was better than overexerting himself now and crashing later. Sleep mattered as much as walking, and he needed to maintain a reasonable balance. Every time he slept more than he really needed, or lingered over a meal, the minutes accumulated. Unless completed with efficiency, every foot repair stop, clothing change, sled adjustment, and snack break could add up to additional days on the trail. Even before Loreen arrived in McGrath, Tim slept only a few hours, resupplied his sled, and set out by mid-morning. He was confident Loreen would arrive safely, and wanted to waste no time. He limited his stay at the warm and inviting residence to less than eight hours.

Although the village of Takotna, with its welcoming volunteers and plates of macaroni and cheese, still lay ahead, Tim's mind was already zooming ahead to possible state of the trail beyond the cut-off to the Southern Route. This seemed to be the default setting for Tim's brain — haunted by anticipations of future difficulties. This mindset kept him focused on the task and allowed him to reign in mental mind games, but it also lent itself to anxieties even when no danger was immediately present. Tim was concerned that there would be no set trail beyond Ophir, and hoped the checkpoint volunteers would have a report. However, it almost didn't matter what they said — the trail is what the trail is, and Tim would proceed regardless.

Tim was pleased to find a snowmobile track clearly following Iditarod Trail reflective markers beyond the Southern Route intersection. He proceeded with purpose, promising himself small rewards — such as a packet of tuna — if he would keep marching for another two more hours. After a short break, he stuffed his outer jacket beneath a bungee cord on top of his sled for easy access when darkness arrived. But when he went to grab the coat an hour later, it was gone. The wind was blowing hard and Tim was certain he'd never see this crucial piece of gear again. But he had to check. He unhooked from his sled and sprinted back down the trail. Twenty minutes later, he spied the jacket tangled in an alder bush right next to the trail. Tim breathed out a sigh of relief. Once again, the Iditarod Trail had showed him a glimmer of mercy, and for this he was grateful.

A few miles outside of Iditarod, a caravan of seven trail-breaking snowmobiles roared past Tim, churning up the existing track to establish a more prominent trail. When he arrived at the dog sled race checkpoint, the trail breakers had just settled into sleep at a shelter cabin. Three cyclists were there as well — Jay and Tracey Petervary of Wyoming and Aidan Harding of England. They had apparently been holed up at the ghost town for two days, waiting for the trail breakers to arrive. There was no track beyond.

At first light, the large crowd was milling about the single-room cabin. The Iditarod trail breakers' snowmobiles required some maintenance, and a part for one of the machines was being flown in on a ski plane. They would not leave until mid-afternoon. Having rummaged through drop bags, restocked his sled, eaten a meal, and dressed his foot wounds, Tim was ready to forge ahead. The cyclists seemed anxious, and not happy that Tim could arrive late, rest, and just continue happily down the trail. After two days of being holed among the collapsed shacks of Iditarod, cabin fever was setting in for the cyclists. While Tim could strap on a pair of snowshoes and work a little harder for a slightly slower pace, the cyclists were all but stuck without a trail. Alternately pushing a bike through deep powder, and throwing it over alder branches, combined with wallowing in thigh-deep drifts is an ugly affair, and forward progress is often best achieved by biding time.

The trail breakers passed Tim again in the mid-afternoon, impressed that he had stayed in front of them as long as he had. Tim reached the Big Yenta shelter cabin after midnight, and sure enough Jay and Tracey arrived shortly after. The husband and wife team was fiercely competitive and didn't want to yield ground to Aidan, so they took a short nap and were back out the door after two hours. Tim got up and left just behind them, but sleepiness swallowed his steps, and he decided to take another two-hour nap in his sleeping bag. Aidan arrived just as Tim was getting up, and Tim noticed that Aidan was in good spirits and fully intending to race the Petervarys.

A clear, crisp day followed, with endless photo ops of expansive vistas, boreal forests, and snow-covered mountains. It was difficult for Tim to imagine any place aside from the polar regions where one could feel this far beyond civilization. Many people would be unnerved by this depth of isolation, but Tim felt fortunate to live in an era when such adventure was still possible. The Shageluk Hills rippled over the horizon, and Tim marched with purpose, determined to push past the village Shageluk and aim for Anvik and the Yukon River before he rested. But darkness once again brought crushing sleepiness. Between flickers of waking dreams, Tim scanned the snow for a place to sleep.

Where there was protective vegetation, there were nearly always moose tracks. He pondered whether it would be better to sleep where he could be run over by a drunk snowmobile driver, or stomped by a territorial moose. Both options seemed just suicidal enough to fuel the adrenaline he needed to keep moving, and he stumbled along until he found a safer-looking strip of woods between swamps.

After a couple of hours, Tim was back on the trail beneath a spectrum of Northern Lights. The full moon sat low on the horizon, shining like a spotlight through the trees and casting heavy shadows on the snow. Raw sleepiness still clung to Tim's consciousness, and a shadow directly in front of him looked so solid that Tim found himself mindlessly stopping to yield the trail to his two-dimensional companion. Even when he acknowledged that this dark figure was just his own reflection, he still found himself chatting with his shadow, making observations about the trail and the mysterious landscape beneath this wash of otherworldly light.

Tim reached Anvik by late morning, stopping only for coffee. He marched through Grayling several hours later without pausing, opting instead to make several miles on the Yukon River before nightfall. Trail conditions deteriorated, but Tim was still in prime physical shape — a few blisters, but no respiratory problems, no pulled muscles, no sprained ankle or frostbite or broken bones. He had nothing to complain about compared to past years on the Yukon River. It was truly as good as it gets out on this ocean of a river, and Tim had enough experience to know when to rest and when to keep marching. Conditions are always bound to change.

The headwind grew fiercer, battling his forward progress. After a two-hour nap on the river ice, Tim was able to push all the way to Eagle Island, halfway up the Yukon River. There was a lull in musher activity at the checkpoint, and a volunteer allowed him to share one of the Iditarod tents. After a few hours Tim was back on his feet, anxious to make some miles away from the river and its relentless wind. Another full day of marching into the wind on soft snow ended with a short nap just twelve miles outside of Kaltag. Temperatures were deep into the subzero range, and Tim knew this would be a restless, shivering stop. But he had the experience to know when his pace would benefit more from a mental recharge than slow sleepwalking. In Kaltag, Tim's drop bag was missing, so he raided the left-behind supplies of the cyclists who had already been through, a few racers who had scratched, and even some mushers' discards.

Unless an obstacle stood in his way, Tim's singular purpose made him unstoppable. A call in to the race director confirmed he was on record pace, and he maintained a routine of marching through the day and capturing short naps at shelter cabins, not even bothering to build a fire in the wood stove because heat was a luxury, not a necessity. He stopped at Iditarod checkpoints to chat with volunteers, eat a hot meal, and call home — but he never lingered long. In Shaktoolik, the race director informed Tim that Aidan had crossed the sea ice following a trail apparently marked by the Iron Dog race. This side trail veered west at the head of the bay and led directly to Elim, bypassing the village of Koyuk. It was a small shortcut, and it skipped a major supply stop, but it did reduce the overall mileage. The race director informed Tim that race rules allowed him to diverge from the Iditarod Trail — in the Invitational, there are no mandatory checkpoints after McGrath. If a racer wants to forge their own way, that's their right and also responsibility. They're free to do as they see fit, but have to accept any setbacks or perils that might accompany a bad decision.

Winds were stiff but manageable as Tim headed toward the sea ice crossing, and a light snow began to fall. Snow usually meant warmer temperatures — something that Tim welcomed amid the dangerous exposure of the Norton Sound. But as soon as he arrived at Little Mountain cabin, skies had cleared and temperatures plummeted. The door to the cabin was frozen shut, and after slamming against the wooden barrier with various body parts and without success, Tim yielded to the ice and set up his bivy on the tiny porch. In the deep cold, he forgot he was wearing goggles when he climbed into his bag. When he poked his head out at first daylight, the humidity inside the goggles froze to a hard ice that he could not scrape away. Winds were directly in his face and the temperature was too low to walk without goggles, so he made do with a tiny, obstructed window of sight near the bridge of his nose.

As Tim made his way around Little Mountain in the fog of his goggles, he quickly lost the trail. He could have removed his goggles at intervals or even walked more slowly to scan for snowmobile scratches on top of the ice, but the surface footing was good and he knew which direction he needed to go. He was too preoccupied to worry about losing the course — frustrations about his goggles consumed almost every thought.

By 10 a.m., the sun had finally warmed the air enough to remove his goggles, and Tim began searching in earnest for signs of the trail. Eventually, he caught sight of something moving to his right — a tiny string of dogs, probably a mile to the east. He revised his course to intersect the dogs' path, merging onto a marked trail about ten miles from Koyuk Bay. Finally, Koyuk was within sight and Tim was certain he had missed Aidan's shortcut, but with the potential time-saver in mind, he decided to continue angling toward Elim with or without a trail. Sure enough, the crust began to soften under the mid-day sun, and soon he was wearing snowshoes and angling north toward Koyuk again.

A mile later, he arrived at Iron Dog trail markers. He recognized a landmark, an outcropping called Isaac's Point, which was about three or four miles beyond Koyuk, and looked to be three or four miles behind him now. He had still probably saved time by cutting his own route, but he now had another forty miles to travel without replenishing his food or supplies. Still, the record remained in reach, and that was what mattered.

He reached Elim after midnight, and volunteers told him there was room to sleep inside the checkpoint. Tim had only slept a couple of hours on the porch of the Little Mountain cabin, and before that only a few hours in Unalakleet. Surprisingly, he did not feel completely exhausted. The store would not open again for hours, but he was determined to keep moving. He scavenged leftover musher food: vacuum-packed lasagna and some candy bars for the trip to White Mountain. Two hours later, he was awake and packing up again. A dog sled race volunteer expressed disapproval that he didn't rest more, but Tim assured her that he would rest once he arrived in Nome.

Beyond Elim, the Iditarod Trail followed the slower and steeper overland mail route rather than the jumbled sea ice, and Tim doubled his efforts to make good time over the sastrugi-sculpted hills. He descended the steep slope of Little McKinley in the late afternoon, and traveled five miles on the sea ice into Golovin. From there, the trail again veered inland, following the shoreline around the bay rather than crossing it. This would add another five miles of difficult travel. An old villager explained that a wind storm had ripped apart the ice in Golovin Bay. Open leads formed and sea water flooded the normally solid surface, creating a chaotic jumble of old and new ice. The obstacles were impossible for dog teams, but the villager took a look at Tim's trekking poles and expressed confidence that a person with walking sticks could make the crossing.

Tim had had enough of the overland route, and no record attempt would be complete without a few risky strategic moves. He headed out across the ice, making good progress for two miles before he arrived at a seemingly uncrossable lead of open water. But as he walked closer, he saw the open water was actually new ice, as clear as glass. On he marched, praying softly that this fresh ice would hold. Evidence of snowmobile tracks had disappeared, and he began to second-guess his bold decision. Crossing Golovin Bay had seemed like a no-brainer in the village, but the term "no-brainer" was taking on a more literal meaning as he skittered across the fragile surface. Still, Tim was committed to forward progress, and continued to make his way around slabs of broken ice. Some were piled as high as houses and appeared as insurmountable as a brick wall, but he always found a way through the mess.

The afternoon sun made him sleepy, and he tumbled a few times when it became difficult to focus on the complex footing. He meandered around the ice chunks like a tiny boat navigating rocky whitewater in a gorge, always hopeful that the next bend would reveal a clearing. Finally, about two miles from the edge of the bay, the chaotic jumble ended in another section of translucent ice, like calm seas after a violent storm.

Tim scuttled over the glare-ice surface and six miles later arrived in the village of White Mountain at the home of Jack and JoAnna Wassillie, a local couple who were fans of the human-powered race and opened their home to exhausted cyclists and runners as they passed through the village. The Wassillies served up a feast of muskox meat and king crab freshly caught through a hole in the sea ice. Despite near-riotous noise levels from JoAnna's sons and grandchildren, Tim slept comfortably in a bedroom. Still, he was up within ninety minutes, calling the race director to check his status. Bill confirmed that Tim was now ahead of Tom Jarding's splits from 2010, which meant he was on overall course record pace. If Tim could cover the final seventy-seven miles to Nome without sleep, he should be able to pull it off.

Tim marched hard through the night. Just before dawn, snow began to fall, and by the time he had descended from Topkok Point to the Bering Sea, winds had whipped up a swirl of new powder. The trail was now obscured, and Tim couldn't locate the base. A musher passed, also off trail, and following her tracks did not seem to help. He wavered back and forth for several miles before he finally reached the welcome sight of the Bonanza Bridge and the roadbed that would lead him into Nome.

When he passed through Safety with twenty-two miles to go, he was still in front of four dog teams. Tim had never been ahead of dogs at this point on the trail, and the checkpoint had always been closed by the time he arrived. Inside the checkpoint was a small saloon, and when Tim requested water, five people sitting around the bar uniformly offered to pay. One man who purchased a bottle for Tim told him he looked like "death," but this characterization didn't dissuade Tim from the task at hand. Knowing he was in front of dog teams gave him new motivation to try to finish in front of at least one musher. Of course, he wasn't racing them head-to-head, as he'd started a week earlier. Still, he would relish in the opportunity to be able to claim a small victory over the huskies, whom he considered his peers.

Even if he looked like death, Tim felt great, so he alternated walking and running. He was now on a road with mile markers, which allowed him to count down the distance, and he was clicking them off every twelve and a half minutes. Sixteen miles from Nome, Phil Hofstetter showed up on his snowmobile to offer a hug and encouragement. As night fell, the lights of Nome began to sparkle. As Tim rounded Cape Nome, the trail softened, forcing him into snowshoes. With the darkness, vivid hallucinations began to fill in the empty spaces. He saw a man dressed all in white, wearing a headlamp and cheering for Tim. But when he passed, the man turned into a distant streetlight. Five minutes later there was another man dressed all in white, who again turned into a streetlight. Tim felt on the verge of passing out, and had to continuously remind himself to put one foot in front of the other. All he could think about was stopping.

Twenty days, seven hours, and seventeen minutes after leaving the Knik Bar, Tim silently dragged his sled along the empty streets of downtown Nome and stood under the Burled Arch. He was still in front of four dog teams, and had set an overall record for a foot traveler on the Iditarod Trail to Nome. As it was, the lead cyclists had only beat him by less than three days.

He unhooked from his sled and lay down under the arch, letting exhaustion settle over his body like a blanket. Finally, he could let go of the hard veneer of single-minded focus on forward progress and let his emotions wash over him like overflow atop an ice dam. As tears streamed down his face, a drunk man staggered toward the arch to try to comfort him. Tim accepted the hug but he needed no comfort. He could not have been happier.

Inundated 13

The year 2012 brought a return to the Northern Route, and Tim was convinced that he could bring the overall foot record down to nineteen days or faster. Nineteen days meant averaging around fifty-five miles per day, dragging a sled through deep snow, up and down mountains, and along frozen waterways for eighteen to twenty hours per day. Although such a benchmark wouldn't be easy, Tim knew a combination of determination, experience, and a little bit of luck with the weather would put him in a position to set a record that few could challenge.

Racers for the tenth running of the Iditarod Trail Invitational enjoyed a friendly start; skies were overcast and temperatures were mild, around twenty degrees. Rookies fidgeted with their gear and paced the snow-packed parking lot near the starting line. Tim had become comfortable with this nervous energy, and enjoyed a restful respite while reclining in the Knik Bar after eating his final pre-race meal. The weather forecast was encouraging, with no indication of markedly cold temperatures or storms in the near future. Initial trail reports were positive, and Tim felt confident that he could go out fast and bank some time early in the race. Any extra miles he could cover in the first few days would be valuable capital to cash in during less favorable conditions.

However, it didn't take long for things to go bad. Just a few hours after the race started under light clouds with no storms in the forecast, the overcast sky darkened and heavy snow began to fall onto the trail. Tim spent much of the first fifteen miles trading the lead foot position with Geoff Roes, who was back to challenge the 350-mile race to McGrath after his failed attempt in 2009. Three years later, Geoff had risen to the top of the sport, having been named Ultra Runner of the Year two years in a row and setting a course record in the most prestigious hundred-mile trail race in the United States, the Western States 100. In fast conditions, Tim couldn't match Geoff's youthful speed, but he had experience on his side. Geoff's resume established him as a favorite in the 350-mile race, but Tim wasn't about to concede the short race just because a semi-pro had joined the field.

As dense snowflakes accumulated on the trail, Tim and Geoff stopped to put on their snowshoes. Although Tim usually gained increased mobility with snowshoes in deep powder, snow was falling at a rate that canceled out any noticeable benefits immediately. They were sinking just as deep as they had without snowshoes an hour earlier. He guessed that snow was accumulating at a rate of two inches per hour, enough to obliterate any sign of cyclists or snowmobiles that may have passed through just minutes before.

Night fell many hours before they arrived at Flathorn Lake, just twenty-five miles into the race. The trail had become nearly indiscernible from the surrounding snow fields. The depth of new snow was approaching two feet, and they were about to cross a frozen lake, with no tree cover to temper the accumulation. Even with snowshoes, Tim and Geoff were sinking up to their knees, and floundered even deeper when they stepped off the trail base, which was impossible to see. Tim looked up through the barrage of snowflakes, scanning the black sky for any break in the clouds. Since there had been no storms in the forecast, it seemed like this should just be an anomaly, a squall, which would taper off soon. But snow kept coming down with no relief in sight.

When they reached an arm of the lake, Tim and Geoff struck out in search of a side trail that would keep them under tree cover. The narrow corridor through the woods would also make the hidden trail base easier to locate. However, Tim could barely maintain forward motion as he punched up a steep embankment, driving his fists into fresh powder with nothing to grasp. Each step sent him sliding back a foot or more, and the prospects at the top of the bank were not much better. The only snowmobile track circled around a cabin back to the lake, and there was no clear evidence of a route beyond.

As they returned to the lake, three more foot racers caught up — Frank Jans of Belgium, a Swiss software engineer living in California named Beat Jegerlehner, and Anne Ver Hoef, who had returned to the race after three failed attempts and was determined not to scratch again. The group of five opted to work together, traversing the lake in a single-file line and taking turns breaking trail. Snow bombarded the flat expanse. Visibility was so bad that the person in front was virtually blind, and those behind floundered outside the path even with deep footprints to follow. The thick powder pulled one of Tim's snowshoes off his foot; by the time he noticed, he feared it might be buried beyond recovery. He called out his distress, and Frank noticed a thin strip of metal poking out of one of the postholes. Frank reached in and retrieved Tim's snowshoe, which he likely would have never noticed if Tim hadn't spoken up right then. It was a lucky break.

On the far edge of the lake, a headlight approached from the direction they were plodding. At this late hour it could only be another Iditarod racer, but why was this person traveling in the wrong direction? Maybe they were the ones traveling in the wrong direction. The group stopped and huddled around Tim, expecting the seasoned veteran to know the way. Tim was certain he did, but the approaching headlight sent conflicting signals. The light belonged to a cyclist — Phil Hofstetter, Tim's friend from Nome — who had entered the lake from a different trail. Pushing a bike without snowshoes, forward progress had become all but impossible for Phil, and he was anxious to find anybody else to help break a path.

Soon enough, the group caught up to other cyclists who had been far ahead in the early hours of the race, only to flounder in the deep snow of Flathorn Lake. More than a dozen cyclists had already quit, turned around, and returned to the start. Those who remained were slower than any of the walkers, who all wore snowshoes and didn't have wheeled anchors to drag through the powder. Phil's headlamp faded quickly in the background, as did the lead cyclists. When Tim looked back, the string of headlights along the lake resembled a mental image he held of lines of climbers scaling Everest in the predawn darkness. Anyone who took their turn up front to break trail became, for the time being, the leader in the race. Tim was amazed at just how much harder it was to break through the fresh powder than it was to follow. By the time he was the fourth or fifth in line, he had to concentrate on slowing down in order to avoid running over the person in front of him. Anytime his effort level became easier, impatience about the slow pace would move to the front of his mind. Still, he couldn't afford to break away from the pack. The energy to sustain this pace without help would drain all of his reserves, and he wouldn't get very far.

By 3 a.m., thirteen hours after the race started, they were still short of the Susitna River, fewer than thirty miles beyond the starting line in Knik. The team of foot racers had swelled to seven, with the lead cyclists not far behind. Exhaustion set in, and several people in the group announced they would stop and camp before they crossed onto the river. Tim didn't want to rest just yet, but he wasn't about to forge ahead on his own. Throughout the early morning hours, several more people joined their encampment beneath the birch trees at the edge of the Dismal Swamp. Others stopped farther back on the trail.

At first light, Anne roused the group. During the night, two cyclists had passed their camp and continued through the unbroken snow on the river. Tim spent some time scouting a path only to discover it dead-ended at a cabin. Rick Freeman, Tim's friend from Pennsylvania who was back in the race for his third attempt — this time with a plan to go all the way to Nome — caught up after Tim retraced his steps. Rick had fallen behind early and bivvied on the lake, but he had been up for hours and made up enough time to catch Tim. Together, the two began reeling in racers. The two cyclists who had pushed through the night were the first to be overtaken. Rick fell back again and Tim caught Beat, Anne, and Geoff. Again, the pack of runners led the race.

By afternoon, they still had miles to reach Luce's Lodge. Tim was incredulous at this reality, as he was used to arriving at this mile fifty-two landmark twelve hours earlier. It was only the first day of the race, and his progress was less than half what it needed to be to even approach the record. Beyond the lodge, the trail became marginally better — at least, there was a trail, thanks to one or two snowmobiles that had traveled between Luce's and Yentna Station. Although less than ten miles up the river, it had taken another small eternity to reach Yentna, so Tim ordered another plate of food and hung up some of his clothes to dry.

Geoff, Tim, and Anne were in the lead. Anne and Geoff indicated they planned to sleep at Yentna Station, but Tim had reached the point where he preferred to nap outside rather than in the stuffy, crowded confines of a cabin or lodge. He decided to press on, hoping the single snowmobile track would continue toward Skwentna.

Perhaps predictably, the snowmobile trail veered off the river after a few miles. Tim was on his own in a deep expanse of snow. He wallowed through knee- to thigh-deep powder, scanning for wooden lath or any sign of a trail base. Breaking trail demanded an enormous well of energy, and he knew his efforts would only hurt him and help the competition. Anyone else on foot could easily catch him by taking advantage of the broken trail. He expected to see Geoff soon. Although Tim was aiming for the thousand-mile record and Geoff was running the 350-mile race, Tim pondered his competitive strategy. Tim had much more experience in this race, but Geoff was a stronger runner. In a head-to-head competition, Tim might give himself better odds in a 350-mile race, but not a five-mile race. If he and Geoff stayed close together, Tim suspected he could not win if the race came down to a finish-line sprint. But if he continued to fight for the lead, he would expend too much energy breaking trail for everyone else.

Sometime after midnight, Tim decided it was time to sleep. He couldn't sleep on the river, as he'd been setting the trail, and any snowmobile that followed his track would surely run him over. He broke through the powder up a steep embankment and set up his bivy sack. After three hours, he returned to his trail. The snow beyond his tracks was still pristine; Geoff hadn't been through yet, nor had anyone else.

Tim remained alone for the rest of the day. The snowstorm had tapered off the previous morning after depositing more than three feet of fresh powder over the region. Skies were clear for the time being, but the damage had been done, and the good weather did nothing to lighten the load. About eight miles outside of the Skwentna Roadhouse at mile ninety, three snowmobiles dragging large trailers passed. Tim was happy for a broken trail, but felt a tinge of resentment that those behind him would enjoy this relief for even longer.

Only a single skier, a European man named Andrea, arrived before Tim checked out of the mile ninety checkpoint in the late afternoon. He led the race through the Shell Hills; Geoff finally caught up while Tim waited for his food order at Shell Lake Lodge, mile 110. Anne showed up while Tim was settling down to rest, but sleep wouldn't come. He didn't want to always be the racer taking the lead in breaking trail before snowmobiles came through, but he hated wasting time. After two hours, Tim told Geoff he was heading out and would bivy farther down the trail.

Snow squalls returned, with driving flakes and thick accumulation, again. Tim couldn't believe it. He marched for two hours until he came to a small stand of pines clustered together tightly enough to temper the snow and wind. As it often did in the quiet wilderness outside of checkpoints, sleep came quickly, and a seeming moment later, Geoff called out to Tim inside his sleeping bag. Geoff fussed with one of his shoes while Tim squeezed his feet into his own frozen shoes, folded the ground pad over the sleeping bag, and stuffed it in his sled under two bungee cords. Geoff was still tying his laces when Tim stepped back onto the trail, ready to go — a turnover that shocked the younger racer. Another Iditarod runner would later comment that Tim could set up a bivy spot, make tea, eat a meal, sleep, and pack up his sled in the same time it took him to fire up his stove. Tim explained to Geoff that mastering the art of an efficient bivy was one of the keys to success. It made more sense to sleep when he needed it rather than forcing a restless recline at a less opportune time, or struggling to stay awake for checkpoints. Geoff nodded his head in understanding.

Geoff forged ahead but eventually stopped for his own short nap, and the two arrived within minutes of each other at Finger Lake. Tim again headed out first, having been told by workers at Winter Lake Lodge that the trail had only been broken about three miles beyond the lake, after which it was probably buried in fresh snow again. Tim resented the prospect of breaking trail, yet he wasn't about to just lounge around lazily and wait for somebody else to take the lead. Sitting idle when it wasn't necessary just wasn't his nature. Geoff told Tim that he only planned to rest a couple of hours, so Tim expected he'd see the young runner again soon.

The broken trail did indeed end in three miles, after which the difficulty seemed to compound. Instead of cutting a straight route, Tim's tracks serpentined widely as he searched for a solid base. Off the trail, his snowshoes occasionally snagged in alder or disappeared into deeper wells of heavy powder. Even several days into this slog, it was still a frustrating realization to discover just how much his progress slowed when he was breaking trail. While taking a dinner break, he was finally passed — to his surprise, by the remaining skier in the race, Andrea. The Italian was skiing with one pole while his other arm hung limply to his side. Andrea said that he had injured his arm in a fall. Geoff would later reveal that Andrea had actually broken his arm, rendering it useless. The resulting pain and difficulty would force him to scratch at the next checkpoint in Puntilla.

Although deep snow and unbroken trails made 2012 a likely year for skiers to dominate the Iditarod Trail Invitational, only two started and none finished. As of 2014, no other skier has participated in the event. Fans of the race often speculate as to why more skiers don't enter the race to Nome, as it seems natural that skiers would be at the forefront of a winter event. A combination of technical trails, often less-than-ski-friendly conditions, lack of snow in some areas, extreme distance, and the fact that the sports of cycling and running have specific ultra-endurance racing disciplines while skiing does not, probably all contribute to the scarce numbers.

Throughout the night, Tim traded positions with Geoff, Andrea, and the Belgian runner, Frank, as each took their own rest breaks. Whoever was up front was breaking trail, and Tim noticed that the less-experienced athletes in front of him often wandered far from where he knew the trail base to be. But at least they were still moving in the right direction. About ten miles from Puntilla Lake, Tim lost all visual clues of the trail and spent an hour floundering until he saw two figures moving parallel across a swamp in the distance. Based on their speed, he concluded they had to be on top of the trail base, and angled his path to intersect theirs. It was Geoff and Andrea. The trio decided it would be beneficial to stick together in route-finding and trail-breaking.

At Puntilla, Andrea withdrew from the race and Geoff wanted more rest, so Tim again took the lead. As he climbed the wind-scoured alpine valley, thin crust and sastrugi dominated the surface. The trail was still invisible, detectable only by the occasional spruce-trunk tripod in an otherwise white expanse. A gray afternoon cast the mountainscape in flat light, and the lack of contrast made travel even more technical. Tim couldn't discern high-cresting sastrugi from a flat slope, and eventually turned his ankle while tripping over another unseen obstacle. His swollen ankle throbbed while he continued to stumble along, not sure if he should start crying or laughing because at least he was making forward progress.

After hours of fumbling in a blank gray slate, Tim heard the distinct whine of a snowmobile approaching. "Finally," Tim thought. "Somebody else will break the trail." The snowmobile driver was an Anchorage journalist named Craig Medred, who was following the race to document it for a local news organization. Craig stopped next to Tim and snapped a photo. The journalist confessed that he didn't know if they were close to the trail base, as he'd simply followed Tim's snowshoe tracks. Tim told Craig he was glad that someone else was going to take the lead for a while. "I'm not going any further," Craig told him. "I just wanted to catch up to you and take your photo, since you're leading the race."

"What the fuck?" Tim blurted out. It was uncharacteristic of him to swear at others, but the news had unleashed all of his pent-up frustrations. "You mean to tell me you came up here, putting in a trail for everyone else, and now you're going to double back and make that trail better for everyone else?"

Craig shrugged. "That's right." With little else to add, Craig turned and headed back toward Puntilla.

Tim pushed through his frustration and groped for perspective. On one hand, it was difficult to reconcile the unfairness of doing all of the trail breaking. But at the same time, it was a unique experience to be standing at the crest of a pass in the Alaska Range, all alone, as one of the first humans to travel up and over the summit that season. While he had openly complained to Craig, the heart of the matter rested in the reality that Tim loved challenging himself against difficult conditions. This was a competition against himself, and he was persevering. Friends often asked Tim what exactly attracted him to the Iditarod Trail, year after year. He never formed an acceptable answer, but the closest he came was professing a love of adversity. Some view this as masochistic, but Tim didn't see it this way — overcoming challenge and adversity always brought a depth of joy.

The Iditarod Trail never failed to provide a worthy adversary. Poor visibility persisted, and Tim punched his way up a steep slope only to realize that he had drifted off route, again. After cresting Rainy Pass, the wind-drifted crust gave way to deep, untrammeled powder, and Tim broke one of his trekking poles after it wedged into the snow and became stuck. Efforts to splint the pole with alder branches and duct tape proved unsuccessful, so Tim would have to go without until he could locate a wooden lath to serve as a pole. Geoff caught up as Tim worked on repairs for his pole and his blistered feet, and remained ahead when Tim stopped to bivy a few miles outside of the remote outpost of Rohn.

Beyond Rohn, the runners were still leading the entire race. With advances in fat bike technology over the years, this prospect had become almost unfathomable — that athletes without wheels or gliding skis could still conquer all others more than two hundred miles into the Iditarod Trail Invitational. Fans of the race speculated about the prospect of Tim Hewitt winning the race to McGrath outright — him, a man in his late fifties, against a hot young running star and a legion of cyclists.

Tim might possibly admit to pondering the same prospect as he chased Geoff into the Farewell Burn. They leap-frogged again while Geoff stopped on the trail for a rest, but Geoff caught back up to Tim by running across the glare ice of one of the Farewell Lakes. Geoff told Tim his ankle was bothering him and it felt better to run. Generally, Tim would only run downgrades because pulling the sled on ascents and flat terrain was so taxing. The drag of the sled meant his running pace was only marginally faster than a power hike, but drained a lot more energy and strength over a long haul. Tim wondered if Geoff could maintain this running pace. There was a better chance than not that Geoff's energy reserve would diminish and he'd slow considerably; maybe Tim could reel him in again by simply continuing at his own pace. He let Geoff go.

A few hours later, Tim indeed caught Geoff as the young runner sat at the crest of a hill, trying to build a fire. It was still snowing, mostly sideways, and yet temperatures were dropping as the wind intensity increased. After more than two hundred miles of snowshoeing through wet powder, Tim's feet were a mess of blisters, and his socks were soaked in water and blood.

Trail conditions began to improve, and the two men traveled in close proximity of each other through the night. Just outside of Nikolai, nearly three hundred miles into the race, the runners finally relinquished the lead to the first cyclist, a Czech named Pavel Richter. The trail was finally solid enough that Pavel could ride his bike. Tim didn't expect this to change. The last remnants of the storm were beginning to fade, skies were clearing, and a deep cold was settling in — conducive to hard-frozen surfaces. For all the battles Tim waged with the Iditarod while breaking trail, it was surrendering just in time to give the cyclists a fast finish. Tim wouldn't win the race outright, and he wondered if he had enough energy left to chase Geoff for the win in the foot race.

Tim left Nikolai just behind the first and second cyclists. A sharp cold had enveloped the Kuskokwim River, down to forty below, and Tim had to move quickly just to maintain a weak hold on his core temperature. After an hour, Tim became so sleepy that he was losing this battle, so he lay down for a nap. In an hour he awoke, wracked with shivering, but he was still deeply fatigued and could scarcely stay awake on his feet. He lay down again to the same fitful shivering, and awoke when Geoff passed. Tim tried to grab a few more minutes of sleep, knowing his crushing fatigue would follow him to Nome if he didn't deal with it soon. This trek to McGrath had demanded too much time, and he would have to make substantially better progress from now on if he still wanted to set a record to Nome. But it had also demanded too much energy, and there was no possibility of maintaining this brutal effort level. A record might still be possible, but he needed rest.

Still, freezing air continued to find its way into his sleeping bag. He couldn't close the vents entirely; doing so would trap all of the moisture from his breath in the bag's insulation, reducing its effectiveness. But the air was too cold to breathe directly, and Tim couldn't sleep.

Geoff was in front, and Tim didn't know how far. He made his way to a trail intersection on the Kuskokwim River. The only broken path went left toward a mining operation, which was located at the end of a plowed ice road about thirteen miles outside McGrath. Just as Tim had suspected, the race would have come down to a finish-line sprint, a runnable half marathon. As it turned out, Geoff ran this section as hard as he could to bring his finishing time under seven days, in fourth place overall and fewer than eight hours behind the first-place cyclist. Tim kept his pace steady and arrived four hours after Geoff without regrets.

In McGrath, Tim learned that the dog sled race trail breakers did not plan to head out for another two days. Two of the cyclists who had arrived before Tim had signed up for the race to Nome, but opted to stop at 350 miles, citing physical exhaustion from the long haul to McGrath and the lack of trail beyond the village. Rick Freeman also called from Nikolai and reported that he wouldn't go beyond McGrath. Tim was already two days behind potential record pace, and waiting another two days for the trail breakers to set the trail would put the Northern Route record entirely out of reach. There was a good chance he'd be alone for the entire distance as well, just as he'd been in 2004.

Bill Merchant's wife, Kathi, who served as a co-race director, asked Tim if he'd consider finishing in McGrath as well. The trail beyond the village had been buried in four feet of new snow, and Tim knew that even the most stubborn determination wouldn't lift him out of waist-deep powder. For the first time since the Iditasport Impossible had launched a thousand-mile race in 2000, no one would attempt the race to Nome.

Unsupported

14

It is not the mountain we conquer but ourselves.

~ Sir Edmund Hillary
Mountaineer

"Ultimate challenge" is an overused cliché in modern adventure narratives, and it's also a lie. No matter how challenging an endeavor, there are always ways to up the ante. "Limits" are a line that will forever be drawn in pencil, waiting to be erased by those who dare to cross once-unthinkable boundaries.

Tim's Iditarod Trail pursuits had been conquered in many ways, but one challenge he had yet to try was complete independence — crossing Alaska with everything he needed to survive for a thousand miles in his sled, with no outside shelter or support. The idea to travel the Iditarod Trail unsupported came from Mike Curiak, an accomplished Iditarod cyclist who had ridden the entire Northern Route without outside support in 2010, completing the bicycle expedition in twenty-four days. At the time, Curiak — a bicycle wheel builder from Grand Junction, Colorado — held the overall record for a human-powered journey to Nome, and had completed multiple rides across Alaska. Curiak rode a custom-made bicycle with twenty-five days of supplies, all together weighing 155 pounds. Curiak was a stickler for detail and spent years refining his system. He still stopped short of Nome on his first two attempts, and finally finished on his third. Curiak justified the grueling process because he had his eyes on an even greater challenge — an unsupported crossing of Antarctica.

The allure of Antarctica had also captured Tim's imagination. A trek across the frozen continent from McMurdo Station — a scientific base on the coast — to the South Pole, and then on to Hercules Inlet through the Patriot Hills would be roughly eleven hundred miles — similar in length to the Iditarod Trail. Very few people, if anyone, had ever made a trek of that distance on foot without support — Antarctic skiers typically employ a logistics provider to leave air-dropped food caches, or take much shorter routes. Tim felt confident that he could cover this distance without aid. But in order to attract sponsors for such an expensive and seemingly impossible expedition, he felt a certain obligation to prove it. Like Curiak, Tim knew Alaska would provide a rigorous training ground.

Even Tim's Iditarod plan would be more than four hundred miles longer than the longest known unsupported trek by a person on foot — a South Pole expedition by runner Ray Zahab, who traveled seven hundred miles from Hercules Inlet to the pole in thirty-three days during the winter of 2008 to 2009. Tim spent months mulling how long it would take him to travel a thousand miles across Alaska with considerably more weight, how much food and fuel he would require, and how many batteries he'd use. Would he even be able to pull a sled up mountains if it weighed more than a hundred pounds? Tim consulted Mike Curiak, who aggressively tried to dissuade Tim from trying. The unsupported bicycle trek had nearly killed him, Curiak said. It wasn't an experience he'd wish on his worst enemy. As it was, Curiak had since decided to abandon his own ambitions to ride to the South Pole.

Still, Tim knew he was capable. This was similar to the flash of inspiration he had experienced in 2000 while running the Badwater 135 in Death Valley. He knew that when he ran with these ideas, incredible experiences would follow. Worried friends reminded Tim that he was nearly sixty, and not as young as others who took on such arduous pursuits. But after twelve years of Iditarod adventures, Tim saw his age as an advantage rather than a disadvantage — experience had hardened his body and sharpened his mind. He understood better than most what such a journey would take.

Preparations commenced, as Tim refined everything he had learned over the years to determine what he'd need for an unsupported crossing of Alaska: a longer sled, a sleeping bag rated to sixty below, and a vapor barrier liner to prevent body moisture from freezing inside the bag's insulation. Spending the entirety of the journey outdoors meant he would have no opportunities to dry his gear; if something became wet and froze, it would stay that way. He added some extra pieces for anticipated wear and tear, such as spare straps for his gaiters. Food was calculated between 5,000 and 5,500 calories per day, and consisted of twenty pounds of peanut butter divided into three-quarter-pound Ziploc bags, twenty pounds of chocolate bars, twelve freeze-dried meals, twelve packets of tuna, twenty-four beef and elk sticks, six bags of candy, twenty-four VitaFuel bars, six bags of freeze-dried fruit, and one bag of Swedish Fish. Also included were four tea bags, which would be reused until they fell apart. He allotted enough fuel for twenty-four minutes of cooking per day — enough to melt a few liters of water and cook one freeze-dried meal every other day. Fuel, food, and batteries were carefully calculated and rationed, and once they were gone, that was it. The potential for running out of food, water, and light would provide ample incentive to keep up the pace.

The loaded sled weighed one hundred and ten pounds at the start of the race. Tim took heart in the knowledge that his food and fuel consumption would reduce Cookie's weight by two and a half pounds every day — although he would learn that these reminders rarely made him feel better.

Tim started his training by lugging a fifty-pound pack around the Laurel Mountains near his home in Pennsylvania. When snow began to accumulate for the winter, he loaded up a sled — first with a fifty-pound bag of dog food, and then seventy pounds. He topped out at ninety pounds for a couple of six-hour pulls through gentle hills, and found he couldn't even come close to keeping up with his wife, Loreen. On flat sections of trail, every step required the effort of climbing a steep mountain. Hills felt almost insurmountable, and even gentle inclines demanded the top end of Tim's aerobic capacity. How would he keep this up for twenty-four days? Was it even possible? Doubt seeped in from every angle, but the only way to answer these questions would be to try.

Loreen would again join Tim in Alaska this year, also with a new ambition to complete the journey to Nome. After finishing the race to McGrath three times, she had amassed the experience and determination necessary for the full distance. However, not long after she made the commitment, her mother died. Loreen stepped in to take care of her infirmed father, traveling to Florida to sell his house and furniture. Loreen's father moved in with them for a few months while they arranged placement in an independent living facility nearby.

Loreen's training suffered amid this setback, and she continued to worry about leaving her father alone for a month while she was in Alaska. Although she looked forward to the escape of the adventure, the danger and difficulties of the Iditarod Trail can amplify physical and mental distress even in the best of conditions. While Tim towed his 110-pound sled, Loreen had her own heavy baggage to haul across the wilderness.

As the 2013 field gathered on the edge of Knik Lake, Tim decided to try and keep pace with the others in the early miles. There were many doubters among the spectators, and he didn't want to give them the satisfaction of watching him struggle. When the race launched, Tim gripped his trekking polls and leaned into a hard march. After thirty meters, he was out of breath, and the strain on his leg muscles was significant. As he followed the other runners up the first hill, Tim could feel severe strain in his knees and ankles. He was at mile one of a thousand-mile journey — not a good place to pull a muscle. Pride is a difficult thing to swallow, but Tim knew it was smarter to ease off the pace than worry about his position in the race. Being passed by every other runner in the field was a deeply humbling experience for this typically dominant runner — enough to make him feel queasy.

Cookie dragged harder than a lead anchor on any incline, but at least the flat sections made her feel comparatively weightless. Tim jogged down the rolling hills of the first miles, and was able to close the gap on some of the runners in front of him. His pattern involved falling back on climbs and catching up by running the flat and downhill segments — a strategy he justified in the name of self-preservation. He needed to utilize gravity by running the descents to make up for time lost on the climbs. He was able to keep pace with Loreen, who appeared distressed from the start. Instead of being happy that her husband was keeping up with her, she was disappointed that he was able to.

As in past years, Tim hoped to share this experience with Loreen. This year she would be going all the way to Nome, and originally he was concerned that he'd never be able to hold her pace, even while predicting that he might catch her near McGrath after his sled lightened a bit and the terrain flattened on the far side of the Alaskan Range. But Loreen had her own goals — to simply finish in the thirty-day time limit. That was six more days than Tim had to spare. When they reached an iconic trail sign at mile eighteen — "Nome, 1,049 miles" — Tim calculated it was about an hour later than usual, when his sled was sixty pounds lighter and Loreen was in better shape. Loreen expressed disappointment at the level of discomfort she was already experiencing so early in their "vacation," but Tim encouraged her not to lose heart. The Iditarod is never won or lost in the first day.

But the first big test came early, when Tim and Loreen reached the "Wall of Death," a somewhat flippant name for a thirty-foot drop onto the Susitna River. It was short but nearly vertical, and Tim attempted to brace his poles against his sled and dig his heels into the snow. When the weight of the sled pressed against his back, he lost traction and broke into a run just as the Cookie Express slammed into the back of his legs. He tumbled backward on top of the sled as snowshoe cleats dug into his back. Still, when the runaway train finally came to a stop on the river, he stood up no worse for the ride. How he wasn't injured in the rear-end collision was a mystery, but the incident served a valuable lesson. It was impossible to outrun his sled; for future steep descents, he would have to let Cookie go first.

As the couple rounded a slough connecting the confluence of the Susitna and Yentna Rivers, Loreen was fading and Tim decided rest was in order. It would be the first night Tim used his vapor barrier liner inside his sleeping bag. On previous trips, he had noticed ice clumps forming inside of his sleeping bag after a few nights without drying. The problem would only continue to compound over twenty-four nights, unless he prevented the moisture of his body from escaping. After consulting several winter camping and expedition experts, Tim settled on what was touted to be the best product available — a Western Mountaineering HotSac, which was designed with a silver reflective coating to increase heat retention. But after a couple of hours inside the bag on the first night, noxious fumes left Tim feeling nauseated. The poisonous chemical smell was enough to cause lightheadedness, but he couldn't let himself fret. Maybe this was just "new gear" smell, and would wear off.

On the second night, Loreen went inside a cabin on the Yentna River to sleep, and Tim opted to wait for her outside. When he awoke, the acrid smell was back, and he noticed that silver dust had accumulated on the outer layer of his clothing. The vapor barrier liner was delaminating — a simple manufacturing defect, but a major aggravator in Tim's position. He worried that the silver particles would cause him to become ill, but he couldn't risk ice building in his sleeping bag by discontinuing use of the shoddy vapor barrier. Tim wondered whether this gear defect would prove to be the unanticipated wildcard that would ultimately take him out of the race.

It seemed like problems were bombarding him from all directions. Pulling Cookie was every bit as difficult as he could have imagined in these early miles on flat rivers, and the climb over the Alaska Range loomed. Loreen was potentially moving too slowly to hold his twenty-four day schedule, but he didn't want to leave his wife behind. A crucial piece of gear wasn't just failing; it was threatening to poison him. And although it had only been two days since he started on food rations, hunger was already gnawing at his stomach. Five thousand calories per day was enough to maintain forward motion, but not enough to remain warm and comfortable. Tim had always considered life on the Iditarod Trail to be fairly simple, but this year most of his thoughts encompassed worries rather than awe and appreciation.

Loreen was struggling with her own pressures — distress about the pace, accumulating fatigue, and guilt about absence from her ailing father. Tim encouraged patience as they pushed through the night after only a short rest on the Yentna River. Loreen went into Skwentna Roadhouse for a meal as Tim waited outside. This would become a pattern for Tim and Loreen — she would step inside for a break that usually included unproductive downtime such as waiting for a meal, chatting with lodge owners and racers, and fidgeting with gear. Tim, without anything else on his schedule besides eating, sleeping, and walking, would squeeze considerably more sleep out of every stop. He melted snow and settled in to add a few more hours to the sleep bank.

The first substantial climbs into the Shell Hills were every bit as difficult as Tim feared. Several ascents were so steep that Cookie's downward pull forced Tim to his knees, and he had to dig his feet into the snow to keep himself from slipping backward. Sometimes he did slide downhill until he managed to self-arrest in deeper snow off to the side of the trail. Still, it was generally forward progress, and Tim knew that any forward progress was good progress.

Midway through the Shell Hills, Tim found a swift-flowing stream at an opportunistic time, as he was nearly out of water. The open stream was guarded by a bank of loose snow and fragile ice nearly six feet deep — too steep to retrieve water with his hands without tumbling into the current. On the fly, Tim invented a water retriever using a Nalgene bottle attached to his trekking pole with bungee cords and caribiners. The device provided a secure hold while fishing for water from a distance — an invaluable tool in his effort to preserve fuel. He filled his hundred-ounce bladder with clear, ice-cold water.

Later that night, Tim left Loreen at Finger Lake Lodge and went to make his camp a few miles up the trail. He expected his pace to slow substantially in the foothills of the Alaska Range, and told Loreen he would see her when she caught up to him. At the Happy River Gorge, he let Cookie go free, detaching his hip belt and pushing the pregnant sled into a free fall down the steep ravine. At the bottom of the final step, he heard a cry from above. Another racer, Beat Jegerlehner, was racing his own sled down to the Happy River. Having finished the trek to McGrath in the difficult conditions of 2012, Beat was making a go for the full distance to Nome in 2013. Tim was happy to have some company for the climb out of the gorge.

When he was still early in the planning stages for this year's trek, Tim figured the climb out of the Happy River Gorge would be his biggest test. The trail cut a direct line out of the ravine, and it was likely the steepest segment of the entire Iditarod Trail. Tim feared he'd simply be physically unable to tow his sled up the canyon wall. There was no room for error — if he lost his footing on the packed snow, he could feasibly slide hundreds of feet back to the bottom of the gorge, dragged like a piece of road kill behind the Cookie Express. No, he had to maintain traction at all times, and so every step would require the utmost precaution. Tim felt embarrassed that Beat would witness this painfully slow procedure, but glad there was at least someone else around to respond to a potentially serious mishap.

Beat reported that Loreen had left the Finger Lake checkpoint at about the same time, and he expected she was not far behind. Tim motioned for Beat to take the lead, reasoning that while anyone who signed up for the race was voluntarily exposing themselves to risks, being mowed down by a human/sled train was not on the list of liabilities that racers should anticipate.

Tim grunted, arched his back, flexed his leg muscles, yanked Cookie an inch or two forward, planted a foot, kicked another step, grunted, nearly slipped, cursed, and maneuvered the sled another hard-won inch. He felt like he was harnessed to a tree, although a tree would be better than Cookie, because at least a tree would anchor him to the mountain if he fell. He leaned forward, pushed all the air out of his lungs in a loud exhale, and took another tiny step. The process repeated with frequent breaks, Tim collapsing to his knees after he had secured his toes inside footholds, arms splayed with fingers clutching the lower half of his trekking poles, and neck arching downward like a broken mule. Beat patiently waited a few yards ahead, displaying visible concern for the six-year veteran whom he considered his mentor.

"Do you actually think you can keep this up all the way to Nome?" Beat asked after Tim rose to his feet again.

"Absolutely," Tim said, but he too was having doubts — not in his resolve, but about his body. The tendons behind his knees and hip flexors were burning in pain, and his right knee responded with electric shocks whenever he pushed down hard. These weak areas had to be babied, which in turn overburdened other parts of his body. There was no way around the amount of work that needed to be done; it was only a question whether his 58-year-old body could maintain the power and flexibility required to do the work. He was already taking large quantities of painkillers, hoping that he'd be able to scale back once muscle and joint pain evened out, which they usually did, eventually. Now he wasn't so sure about this year. He had a finite number of pills as well, and at this rate his supply wouldn't be nearly enough.

High on a bluff above the river valley, Tim told Beat to go ahead so he could wait for Loreen. Tim was exhausted from the climb but reluctant to stop as well — wet snow was falling in large chunks, and accumulating on his sleeping bag. If he waited too long, the moisture would soak through to the insulation. He ate a few Clif Shot Bloks, a gummy energy chew that he used to spur muscle recovery. While gnawing on the frozen mass, a brand new crown broke off one of his teeth, leaving the stub in his hand and raw nerves exposed. What more could go wrong? But in the scheme of a thousand miles of potential dangers, this wasn't a big deal. He put the broken crown in the tiny wallet that held his emergency cash, driver's license, and credit card.

Several inches of heavy snow had accumulated on the trail by the time Loreen caught up to Tim and then stopped to rest for an hour herself. The wet snow on his sleeping bag and deteriorating trail conditions compounded Tim's frustration level. Although his rational side warned him not to get worked up over the things he couldn't control, he also knew that the clock was ticking on his twenty-four days' worth of provisions. Any setback to his progress further diminished his chances of finishing. He could always go inside of a cabin to dry gear or a village store to buy more food, but he couldn't give up on his unsupported effort now. He had already suffered inordinately in these first one hundred and fifty miles compared to a typical year, and he didn't want all of that effort to be in vain. "In for a penny, in for a pound," he thought.

The twinkle of lights outside Puntilla Lake Lodge appeared through the snow-flecked darkness at 1 a.m. Tim asked Loreen how long she planned to sleep. She replied tersely that she would stay as long as necessary. Tim sensed the tension and didn't press for anything more. Loreen went inside and Tim settled down beside a cluster of spruce thirty meters from the hut. Loreen emerged at

4 a.m., and Tim told her to go ahead. He liked letting Loreen take the lead because it gave him a target to reel in, taking his mind off the slog by turning his focus to a "race." He took his time packing up and began the long climb toward Rainy Pass. Stars twinkled in an ink-black sky, but the only signs of life amid an expansive emptiness were the beams of tiny headlamps in the distance. Loreen and two other foot racers, Marco Berni and Steve Ansell, were making their way up the broad valley.

Tim hopscotched with Loreen and the others several times before he and his wife settled in for a short nap. Loreen often had difficulty consuming food while she walked, because nausea would set in and force her to stop eating. Determination pushed her forward through these bouts of sickness, and she would continue walking until she simply ran out of gas. Tim knew it was useless to encourage her to continue in this state; it was more time-effective in the long run to stop and refuel the tank. After eating a few bites, Loreen collapsed on her duffel like an animal carcass draped over a sled, covering herself with her down parka. With this method, she could take short naps without the time-consuming chores of breaking camp. However, chill sets in quickly once activity ceases. After twenty minutes, both of their core temperatures had dropped enough to awaken them in a fit of shivering.

The climb plodded on, step by hard-won step. Tim engaged in a constant tug-of-war with his sled, yanking hard against its downward momentum. Every few steps, his racing heart forced him to lean forward and rest his hands on his knees until he could catch his breath. A flock of well-camouflaged ptarmigan suddenly erupted from the brush, breaking the tense silence. Tim watched in awe as their feathers beat against the snowy background in a frenetic contrast of white on white. It occurred to him that Cookie's workload was muting the fun he normally enjoyed on the trail, adding so much hardship to the equation that the whole experience felt off balance. Even in decent trail conditions he felt like he was barely moving. And more worrisome, Loreen was still falling behind.

Rainy Pass marked a respite from the endless climbing, but the workload remained constant. With Cookie nipping at his heels, Tim quickly realized that unhooking the sled and letting it precede him down the mountain was the best strategy. Even then, Cookie frequently tugged him off his feet, then continued to pull his body down the slope as he dragged his heels in the snow until friction finally stopped them both. It was terrifying, tendon-straining work, and he still had to hook back into the hip belt for flatter sections. Toward the bottom of the cascading gorge, the trail jutted up several steep climbs to veer away from the fast-flowing Dalzell Creek. Loose snow covered the surface of the trail, and alder branches tangled in his snowshoes. Loreen, who did not unhook on the descents, tumbled into a face-planting somersault while trying to outrun her sled. She was uninjured, and the incident provided much-needed comic relief.

At Rohn, the checker Rob came outside and wrapped his arms around Tim, congratulating him on completing two hundred miles of his attempt to haul a house trailer to Nome. Tim left Loreen and the other racers at the wall tent, and settled down in a nearby stand of spruce to cook a freeze-dried meal. Tim savored the smell of teriyaki chicken as he waited for the meal to cook; he had been fantasizing about this moment for most of the day. Food was beginning to dominate his thoughts, and was tormenting him nearly as much as agony about the sheer workload his pregnant sled demanded. Every day his sled became lighter, and every day Tim was sinking deeper into calorie deficit. The rehydrated morsels of chicken and rice settled into his stomach like a warm hug, inviting Tim into a peaceful sleep.

The next night, Tim and Loreen would aim for Bison Camp, the cluster of tents halfway between Rohn and Nikolai where Tim was forced to withdraw from the race with severe bronchitis in 2006. The remote encampment had since fallen into disuse; although bison still flourished in the region, the number of hunting clients had fallen through years of economic downturn and rising fuel costs. The tents were locked now, but the site was near the halfway point between Rohn and Nikolai, and would provide a benchmark to reach by nightfall.

The Farewell Lakes region was again nearly devoid of snow. The canyon slopes beside the South Fork of the Kuskokwim River were also subject to frequent wildfires. Skeletal trunks of scorched trees stuck out like broken toothpicks that had been haphazardly stabbed into a bed of dry grass. The trail rolled along short but steep hills, and the minimal snow had become icy on the south-facing climbs. Tim had to kick steps just to keep Cookie from pulling him backward, and then yank the stubborn sled through bare patches of dirt at the top. The hills put unmanageable strain on his hamstrings and knees, and he fretted about blowing out a knee. Loreen maintained a lead on the frequent hills, and Tim would often arrive at the crest of a climb to see his wife making her way over the next horizon.

A short distance past Bison Camp, Tim and Loreen set up their camp on a snowmobile track just off the main trail. Amid a swirl of snow and fierce gusts of wind, they propped up their sleds as windbreakers. Tim shook out his noxious vapor barrier liner and turned it inside out, as he'd been doing for several nights. The strategy provided some relief from the fumes, and he no longer felt anxious about sharp metallic dust clogging the insulation of his sleeping bag and creeping into his lungs. He'd been collecting water at streams, so there was no need to melt snow, and there was no hot meal for tonight. Removing only his down parka and outer gloves, Tim crawled inside still wearing all of his clothing, balaclava, and even his headlamp. A mere ten minutes was all it took for Tim to transition from walking to snoozing.

Three hours later, Tim awoke from deep sleep to the sound of shrieking — only to realize that the shrieks were his own screams. His head was a fog of confusion, but he distinctly heard close-range growling, barks, and howls. Something was scratching at the snow mere feet from his sleeping bag, and Tim knew it had to be a pack of wolves converging on their camp. He sat up and shouted aggressively, "Hey! Hey! Hey!" and continued shouting as he thrashed around in his dark cocoon. The exit zipper angled from the side of the bag to the breathing tube, and moisture from his breath often froze it shut. He jiggled the frozen zipper frantically as growling and scratching noises echoed in the darkness. His wife was sleeping right next to him and he had no idea whether the wolves were attacking her. He screamed and thrashed until finally the zipper released and he thrust his face into the darkness.

Gulping frigid air into his lungs, Tim scanned the area for signs of the wolves, but saw no movement. He found his headlamp where it had fallen in his bag, and pointed the beam toward the forest. The snow surrounding their camp had clearly been trampled by something other than human feet, but the creatures were gone. Loreen was sitting up as well, and said she was all right. As they spoke, the howling and barking started again, this time moving away from them. A pack of wolves had likely happened on their camp while traveling, checked out the anomaly, and decided it was not something to bother with. Still, Tim and Loreen were badly rattled. They packed up in record time and marched quickly down the trail, away from the direction of the fading howls.

Days later, Tim would recount this story and learn that an aerial photographer had spotted a massive pack of wolves in that same area — possibly more than a hundred animals. The pack that encountered the Hewitts were likely just investigating strange-smelling clumps on the snow, and Tim was grateful that these animals capable of ripping them apart in seconds had chosen to leave them alone.

During the long slog into Nikolai, Loreen began to make more frequent noises — not yet audible complaints, but communication enough that she was not in a good state to continue on to Nome. Tim wasn't sure whether to encourage her or voice his own concern about the prospect. There were a lot of unknowns beyond McGrath — the weather and trail conditions would undoubtedly become worse, and he would likely reach a point where he just didn't have the fuel and food remaining to wait for her. He was confident in his wife's abilities, but still uneasy about leaving her alone, especially for so many miles, when she was already so clearly struggling with physical distress.

He felt sadness that the sublime beauty of the Yukon River, the Blueberry Hills, the Norton Sound, and the Gold Coast would not be shared. Loreen briefly expressed anger at Tim's decision to go unsupported, which she argued took the fun out of the journey for both of them. But beyond Nikolai and into McGrath, she mostly remained quiet, and Tim understood the depth of frustrations communicated by her silence. By the 350-mile mark, she had made up her mind. Her energy reserves were exhausted. Her race would end in McGrath.

As Loreen stepped into the inviting warmth of Peter's house, Tim spread out his sleeping bag a few meters away in the yard. He told his wife that he planned to leave after four hours, and hoped with a glimmer of optimism that she might change her mind and come out to join him. After he awoke, Marco Berni walked out the front door and announced that Beat would follow shortly. The tall and lithe Italian congratulated Tim on being "a very strong man." Loreen never did emerge from the house, probably sound asleep under a week of exhaustion. Tim wondered why she didn't come out to see him off, but perhaps the reality of remaining behind was too difficult to face at the moment. With McGrath as nothing more than a waypoint, he had no reason to stay, so he packed up and continued on his seventh attempt at Nome.

Stretching the Limit

15

*I don't want to get to the end of my life
and find that I lived just the length of it. I
want to have lived the width of it as well.*

~ Diane Ackerman, Poet

With his wife safely resting in McGrath, Tim now only had himself
to worry about. Vicariously he felt disappointment, similar to what Loreen must
have been feeling about ending her journey. He also felt curiosity about whether
Beat would decide to continue on to Nome, and camaraderie with Marco, who
was just ahead on the trail. Mixed in this cocktail of emotions was concern about
the soft trail conditions and equal parts excitement and dread about the many
miles in front of him.

Perhaps overwhelming all these emotions, however, were the encompassing
demands of his physical needs. Tim's thoughts often fixated on his next meal. It
was nearly 2 p.m., which meant the beginning of a new race day, and this day
brought an allotted freeze-dried dinner. As he trekked through Takotna, the
next village beyond McGrath, Tim passed Marco's sled parked outside the community center. Takotna was a heralded checkpoint in the dog sled race, and its
volunteers were known for hospitality and gourmet dinners. Tim envisioned the
warm interior of the building and all of the wonderful foods contained between
its walls — steak, fresh bread, cold beer, hot coffee. "That lucky dog," Tim
thought of Marco. But he chose not to dwell on it — such thoughts could eat
a hungry man alive. Instead, he continued walking and nurtured anticipation
about his own packaged meal.

When he moved through the next checkpoint of Ophir, volunteers there emerged from the lone habitable cabin in the gold mining ghost village to welcome Tim to town. These commercial airline pilots, who arrived in their private ski planes, manned the checkpoint. Several already knew about Tim's unsupported effort and teased him with invitations to come inside for a prime rib dinner. After a few minutes of conversation outside the cabin about Tim and Loreen's wolf encounter, he headed down the trail.

During the past few days, temperatures had fluctuated wildly between subzero and near freezing — conditions that disrupted winter's usual suppression of groundwater. The trail surrounding the remote ghost town had been inundated with overflow where newly open streams gurgled over the snow. The water refroze into angled ice, which dipped into puddles that were both insulated from freezing and hidden from view by a blanket of snow. Tim tiptoed through these glaciated sections of trail, as though side-stepping the edge of a dangerous waterfall. Screws in his shoes held him to the slanted ice, barely, as Cookie dragged through slush beside the trail. The prospect of falling into open water was unnerving, but at least he could scoop some slush to refill his drinking water supply.

Night fell as Tim neared the intersection where the Northern Route and Southern Route split. There, he would turn left toward the longer and more difficult Southern Route, making his way across the barren expanse of Beaver Flats toward the Shageluk Hills. But before then, he would sleep. Tim remembered an idyllic forest near this intersection, a dense cluster of healthy spruce trees surrounding pillows of deep snow. There he would find relative shelter from the wind and unobstructed views of stars upon stars in the sky. The thought of spreading out his sleeping bag in this familiar spot brought a warm sense of comfort. Happy emotions overshadowed any remnant wistfulness about leaving behind the possibility of a good meal, a warm space to sleep, and friendly company in Ophir. He was at home in these woods, perhaps even more content than he would be if he were returning to a warm bed. At once he recognized these emotions as bizarre — more animal than human — but he didn't push them away. It occurred to him that an excellent spot for him to rest would be equally inviting to a mega-pack of wolves or territorial moose. Still, the primary need for sleep spoke louder than more useless human anxieties, and the thought faded like a whisper in the wind. Tim was too tired to care.

The following morning started out favorably, with light winds and temperatures around ten degrees. The trail beyond the intersection had been packed down by snowmobiles, and Tim could see tracks from the three cyclists who were in front of him. He saw no footprints, which meant the cyclists were still riding their bikes — a good sign. This had been his largest worry of all — that he would have to break trail for many miles with his pregnant sled. Marco was still behind him, which meant Tim was leading the foot race. Always a competitor, the prospect of winning was meaningful, although he viewed Cookie as his true adversary. The only way for him to actually "win" would be to tow his sled the entire distance without resupply, and without stepping indoors. Everything else was losing, no matter where he finished in the race.

By late morning, temperatures had climbed above thirty-two degrees. Although warm days sound like a good thing, the realities of a mid-winter thaw in Alaska are anything but positive. The snow on the trail became softer, slowing progress. Snowmelt and sweat soaked into Tim's shoes, rubbing like sandpaper against his already raw feet. Groundwater seeped from its winter confines, and some of the valleys were inundated with urine-colored overflow. Brackish water flowed over brown ice, and the resulting streams of slush were too wide to cross without leaping. Tim lumbered into a running jump, knowing he would need to lunge forward as soon as he landed so Cookie wouldn't yank him backward into the slurry. His foot broke through the ice before he launched, so instead he fell onto his arms in the middle of the stream, sinking up to his elbows in ice water. His right hand landed on hard ice, with enough purchase that he was able to lift his body to a tripod position, keeping his legs out of the stream.

It was a brief mishap, but now all three layers on his left arm were soaked, as were the front of his Nano Puff jacket and his right foot. Tim felt disgusted, but at least temperatures were above freezing, meaning wet clothing was uncomfortable but not a disaster. He was approaching Beaver Flats, a barren pocket of the Interior where spindly spruce grow only near river banks, and windswept hills are covered in ankle-twisting clumps of grass. This meant he needed to take advantage of any tree cover while it still existed. Tim stopped at a sign marking the intersection to Tolstoi Cabin to cook and dry out his wet clothing as much as possible. He removed his upper layers to wring them out before putting them back on, hoping body heat would help dry them as he rested. He hung his socks, one wet liner glove, and a mitten over the thin aluminum windshield surrounding the stove.

Once he removed the following day's allotment of food from his sled, Tim sat on top of the duffel to rest while he melted snow over the stove. Since he had already taken off his top layers, he didn't give any extra thought to the position of the hose that led from a hundred-ounce water bladder. The hose ends in a valve that requires biting to release water, along with a shut-off lever to prevent accidental drainage. This was useful for sleeping, as he needed to keep drinking water near his body at all times to prevent it from freezing. He was meticulous about closing and then double-checking the valve before he crawled into his sleeping bag. However, he didn't have a habit of closing it during the day, when ice could form around the opening and make his drinking water less accessible.

After several minutes of patiently scooping cups of snow into the pot, Tim noticed that his butt felt wet. At first he brushed it off as water from his wet shirts seeping into his pants, but then an internal alarm went off — this was much too wet. He jumped up as though his pants were on fire, but was too late. He had been sitting on the bite valve of his water bladder, which was now nearly empty. Almost a hundred ounces of fluid had drained directly onto his sleeping bag, down coat, and extra clothing. This was not a small mishap; this was a major mistake.

Tim's head spun. He wanted to vomit, but all he could do now was act in the most logical way possible. He gently removed the sleeping bag and shook off the water that had pooled on top of the bag. He hoped its water-resistant fabric had worked as advertised, and not let too much liquid seep into the down insulation. He did the same with his down coat. As he shook out the standing water in the duffel, he smelled the distinct aroma of something burning. Amid the panic of the water disaster, he didn't notice the heat from the stove burning holes into the thumb of one of his liner gloves, and both socks. Just when it seemed like his situation couldn't become any more awful, it had. He was wet, frustrated, fretting about all the fuel he had wasted in this process, physically exhausted, and emotionally broken.

And it kept getting worse.

The arid climate of Beaver Flats, combined with constant wind, erased snow from the ground. There was no defined trail to follow over a minefield of bowling-ball-sized tussocks laced with ribbons of wet ice. Tim knew that to stay on track, he needed to keep the distant mountains to his right, and the occasional log tripod on his left. As he stumbled through the obstacle course, seven snowmobiles from the Iditarod trail breaking crew blazed past him with little more than a head nod. Ten minutes later, three more snowmobiles passed — amazing to Tim, as he hadn't seen anyone since he had left Ophir. These drivers stopped to chat — they were all large men decked out in camouflage suits, and said they were spectators driving out in front of the dog sled race. With temperatures this warm, their more aggressive style of driving was doing a number on the Iditarod trail breakers' work, tearing up what little was left of the trail surface. If the trail had been difficult for a man on foot before, it would be nearly unnavigable now.

The drivers described Beat and Marco traveling together a few miles back. The news heartened Tim — he was glad Beat had decided to continue to Nome, and hoped to have company soon. But as he watched the three men disappear over the next hill, carelessly tearing up what little trail there was to follow, Tim felt overcome with the weight of it all — the deteriorating trail, his fatigue, his hunger, his wet clothes and burnt socks and possibly soaked sleeping bag that might no longer keep him warm at night.

With shaking hands, he unhooked his sled right there and removed the sleeping bag, assuring the logical side of his brain that a mid-day nap was in order — he needed to spread out the bag to dry while the day was still warm and sunny. He draped it over himself and curled up on his ground pad next to all of the food he had cordoned off for the day. Included in this pile was his special bag of Swedish fish, the one treat he was saving to celebrate his arrival at the Yukon River in a couple more days. Without a second thought, Tim grabbed the candy and devoured every last one, all of his Yukon Fish, and then moved on to most of the food he had allotted for the next twenty-four-hour period.

The last morsel of remaining food was another treat he had been saving, a bag of pistachio nuts. Tim ate half of those as well. He agonized about Loreen, that maybe he hadn't done enough to encourage his wife. He felt defeated and vulnerable, wrestling between his logical and emotional sides — the angel and devil on his shoulder. One demanded he pick himself back up right now, and another told him to concede, that enough was enough, and he should just lie there until it somehow all went away. Tim knew that the first voice was the right one, but the mind and body are sometimes two separate entities at war with each other. His body and leaden emotions needed to regroup somehow, and he was too weak to wage the necessary battle against apathy just yet. After an hour wasted, Tim finally regrouped, packed up his stuff, and returned to the trail.

As darkness again enveloped the wind-scoured hills and anemic forests, Tim held out hope that the trail conditions would improve. The temperature dropped, but only a few degrees. It was still warm enough that snow on the surface remained soft and sugary. He opted to take another nap, hoping that several hours of sleep would position him for travel in the coldest part of the night. But after four hours, trail conditions were still bad and Tim resigned himself to the reality that they were not going to improve. Still, he felt markedly better after resting longer in the past twenty-four hours than he had yet in the race. He wondered how much fatigue had factored into his Yukon Fish meltdown. The well-intentioned treat was gone and now he could only chuckle about devouring them without enjoyment while he was so upset. A man who can't laugh at himself has no power over his mistakes.

Tim relished this healthier outlook but struggled to hold onto it. The trail-plundering snowmobilers ripped past him again in the morning. He weaved around their tracks to locate a firm base for walking, but there was simply nothing there. The hills were only beginning now, each one small but mercilessly steep, rippling toward the remote village of Shageluk for many miles. The combination of soft trails and Cookie-induced backward gravitational pull made it impossible for Tim to power up these short climbs as he had in the past. Every thirty seconds he had to stop marching to catch his breath, stooping with his hands on his knees to calm his racing heart, and scooping handfuls of snow into his mouth. Eating snow kept his throat moist, provided some hydration, and helped cool his internal engine. Even at temperatures below freezing, a human can overheat while pulling a heavy sled up a mountain.

His feet were commanding more attention as well. Instead of fixating on hunger or the terrible condition of the trail or the obese sled Cookie, blisters were beginning to take the main stage in his thoughts. It was evident that the warm afternoons were causing his feet to sweat more profusely, and both heels had bulging blisters larger than quarters. Puncturing blisters had become a regular occurrence, and swelling around the edges indicated that he would soon have to start taking antibiotics to ward off infection.

Each hilltop brought sight of yet another mountain to climb, another Sisyphean battle. Economic stimulus money had spurred the building of more shelter cabins on the trail, complete with tree-mounted signs announcing their approach — thirty miles, twenty miles, ten miles. Tim would guess the time it would take to reach these benchmarks based on distance, and be dead wrong every time. The time to cover a certain amount of miles always took at least twenty-five percent longer than he expected, until Tim couldn't bear his own predictions any more. This journey was simply going to take as long as it took, no matter how much his twenty-four-day deadline protested. At the top of one hill, Tim caught sight of another group of snowmobiles that had passed him earlier, idling just beyond the Moose Creek shelter cabin. This is where Tim would encounter the rushing overflow that required three trips through thigh-deep ice water to cross. Sleep would again bring brief respite from the relentless effort, but daylight — along with warm temperatures, soft trails, and endless hills — would return again.

Each morning also brought renewed anticipation of 2 p.m. That was the moment the race clock flipped over to a new day, and Tim was free to dig into another twenty-four hours' worth of rations. As this heralded hour approached, Tim noticed the first dog team of 2013 charging toward him. The dogs moved like race horses in full gallop; Tim had never seen a sled dog team move so fast outside the start of sprint races in downtown Anchorage. The musher was leaning into the uphill side of the trail, angled enough that the downhill runner was suspended off the trail. Tim dove off the trail just as Martin Buser, a good friend with whom Tim had talked nearly every year, raced by in first position. In previous years, Martin had always stopped to greet Tim with a piece of chocolate or smoked salmon. On this day he was truly in a hurry, but he yelled something as the team blurred past. Tim marveled at this flash of excitement as he watched the team disappear over the crest of the hill. As he stepped out of the bank to return to the trail, Tim noticed a package of gummy bears lying in the snow. Martin hadn't forgotten Tim — he had just conducted a drive-by greeting this year.

Tim was thrilled but torn. He wanted those gummy bears more than anything; he was starving. But if he let himself devour them, then all of his grueling work would be for naught. Unsupported was exactly that, and anything else would mean all of this was wasted effort. Anger bubbled through his excitement, and he stomped over the package of candy and let Cookie crush them as well for good measure.

He immediately realized how childish it was to be angry at a man who had no knowledge of these self-imposed restrictions, and who was just trying to be friendly. He marched and tried to push the gummy bears out of his mind, and soon came upon a Ziploc bag of chocolate. Damn that Martin Buser. Now Tim couldn't contain his anger. What kind of sick joke was the musher playing? Taunting a starving man with food he could not eat was like waving a steak at a lion in a cage. Tim knew it was irrational to feel so upset; Martin's unappreciated gesture wasn't a test, it was simply kindness. When a third bag containing nuts appeared on the trail, it was almost too much to bear. But there was nothing Tim could do. He marched his sled straight over offerings that were as valuable to him as gold, and took heart in the notion that Beat and Marco weren't far behind and could appreciate these treasures.

For hours, Tim obsessed about the gummy bears, chocolate, and nuts. They became a specter hanging over his shoulder, the cackling devil behind the eerie moans of the wind. Hours later a second headlight appeared from behind. This time it was Aliy Zirkle, a female musher with whom Tim had also become acquainted. She once retrieved a trekking pole he had dropped on the trail, and always took the time to stop and chat. She passed Tim on a steep downhill near one of the new stimulus money safety cabins. Tim caught up with her as she tended to her dogs outside the cabin, a necessary stop even as she chased leader Martin Buser into Shageluk. Tim felt heartened by this encounter, and hoped either one of his friends would win the Iditarod. He marched for another hour before reaching another inviting bivy spot in the woods. The air tasted moist, almost like spring, and Tim knew the warming pattern was picking up strength.

The next afternoon, snow flurries deteriorated into spitting sleet, followed by freezing rain. Tim was incredulous — rain, in the Interior, in early March? His gear system wasn't designed to hold off rain. If his duffles absorbed water, all of the gear inside would become wet as well. He carried a single trash compactor bag for this purpose, providing the only layer of protection between his crucial survival gear and the hateful moisture falling from the sky. Tim's self-imposed rules also dictated that he could not build fires, since there were no trees in all of Antarctica. But it also rarely rained in Antarctica, and Tim had no other recourse to dry wet gear. Tim had only body heat to dry clothing, and wet clothes sucked precious calories from his deteriorating body.

The rain mix pelted him for most of the day, continuing into the early hours of the following morning. It was too wet to camp, and chills would sink in from his damp clothing if he stopped for even a short time, so he continued marching. The surface snow was saturated with moisture, causing Cookie's drag to feel much heavier than her already obese eighty pounds. Tim passed through the village of Shageluk and kept on marching, stopping at the top of an embankment thirty feet above the river. He felt immutably miserable, and decided some kind of reward was crucial. He pulled the duffel bag out of its trash-bag shell and took out a bag of dried peaches. His soaked feet were throbbing in pain, and if he could only take the weight off them for a few minutes, drain his blisters, and eat some food, he was bound to feel better.

As he savored the last wonderful morsel, he felt a truly terrible sensation — cold water seeping through his pants. His fingers went limp and the empty peach bag tore away into the wind as Tim stood up, utterly dumbfounded. How could he have possibly been so stupid? Sure enough, he had again sat down on the bite valve of his hydration bladder, draining water into his duffel once more. He had been enjoying the peaches for ten minutes, which was plenty of time for all of the water that had pooled on top of the duffel to seep into the bag. More had run down the insides of the duffel onto a pair of thick fleece pants at the bottom of the duffel that Tim reserved for the coldest weather. The pants were saturated, as wet as they would be if he threw them in a lake. Tim wrung them out and then shook out his sleeping bag once again. And, of course, he was again completely out of water.

As low as Tim had been when he devoured his Yukon fish two days earlier, this was markedly worse. He wasn't just miserable or wallowing in self-pity — he was consumed with rage at himself. Standing to brush away all of the excess water had ignited a spectacular flash of pain from his feet; now that he had drained the blisters, the raw sores pushed against his shoes, and walking would be agony. His feet were soaked, his clothing was soaked, his sleeping bag was soaked, the trail was soaked – and Tim was nearly paralyzed by the weight of his predicament. Tears streamed down his cheeks as he stared toward the empty horizon. Shageluk was still almost in sight directly behind him, but quitting never crossed Tim's mind. There was only one thing he knew how to do when everything seemed absolutely hopeless, and that was to keep moving.

And through that determination, bright spots slowly began to return. The sky had lightened some, and it looked as though the rain was finally tapering. Tim removed the duffel from its trash-bag liner and stretched out the fleece pants over the top to dry. But after the sun set, a sinister darkness settled, signaling another drop in the cloud ceiling. Sure enough, the rain returned. Tim needed water and a meal, and no longer saw much point in zealously protecting his gear from the moisture. He found a well-protected wooded section and pushed Cookie into the deep snow, then tossed his duffel to the side and collapsed on top of the sled. He slithered into his sleeping bag with the vapor barrier inside and the trash bag pulled over the bottom. There, he fired up his stove. As he was cooking, a drunken Native pulled up on a snowmobile and urged Tim to have a nightcap with him. Tim was in no mood to explain his unsupported ethic to a drunk, so he simply refused multiple demands until the man went away.

Tim slept for a few hours, wakening several times to what sounded like pouring rain but was in fact ice pellets, and finally to a fresh coating of snow. It took all of his willpower to wedge his raw feet into now frozen saturated shoes. Once he completed the task, he realized that he had put the wrong shoe on both feet. He hadn't done something like this since first grade, and the absurdity of it caused him to break out in a fit of cackling laughter. In a few hours he had shifted from hopeless sobbing to uncontrollable laughing. Was he losing his mind? It was a valid question.

He hobbled to the far end of a swamp, where he could see the headlamp of a musher a few hundred meters back. He stepped off the trail and rested his hands and chin on his trekking poles for the minute it took for her to approach. The musher's dogs blazed past without even a sniff in his direction, but the woman let out a loud yelp when Tim said "Hello."

"You're real!" she exclaimed. "I thought you were a tripod."

"I feel like a tripod," Tim replied, and they both laughed. Tim's feet had started to feel marginally better, and the dip in temperatures brought an energizing chill to the air. Tim came upon a pair of handmade gloves with a fur ruff and intricate bead designs. Whoever lost these mittens was likely long gone, and his unsupported ethic meant he could not use them during this trip. Still, they were too beautiful to leave discarded on the trail, so Tim packed the treasures beneath his duffel bag, filled with gratitude at the small turn of fortune. This emotional roller coaster was more dramatic than any Tim had ridden before, but at least things were currently on their way up.

Of course, roller coasters have a way of plunging steeply right at their apex. When Tim arrived at the village of Grayling on the Yukon River, the sky had darkened again, and snow flurries swirled around his face. In the flat light, it was difficult to judge the rate of accumulation, and Tim maintained optimism that it was minimal until a snowmobile driver passed and disappeared all too quickly — indicating a wall of falling snow. The dancing flakes mesmerized Tim, who was already sleepy, but he knew if he stopped on the open river he would soon become buried in snow and vulnerable to being run over by anyone who passed. Temperatures remained warm, and the new snow melted on contact. Finally, Tim decided that no one in their right mind would leave Grayling in a full-fledged blizzard, and made his camp a few meters off the trail. He used a trail stake and two trekking poles to create a frame, and draped the garbage bag over the top as something of a tent for the head of his sleeping bag. When he woke up two hours later, several inches of snow had accumulated on the foot of his bag.

The trail was all but invisible, a shallow indentation in a flat, white sea. Tim slogged forward in his snowshoes for several hours until it became apparent he would not make it to dawn without falling asleep on his feet. He again set up his makeshift tent and collapsed into dreamless oblivion, awakening once more to full daylight. At first Tim was livid with himself, thinking he had slept all night long. He had no recollection of getting up, moving several miles down the trail, and stopping again. The realization that he had made two camps didn't come to him until later, while he was still stewing with frustrations about wasting time.

Skies cleared, but not in time to save the trail from being completely buried. Mushers would pass through, but for the most part these conditions wouldn't change, and Tim just had to accept that he would continue to move at a glacial pace for the next 120 miles up the frozen Yukon River to the village of Kaltag. Clear skies also ushered in cold air that Tim had wished for days earlier, and temperatures dropped precipitously. His joints ached and fingers went numb, indicating it was at least twenty below zero. He wanted to put on his fleece pants, but the wet garments had frozen solid. He beat the pants against his body until he could pry apart the fabric enough to pull it over his legs, but the pants remained stiff and cold. Tim questioned the wisdom of using ice pants to warm up, but reasoned that even frozen insulation would still prevent heat from escaping.

There was no avoiding the fact that he needed more warmth now; the fourth toe on his left foot was starting to sting. Years ago, the toe froze to his sock and developed a black patch of frostbite. Tim had removed the dead skin with his Swiss Army Knife. Ever since, that frostbitten toe has served as his canary in a coal mine — the first appendage to alert him that his body temperature was dropping too low.

Tim made camp at sunset. That night he indulged himself by dumping some broken chocolate pieces into a cup of boiled snow, for his first hot chocolate of the journey. The sweet, watery drink slid down his throat like nectar. It was, without hyperbole, the best thing he had ever tasted. Just a few sips ignited a warmth and vitality that few would understand, a sense of almost superhuman energy. The pink sky blazed overhead, painting the ice-scape of the Yukon in soft pastels. Tim smiled to himself at the thought that any person in their right mind would have quit days ago, and they would have missed this incredible adventure. This was, indeed, a most wild emotional roller coaster.

When he awoke, it was colder than it had been yet. Tim emerged from his sleeping bag to greet the frigid air like an old friend. He knew this cold, and he knew how to handle it. He sprang from the bag and wrestled his pained feet into shoes as quickly as possible, not fussing with adjusting anything correctly or even tying the laces. All of that could wait a few minutes, but for now he needed to cram everything into his sled and start moving within minutes of emerging from his sleeping bag. Experience taught him that generating new body heat was more important than fussing with gear or ensuring everything was in its proper place. Once core temperature drops at thirty below, it's extremely difficult to recover. There is a thin margin between stopping to tie shoes, and putting one's life in peril.

His pattern had become to sleep in the early hours of the night, and move through the pre-dawn hours. In this deep cold, there was no moisture in the air to obscure views. The Northern Lights appeared in three-dimensional waves, dancing through a high-definition sky. Tim stumbled through the bad snow until sleepiness overtook him again, and he succumbed to another short nap. It was so cold that the screen on his watch went blank, and wooden trail stakes were thick with frost. It was even too cold for wind, which was a welcome development from typical Yukon conditions. Tim preferred extreme cold to near-extreme cold with wind. His tell-tale toe screamed out frequently and he had to sleep in every stitch of clothing he had brought. But he had gotten his wish — a respite from the rain — so he didn't complain.

Then, of course, the wind picked up. There would be no more breaks to eat because he could no longer remove his gloves for even a few seconds, and he had to pull goggles over his balaclava to protect his corneas from freezing. For hours he marched without stopping until he came to a long bend in the river, where the trail crossed an open expanse of ice. He had been following the right bank for miles, and the trail had become firm enough that he had been able to remove his snowshoes a few miles back. Where the trail again crossed over the river, the wind had swept packed snow into drifts; some were high enough to bury the trail markers. From his vantage point, this appeared as a seemingly uncrossable barrier, and Tim once again stared blankly over the horizon, dumbfounded. He unhooked from his sled, sat on his duffel, buried his head in his mittens and sobbed. For the third time in this journey, he was in the midst of an emotional meltdown, releasing a surge of hopelessness and despondence as paralyzing as any he'd experienced. And yet, the only thing that was wrong were deeper snowdrifts across the trail. Tim stopped to eat some peanut butter and had an epiphany — he just needed to put the snowshoes back on and keep walking. The fact that this came to him after a bout of despair, and wasn't obvious in the first place, was disconcerting. Frightening even. Whether malnourishment, exhaustion, or stress, it was clear his thinking was severely impaired.

For the past several days, Tim's pace had been far below the average he needed to maintain for a twenty-four-day finish, and the looming deadline added to his stress. Several miles outside Kaltag, Tim found several packages of fruit snacks apparently dropped by a musher. Most of the packages were crow-pecked, but all still had at least a few candies inside. Tim decided to throw them on his sled as an emergency ration, and eat them after finishing if he was successful. Later, he decided that carrying these fruit snacks was a mistake, and that they should be deposited outside of the Old Woman Cabin. Tim had nothing to leave for the legendary ghost of the Old Woman, and figured these fruit snacks would suffice. As it turned out, they became an offering to his competition — a day later, Beat and Marco found the snacks and devoured them.

Tim lingered outside the buildings of Kaltag only long enough to call Loreen. Trail conditions had improved and Loreen assured him that he was still on pace, but Tim knew that just one more storm or wind event could set him back permanently. Cookie had lost about fifty pounds since the start of the race; at sixty pounds, she was still a heifer. Still, after hauling 110 pounds, sixty seemed almost svelte to Tim.

Darkness fell on another clear, cold night, and Tim set up camp on the access trail to the Tripod Flats shelter cabin. Before dozing off, he set three alarms on his watch and pressed it directly against his ear, held in place by the tight fabric of his balaclava. Most people would consider sleeping with a watch pressing into their head to be extremely uncomfortable, but Tim no longer cared. He was used to being uncomfortable. Discomfort was his baseline state on the Iditarod Trail. Given that the alternatives were pain and danger, he welcomed simple discomfort and became a decidedly low-maintenance guy as a result.

His feet had long since passed the point of discomfort. In the morning, he pressed the tender flesh into concrete-hard shoes, and then hobbled the first few steps with electric shocks of pain tearing through every nerve. Throbbing took over the initial shock, with a sharp soreness that continued to radiate from each infected blister. He thought his feet would become better as he walked, that numbness would take over, but some mornings relief just didn't come. At the top of the day's first hill, Tim detected an urgent need to stop and drain the blisters. Wind was howling over the exposed ridge and the temperature was at least twenty below; exposing the raw skin on his feet to these temperatures for even a few seconds meant another hour of hard marching to bring his body temperature back from hypothermia. But the alternative was remaining hobbled in pain, and moving at a snail's pace, he felt he had no choice.

The wind gathered strength throughout the frigid day, until gusts were approaching hurricane force. However, the wind was blowing in the general direction he was traveling — an almost unmanageable tailwind. Seventy-mile-per-hour gusts shoved him toward Unalakleet, and for the first time in this heavy-weight expedition, Tim ran. Running created more agony than pleasure. Snow drifts were hidden beneath a crust that sometimes held his weight, and sometimes did not, resulting in ankle-twisting steps at unpredictable intervals. He tried snowshoes for a while, but the pressure on his raw feet increased the pain scale to the level of a crushed bone. The edges of each snow dune were soft but the middles were generally solid, so Tim simply took giant steps to effectively leap from the crest of a drift, back to the trail, and onto the next dune.

The hurricane blast continued without relief through Unalakleet and onto Shaktoolik, a huddled strip of a village built on a thin spit of sand between a flat swampland and the Bering Sea. A wooden snow wall did little to temper a ceaseless Arctic wind that funneled through the valley, and Tim couldn't imagine a worse place to erect a village. He made a quick phone call to Loreen from a borrowed cell phone and fought the gale toward the Norton Sound. Tim had made six crossings of the sea ice with varying degrees of difficulty, and knew to always brace himself for the worst. Although the winds raged, this crossing was relatively mild — or perhaps he was simply more weathered, with expectations hardened by experience.

As Tim crossed through Koyuk and pulled his still-hulking sled along the coast, he began to have more encounters with other humans. A thin, short Native man driving a snowmobile pulling a traditional dog sled with two children stopped to chat. The man, who was close to Tim's age, said he was taking his grandchildren to visit their grandmother. He told Tim that he loved to walk and was proud to stay in shape because Natives historically walked great distances. Later, Tim talked to a gold miner who urged Tim to sleep in a shelter cabin, reasoning that "when you get old, you have to be kind to yourself and cheat a little." Tim laughed and told him he was far too deep in this game to start cheating. As he left the village of Elim, a snowmobile drove toward him. The driver introduced himself as "Top Hat," the postmaster of the village, and said he raced out there to stop Tim from leaving town without his resupply package. Tim had to explain that he had sent no supplies ahead, and the packages belonged to others still behind him.

It was a strange dynamic in an unsupported, solo journey to talk with others who were going about their comparatively normal lives. A young couple was awestruck because Tim had traveled all the way from Anchorage, a place that they had never visited. They, like many other young residents of rural Alaska, had never ventured more than a few hundred miles from their villages. Later, Tim watched children ride sleds down a river bank as he climbed up. The play appeared simple, and their cries were of sheer joy. Tim thought about how different their childhoods were from his children's, or his own. For most people, the world is becoming smaller and less mysterious. And yet, it was still possible to live in a small world full of surprises.

Tim started the long climb toward Little McKinley. He was hungry but unwilling to cheat on the next day's food, so he waited patiently for 2 p.m. to bring a freeze-dried meal and melted snow for drinking water. As darkness fell, winds became progressively stronger, and Tim caught himself sleepwalking frequently, moving slowly and lapsing into shivering as a result. Tim noticed that as he got closer to Nome, he required much more sleep and seemed to have more difficulty maintaining his core temperature than past years. Calorie intake was far below levels needed to sustain equilibrium, and Tim's body was eating away at itself just to keep going. The result was less energy for heat, and more pronounced exhaustion, compounding by the day. He was wasting away.

Before Golovin, Tim passed the time calculating and recalculating his remaining food until he decided he had an extra half pound of peanut butter to spare, on top of his daily ration. It must have been designated for the first day on the trail when Tim had little appetite. Ten minutes after passing through the village, he sat down to eat the extra peanut butter and made a cup of hot chocolate with most of his remaining chocolate supply.

The final seventy miles into Nome were the home stretch, when Tim typically broke out all the stops to finish as quickly as possible. With less than two days to go, Cookie was finally down to her usual trail weight of forty or so pounds, and Tim had enough batteries left over to run his headlight on high. It felt invigorating to move through the night with extra light, as though he had taken in an extra shot of caffeine. In past years, he ran much of this stretch of trail, and thought the burst of energy would spur a faster pace. This year, however, his legs balked at every attempt to run. The willpower was there, but the ability was just gone. His muscles were simply too weak, and he was too tired.

One big concern was the Salomon Blowhole, where concentrated winds could make it impossible to stop or even stand. The blow could last for many miles and hours. He had nearly succumbed to blowhole winds three years earlier, and wasn't sure he had the strength to fight them this time around. There were still fifty miles between him and Nome, and his entire energy reserve would have to be derived from his remaining food — one packet of tuna, one freeze-dried meal, a few broken pieces of chocolate, one VitaFuel bar, one piece of jerky, and one bag of creamy peanut butter. It was 1:30 a.m.; in twelve hours, the twenty-four day mark would arrive and Tim would be out of rations. He decided to shore up his strength by stopping to cook and melt water one final time, and push as hard as he could through the final miles to Nome.

As Tim crested the final hill of the trip at Topkok, he saw a headlamp approaching from the other direction. It belonged to Billy Koitzsch, an Anchorage cyclist who was attempting an historical first by riding his bike a thousand miles to Nome on the Iditarod Trail, and then a thousand miles back to Fairbanks on the Iron Dog route. Billy had lost one of his toes to frostbite one year earlier, and would need to have another amputated at the end of his 2013 expedition. Tim felt a strong bond with others who traveled the trail under their own power, and a mutual respect for what they had all endured. He asked Billy if his frostbitten extremities hurt, to which Billy replied, "Every step." Billy unzipped his bright-red jump suit to reveal a .44-caliber pistol and flare gun strapped to his chest. Billy was deeply afraid of wolves, enough to justify arming himself with several pounds of cold metal. Tim could only laugh, and was grateful to receive a report that the final forty-five miles of trail were still good as long as the weather held out for one more day.

Not long after he passed the Topkok safety cabin, the wind became more threatening. Gusts kicked up clouds of snow, obscuring views of Cape Nome. Uneven blasts of wind caused Tim to feel disoriented and dizzy. His body fat had deteriorated to the point that any gust would sap heat from his core like a vacuum, forcing him to start jogging on wobbly legs. As he stumbled against the fierce crosswind, he caught a glimpse of a medium-sized animal running toward him near the trail. As it got close it spotted Tim and ran off the trail, yielding to the larger human. It didn't run like a fox or wolf — more like a raccoon or a groundhog. Since those weren't possibilities Tim decided it had to be a wolverine. It was a rare sighting, so he pulled out his camera to take a photo. This was another uncharacteristic lapse in judgment; Tim knew better than to remove a glove and expose his hand to strong subzero winds. In the time it took to capture two snapshots, three fingers turned white; he wouldn't recover the feeling in these extremities for more than three months. And he didn't even get a good photo out of it.

The wolverine sighting felt like a mirage, and Tim's hand burned in the aftermath of something that may have not even happened — he could no longer be sure. He felt frightened — not because snow was blasting him in the face and wind-chills were south of fifty below, but because he hadn't appreciated the gravity of these conditions. His judgment was clearly impaired, and he no longer knew whether he could trust himself to make good decisions, just as he couldn't necessarily trust his weakened body to maintain its warmth.

Tim felt relief when he passed the darkened buildings of Safety — this meant he had crossed the blowhole safely — with a few frozen fingers, but at least he was still alive. Anxieties could now turn to his food supply. He had eaten everything but one packet of tuna, and still had twenty-five miles — a seemingly insurmountable distance — to travel. He was used to running this section at four to five miles per hour, but his weakened legs now struggled to maintain a three-mile-per-hour pace. He did the math and determined that at best he would arrive in Nome after 2 a.m., and it seemed better to sleep and finish in the morning. Fourteen miles from town, he spread out his sleeping bag for what he hoped would be the final sleep of the journey.

He awoke at 4:30 a.m. and packed up one last time. Eleven miles from Nome, the city lights came into view. Tim decided to celebrate with the packet of tuna; the air was so cold that the packaging peeled apart at its seams. It took a half hour of gnawing to consume the frozen fish brick, Tim clutching at it with fingers still burning from the wolverine photo shoot, and wondering how many wash cycles it would take for his mittens to no longer stink. Still, each ice-flecked chunk tasted wonderful.

Twenty-four days, twenty hours, and thirty-one minutes after leaving the Knik Bar, Tim walked down Front Street for a seventh time and stood beneath the burled arch. It was mid-morning and his friend Phil would still be at work, so Tim crossed the street and pulled Cookie up the metal steps of the visitor's center. To the consternation of a volunteer, Tim stood near the doorway and began peeling off clothing, tossing the burned liner gloves and socks in the trash.

Inside the restroom, he removed the underwear he had worn from the start, now riddled with holes, and also dumped them and all of his trash. He looked at his face in the mirror for the first time in weeks. The ashen figure hunched over the sink was unrecognizable. Hollow eyes gazed out of a sunken face chapped with windburn, and he saw a patch of black frostbite on his nose. Wrinkled skin clung to his cheekbones, and clumps of silver hair were matted against his skull. If his face was startlingly sickly, his body looked even worse — sharp angles of his skeleton protruded from what was left of his flesh. The 137 pound person in the mirror looked like a weak old man nearing death, not someone who had the strength to pull more than a hundred pounds of supplies a thousand miles across Alaska. His body had paid a price for this challenge, but his smile was unmistakable — the physical evidence of a joy that had surmounted all suffering.

He sat at the visitors center drinking warm coffee and regrouping before he found the energy to venture next door to a cafe for a Bering Sea Burger — a double cheeseburger with two fried eggs and bacon on top — along with two Diet Cokes and fries. Tim devoured the meal while staring out the window at the frozen Bering Sea in quiet contemplation, and then walked over to a store to quell a demon that had been haunting him since Martin Buser had passed him on the trail weeks earlier. He left the store forty dollars lighter with an armful of candy, topped with the gummy bears that had been calling his name from this vast distance.

Tim was the first runner to reach Nome that year, winning the Iditarod Trail Invitational as he had in many past years. He had completed one of the longest known unsupported journeys on foot in modern times, and, most importantly, proved again to himself that he was up for any challenge. He had conquered the weakness within.

Epilogue

16

We shall not cease from exploration.
And the end of all our exploring will
be to arrive from where we started, and
know the place for the first time.
> ~ T.S. Eliot,
> "Little Gidding"

After the unsupported journey of 2013, Tim was almost convinced that everything else would seem easy — almost. A sub-twenty-day finish remained elusive, and a race on the Northern Route would be an opportunity to try. Tim set his sights on 2014.

Recovery from pulling a hundred-pound sled across Alaska was slow, and Tim's right knee was hobbled for most of the year. Two significant meniscus tears required surgery in December. His surgeon did say that the trauma was the only thing holding back an otherwise healthy knee — more than a hundred thousand lifetime miles had resulted in little negative impact on the joints. The surgeon gave the go-ahead for another thousand-mile journey by requesting a postcard from Nome.

Still, pain from the injury and recovery from surgery limited Tim's training before the February start date. Loreen also wanted to try for Nome again in 2014, and reduced life stressors allowed her to focus more directly on her training. She was ready, while Tim's fitness was not as sharp as it could be. He planned to start the journey with Loreen to gauge his capabilities, and then decide whether his knee would allow a record attempt, or whether this would be the year to finally share the entire journey with his wife.

Conditions on the Iditarod Trail are never predictable, but 2014 was a particularly odd year for winter weather. A shift in the jet stream pushed a "polar vortex" of Arctic air deep into the southern latitudes of North America, leaving Alaska warm and dry. A long January thaw, followed by several sunny weeks without precipitation, had scoured snowpack from much of the state. Although there had always been dry sections of trail, this year promised trail conditions that resembled early summer more than mid-winter. Tim wasn't sure how to manage dozens or possibly even hundreds of miles without much snow.

As he had in past years with Loreen on the trail, Tim made the decision early to stick with his wife. The bizarre low snow year created mostly favorable, hard-packed trail conditions. Still, a rainy day over the Alaska Range, followed by fifty miles of snowless dirt and tundra, created new challenges en route to McGrath. Tim's recently repaired knee ached throughout each day, and throbbed at night. Loreen struggled with nausea and edema, but finally began to find her stride as they neared the 350-mile mark. Although Tim remained undecided about chasing the record even as they neared McGrath after seven days, he knew he wasn't capable of leaving his wife behind. She showed impressive resolve to complete the distance, and he knew that working together would boost her chances of reaching Nome. This would be Loreen's year.

Leaving McGrath, the couple traveled in close proximity to Beat Jegerlehner, who was making his second bid for Nome. The taiga of the Northern Route is characterized by squat, anemic spruce trees. Nights were clear and cold, but hospitality was particularly warm this year. After his unsupported trek, Tim had gained new appreciation for eggs and coffee breakfasts, wood-heated shelter cabins, company on the trail, and friendly dog sled race volunteers who this year seemed willing to bend over backwards to provide cots and meals to the Iditarod walkers.

Of course, traveling with others also brought its own trials — misaligned sleeping patterns, frustrations with a slower pace, and shared miseries. The group made their way through the wind tunnel of the Yukon and onto the storm-blasted Kaltag portage. A large storm dumped several feet of fresh powder onto the previously ice-covered trail. This swift change in conditions slowed their pace and forced snowshoe use for most of the last three hundred miles to Nome. Due to the low snow conditions prior to the storm, the established trail was anything but direct — the group was meandering over tundra and taking the long way around bad ice on the frozen bays.

Loreen fought valiantly through the difficult conditions, but began to falter during a series of steep rolling hills before Topkok Point, about forty-five miles from Nome. The relentless climbs were like monsters guarding the castle of the finish, stymying forward progress. Loreen requested a break, and Tim decided to walk ahead to the Topkok shelter cabin to melt snow. He marched up another thousand-foot summit, and paused to gaze across the frozen plain of the Bering

Sea. Somewhere out there was Siberia, Tim realized, an entirely different realm just beyond this white expanse. These interwoven connections to the remote corners of the world never ceased to evoke the divine.

At the cabin, Tim waited for Loreen for more than two hours. She trudged through the wooden door looking worse than any other time Tim could remember — swollen face, cloudy eyes, a fatigued expression, and a forced gait. A half-hour nap and hot meal did little to aid in her recovery. Loreen was absolutely spent, here, less than forty-five miles from Nome.

She forced herself out of the cabin, but sugary trails put up their own walls of resistance, and their snowshoe-anchored pace dropped from slow to slower. Tim knew Loreen needed more sleep, but feared stopping. Skies overhead were calm and clear, but they were still about two dozen miles from Safety, which meant they were still in the blow hole danger zone. Blow holes did not need overcast skies or winds to ignite their fury. They were unique micro-climates, driven by forces so unpredictable that even locals couldn't see them coming. In times gone by, such phenomena were attributed to an angry god.

Knowledge that a blow hole could activate at any time made stopping a risk, but Tim and Loreen's forward progress had become so slow that it constituted a waste of time. The trail paralleled a bluff fifty feet over the frozen sea; Tim wandered to the edge to scout for a nook that would keep them protected from a blow hole. Loreen nervously questioned whether it was safe to stop.

"It's a horrible idea," Tim answered matter-of-factly. But he wasn't sure they had a choice. He'd crunched the numbers in his head, and knew that if their progress continued to decline at this rate, they would be worse off than if they stopped. Loreen typically experienced energy surges after breaks, which meant proper rest was more likely to increase the overall pace, resulting in reaching the end of the danger zone faster.

Tim checked his GPS and discovered that the Bonanza Bridge — a place where the Iditarod Trail intersected with a road to Nome — was just three miles away. There, they were likely to find a safer wind break. The road was unmaintained in the winter, but the surface was often black ice. At that point, they'd be traveling southwest, and the wind would likely be at their backs. Loreen vowed to pick up the pace. Emotionally, she was boosted by the prospect of sleep followed by potentially easier travel, and did successfully increase her speed.

At the bridge, they crossed over the road and found a sheltered clearing that the wind had carved out of the snow beside the bridge abutments. They agreed to sleep for five hours, but when Tim's alarm went off, Loreen asked for one more hour. He failed to hear the second alarm, and didn't wake up until they had rested for nearly eleven hours.

Tim couldn't help but feel a tinge of frustration about sleeping in, but it was the best thing that could have happened. Loreen seemed fully recharged — a new person brimming with excitement and vitality that Tim hadn't seen in his wife in days. The black ice conditions on the road did not last long. Deep wind drifts took over, and they were soon wearing their snowshoes again as they battled through waist-deep piles of snow. The difficult trail conditions didn't seem to faze Loreen anymore; through a combination of her fierce determination and the mental reset of rest, she had made a remarkable comeback.

It was early spring in western Alaska, and the last wisps of pink sunlight still colored the horizon when Tim and Loreen walked side by side down Front Street in Nome, arriving at the finish at 9:59 p.m. In twenty-six days, seven hours, and fifty-nine minutes, Loreen had become the third woman to complete the thousand-mile journey across Alaska on foot, and had shaved more than four days off the women's record. Her finishing time was also faster than Tim's first journey to Nome. Tears streamed down Loreen's face as she unhooked her sled and stepped onto the snow-covered platform beneath the Burled Arch. Tim could not have been more proud of her.

A small group of supporters and passersby cheered while Tim and Loreen shared a long embrace. Photo flashes lit up the darkening street, and Tim held up his fingers to illustrate each successful arrival in Nome — eight, now. He was running out of fingers to mark these journeys. In many ways, 2014 had been as challenging as any other year — and just as rewarding. Tim thrived in conquering adversity, but perhaps even more so, he enjoyed helping others meet these challenges and exceed their greatest expectations. His wife was more powerful than she imagined, and now, standing side-by-side with her accomplished husband in Nome, she had gained a deeper understanding of her own strength and potential.

Even as he closes in on sixty, Tim's hunger for challenge and adventure only continues to grow. He is still pursuing ambitions to travel to the South Pole and then return to the coast on a journey that, if successful, would establish several new unsupported distance and speed records in the prestigious world of polar exploration. Funding remains the major obstacle to a South Pole expedition, and whether or not he'll ever have a chance to try is uncertain.

Still, Tim has no intention of stopping his succession of Alaska journeys at eight. Even on the cusp of official senior citizenship, Tim knows his body is still capable of breaking the Northern Route record if he remains determined and patient. He is also considering the possibility of riding a bike to Nome on the Southern Route. As it stands, the bicycle record for this route, set by Jay Petervary in 2011, is seventeen days and six hours — a mere three days faster than Tim's foot record. Although he'll always be a runner at heart, Tim also wonders what he could accomplish with a set of wheels. There's only one way to find out.

Through all of his journeys, Tim has amassed a wealth of trail knowledge that, when condensed and simplified, resembles a list of instructions for life. The following, in his words, are Tim Hewitt's lessons from the Iditarod Trail:

✳ People are resilient and can do much more than they think. The mind places limits at a much lower level than your body requires.

✳ Everyone's perception is different. What scares me may have no impact on you.

✳ Sleep deprivation has profound negative effects on thinking.

✳ Food is fuel.

✳ Problems are solvable with thought.

✳ Challenge motivates people and brings out their best.

✳ Patience reduces anxiety.

✳ Familiarity reduces anxiety.

✳ Experience reduces anxiety.

✳ The unknown calls us. We all desire adventure, even if we resist.

✳ Some people are more comfortable having somebody else to share in decision-making and for company, while others are not.

✳ Traveling alone is simpler and faster. Traveling with anybody else makes you morally responsible for them and limits your speed to that of the slowest companion.

✳ No matter how good or bad you feel, it will change. The human body is never at status quo.

✳ The weather is never at status quo. When it is good or bad, it will change.

✳The trail is never at status quo.

✳ Managing your body and addressing its needs is critical in a multi-day event. Thinking and making the correct decisions for you alone is determinative of whether you will finish.

✳ People on snowmobiles lie about distances. People will give you a wrong answer to a question before admitting they don't know the answer.

✳ You must be at peace with yourself.

✳ What makes me happy would make most people miserable. The opposite is also true.

✳ Everybody has something that is important to them, but that may seem inconsequential to others. Listening to locals talking about hunting, trapping and fishing, I've realized that this is not sport but life for them. I have learned to appreciate how easy many of us have it. When I returned from the unsupported journey, I marveled at the convenience of heat, light, and food supplies. Just being able to do nothing is a luxury we don't appreciate enough. We have so much more than so many in remote villages, which would result in guilt if I thought those people were missing anything. But really, they aren't.

These trail lessons loop back to philosophical questions about how to create a meaningful life. Through individual circumstances and hard work, Tim has achieved comfortable standing in a conventional modern lifestyle. He could choose to sit back and reap these benefits without ever having to endure the pain and difficulties of heavy labor and bodily discomfort, or the wrath of nature.

And yet he seeks this out, year after year. He not only eschews the conveniences that many take for granted, but he invests extra time and resources to voluntarily encounter hardship. The intangible gains extend beyond money, power, and fame, circling all the way back to the values on which humans built civilization: appreciation for the land, respect for the forces of nature, perseverance, ingenuity, kindness, and curiosity.

In modern times, there are those who would discount such adventures as "frivolous," "crazy," or "irresponsible," because a lawyer in Pennsylvania does not need to cross the frozen wilderness to survive or provide for his family. But, in many ways, Tim is simply doing what humans have always done … that very thing that makes them human: exploring and learning. This is why, as long as there are people, there will always be adventure. And there will always be adventurers like Tim Hewitt, who harbor such enduring appreciation for life that even the worst life can offer — blasting storms, searing cold, loneliness, fear, and pain — will never deter them from exploring the edges of the known world, always searching for the universe beyond.

Tim and Loreen Hewitt on the Iditarod Trail in 2011.

Self-portrait by Tim Hewitt

Tim and Loreen Hewitt travel together in 2011.

Photo by Mike Curiak

Tim Hewitt falls to his knees while dragging his 110-pound sled up the Happy River Steps in 2013.

Photo by Beat Jegerlehner

Tim Hewitt approaches the village of Shaktoolik in 2014.

Photo by Beat Jegerlehner

Tripods mark the Iditarod Trail toward Golovin Bay.

Photo by Beat Jegerlehner

Tim and Loreen Hewitt rest at the school in Shaktoolik.

Photo by Beat Jegerlehner

Tim Hewitt makes his way across jumbled sea ice outside of Koyuk.

Photo by Beat Jegerlehner

Tim and Loreen Hewitt embrace under the burled arch in Nome.

Photo by Beat Jegerlehner

References

• The official race map of the Iditarod Trail, released in 2008 by the Iditarod Trail Committee, can be found at http://iditarod.com/race-map.

• The estimated distances of the Iditarod Trail, as established at the beginning of the dog sled race in Willow, Alaska, can be found at http://iditarod.com/about/the-iditarod-trail.

• Human-powered records on the Iditarod Trail, as well as all past finishes of both the 350-mile and 1,000-mile races can be found at the Iditarod Trail Invitational Web site, http://iditarodtrailinvitational.com.

• Historic information about the Iditarod Trail and the 1925 Nome serum run were drawn from the official Iditarod Dog Sled Race Web site (http://iditarod.com/about/history), Wikipedia (http://en.wikipedia.org/wiki/Iditarod_Trail_Sled_Dog_Race), and *The Cruelest Miles: The Heroic Story of Dogs and Men in a Race Against an Epidemic* by Gay Salisbury, and Laney Salisbury (W. W. Norton & Company, 2005.)

• Notes about the establishment of human-powered racing on the Iditarod Trail were drawn from the Alaska Ultra Sport Web site, (http://www.alaskaultrasport.com/race%20history.html.)

• Information and quotes about Joe Redington were drawn from *Father of the Iditarod: The Joe Redington Story* by Lew Freedman (Epicenter Press, 1996.)

• All information about Tim Hewitt and his journeys across Alaska were drawn from notes and recollections compiled by Tim Hewitt. Names of people and places were drawn from his notes and confirmed by race sources.

Photo by Mike Curiak

Tim Hewitt and Jill Homer near Rainy Pass in February 2014.

Jill Homer grew up in Salt Lake City, Utah, and graduated from the University of Utah with a degree in journalism in 2000. She began her career working in community weekly and daily newspapers. In 2005, she moved to Homer, Alaska, to pursue adventure in the Last Frontier. She never viewed herself as an athlete, but she was looking for a unique kind of challenge, and an esoteric sport called snow biking fit that description. A couple of years worth of (mainly mis) adventures landed her in the 350-mile Iditarod Trail Invitational in 2008. The unforgettable experience was the genesis of her first book, *Ghost Trails: Journeys Through A Lifetime.*

Although she was often less than a half day in front of Tim and Loreen during her 2008 ride, she didn't officially meet Tim until she returned to Iditarod Trail in 2009. After stepping in overflow on Flathorn Lake, she developed serious frostbite on her right foot. She was holed up at the Yentna Station checkpoint, mulling whether the injury and potential consequences would prevent her from continuing in the race. Tim Hewitt approached her and said, "You know you can't go on." She still credits Tim with persuading her out of an extremely bad decision.

After moving to California and establishing a career as a freelance writer and journalist, Jill returned to Alaska in 2014 to attempt the 350-mile race to McGrath on foot with her partner, Beat. She enjoyed many memorable adventures while dragging a sled along the Iditarod Trail with Tim and Loreen, before bidding goodbye to the group in McGrath as they prepared to go on to Nome.

She currently lives in Los Altos, California.

Other Books by Jill Homer

Jill Homer has an outlandish ambition: a 2,740-mile mountain bike race from Canada to Mexico along the rugged Continental Divide. *Be Brave, Be Strong: A Journey Across the Great Divide* is the story of an adventure driven relentlessly forward as foundations crumble. During her record-breaking ride in the 2009 Tour Divide, Jill battles a torrent of self-doubt, anger, fatigue, bicycle failures, crashes, violent storms, and hopelessness. Each night, she collapses under the effort of this savage way of life. And every morning, she picks up the pieces and strikes out anew in an ongoing journey to discover what lies on the other side of the Divide: astonishing beauty, unconditional kindness, and boundless strength.

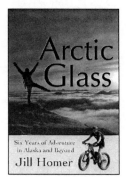

Arctic Glass: Six Years of Adventure in Alaska and Beyond compiles the best essays of "Jill Outside" from the thousands of posts that have appeared on the Web site. The essays chronicle the adventures of an unlikely athlete who takes on harsh challenges in the frozen wilderness of Alaska, the Utah desert, and the Himalayas of Nepal. Endurance racing, overcoming challenges, and self-actualization amid stunning outdoor landscapes are common themes in these vignettes about "The Adventure of Life."

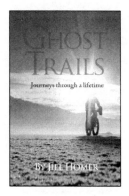

Ghost Trails: Journeys Through a Lifetime is the inspirational journey of an unlikely endurance athlete locked in one of the most difficult wilderness races in the world, the Iditarod Trail Invitational. Through her struggles and discoveries in Alaska's beautiful, forbidding landscape, Jill begins to understand the ultimate destination of her life's trails.

Avaiable from Amazon, Barnes & Noble, iTunes and other online retailers.

CPSIA information can be obtained
at www.ICGtesting.com
Printed in the USA
LVOW12s2349121217
559561LV00010B/316/P